Managing Multimedia

Project Management for
Web and Convergent Media
Book 2 – Technical Issues

Pearson Education

We work with leading authors to develop the strongest educational materials in computer science, bringing cutting-edge thinking and best learning practice to a global market.

Under a range of well-known imprints, including Addison-Wesley, we craft high quality print and electronic publications which help readers to understand and apply their content, whether studying or at work.

To find out more about the complete range of our publishing please visit us on the World Wide Web at: **www.pearsoned.co.uk**

THIRD EDITION

Managing Multimedia

Project Management for Web and Convergent Media

Book 2 – Technical Issues

Elaine England
and
Andy Finney

 Addison-Wesley

An imprint of PEARSON EDUCATION

Harlow, England ■ London ■ New York ■ Reading, Massachusetts ■ San Francisco
Toronto ■ Don Mills, Ontario ■ Sydney ■ Tokyo ■ Singapore ■ Hong Kong ■ Seoul
Taipei ■ Cape Town ■ Madrid ■ Mexico City ■ Amsterdam ■ Munich ■ Paris ■ Milan

Pearson Education Limited
Edinburgh Gate
Harlow
Essex CM20 2JE
England

and Associated Companies throughout the world

Visit us on the World Wide Web at:
www.pearsoned.co.uk

First published 1996
Second edition 1999
Third edition 2002

ISBN-10: 0-201-72899-0
ISBN-13: 978-0-201-72899-6

British Library Cataloguing-in-Publication Data
A catalogue record for this book can be obtained from the British Library

Library of Congress Cataloging-in-Publication Data
England, Elaine.
   Managing multimedia : project management for Web and convergent media / Elaine
   England and Andy Finney. – 3rd ed.
       p. cm.
   Includes bibliographical references and index.
   ContentsL Book 1. People and processes – Book 2. Technical issues.
   ISBN 0-201-72898-2 (Book 1) – ISBN 0-201-72899-0 (Book 2)
     I. Multimedia systems.   I. Finney, Andy.   II. Title.

   QA76.575 E56 2002
   006.7–dc21

                                                                          200206364

10 9 8 7 6 5 4
07 06 05

Typeset by 63
Printed in Great Britain by Henry Ling Ltd., at the Dorset Press, Dorchester, Dorset

Contents

■ Who are they for?

These books provide a background to the management tasks you will need to use when developing multimedia projects. Book 1 takes the perspective of managing people and the production processes, and Book 2 covers the relevant technical issues. They are aimed particularly at people wishing to adopt the role of managing a new media development team. In this context multimedia development includes online projects for the World Wide Web or interactive television (iTV), or offline using CD-ROMs or any other appropriate interactive medium. Previous editions have proved useful whether the readers were already working in the industry or were studying ready to join it.

There are a variety of titles that are used to denote the team leader role – producer, managing editor, analyst, or senior software engineer, for example. The term 'project manager' is used here because it is a neutral term, which does not betray any media origins, since new media is produced from a fusion of talents across several media.

The role of 'account manager' is another term that is met in new media companies. The differentiation of a project manager and an account manager in terms of what they do in new media projects tends to be ill-defined. The account managers appear to have more direct contact with clients at the initial stages of the project and can begin the project definition phase and then pass it over to the production head of project. They may keep a general eye on the project progress and might be brought in during the project if there are any discrepancies. We will concentrate on the project manager role rather than account manager but we cover the definition phase of a project as if the project manager carries it out or when necessary uses specialists to help with the definition.

Our emphasis in the two companion books is the adaptation of project management theory and practice to multimedia projects. This approach offers insights to help you keep control of projects. Interactive media projects are notoriously difficult to keep within time and budget because there are so many variables. These books analyse all the variables within projects from clients to techniques; from team members to applying project management principles.

The material in Book 1 concentrates on the people and processes involved in the definition and production of a project. It follows the life cycle of a project. It broadens the understanding of the multimedia context for those with a single specialization such as programming or graphics, while giving a practical business and management slant for others. It also covers emerging trends in areas that although peripheral to the main processes at the moment, may become mainstream in the near future. This extra material is designed to help the self-development of multimedia project managers. Book 2 focuses on the media platforms and production processes. These have expanded quickly over the last couple of years and for this reason warrant a separate book for this edition.

These companion books will also prove useful for those commissioning new media, since the client's roles and responsibilities are defined in parallel with the project manager's. Book 1, *People and Processes*, clearly identifies the phases of a project and acts as an introduction to the process. Book 2, *Technical Issues*, can help those people commissioning projects increase their understanding of the range of existing interactive media and emerging interactive media. It can help them make the appropriate media choice for a particular purpose. It also covers the production processes so that commissioners know what will be involved and the choices they will need to make on quality levels.

■ The structure of the books

In *People and Processes*, Book 1, the core chapters are organized around the development of a project from initiation to completion. Administration, management and production processes are interweaved, reflecting the way they happen during a project. Because some phases occur simultaneously, the linear nature of the chapters misrepresents the overall process to an extent. However, we have tried to cover all the phases for developing a team-based, client-driven, commercial project. Initial chapters offer background insights into the theory of project management and how it relates to interactive media project management. The self-development chapters predict and cover salient issues for project managers to get up to speed with emerging issues and top up their knowledge. In *Technical Issues*, Book 2, the core chapters address the technical media issues and the associated production issues. They have a common structure with the chapters in Book 1 providing a consistency and integrity across the writing. These core chapters cover a project production process that uses the equivalent of some original video footage, a range of audio assets, commercially sourced and in-house-produced graphics, and text content.

We use a client-centred commercial project as the default in both books because it needs the greatest number of tasks and resources and involves all the management processes relevant to client, team, application development and budget management. There are, however, many varieties of projects, so the readers will need to select and apply the relevant sections according to their particular requirements. All projects need certain management processes but these processes can be streamlined if any of the following apply: you are working alone, no money is changing hands, you do not have a specific client, you do not have to clear rights in materials, and you are not using audio or video in the application.

Some readers of previous editions have asked for a definition of commercial versus non-commercial projects. Commercial as applied here implies that money changes hands for the exchange of services and goods: time and effort is accountable and budgeted against monetary return. This would include projects done for charities if not done voluntarily, for example. There are other types of multimedia projects. Some types of research, student assignments and self-development projects are examples of non-commercial projects.

Projects that don't require a team can of course be commercial. One or two multi-skilled individuals can produce excellent projects alone and would need many but not all of the aspects covered here. If you are working on these types of project you may not have as many administrative and legal aspects to cover as in team-based projects, but many will be the same, albeit on a smaller scale.

Website projects can use just a selection or all of the media, depending on the specific project but as the bandwidth available increases the media choices become more fluid so we cover all media in case the project demands them. Multimedia games and entertainment titles tend to have a different development cycle because they are driven by different tools such as games engines, need different skill sets and are market driven. International projects have more phases, and are referred to when appropriate.

For those who work in small companies with smaller, more contained new media projects, we have included a new chapter (Book 1, Chapter 13) focusing on the appropriate business imperatives and risks. The business case should help to guide your approach to managing projects. This covers the same core principles as the project life cycle chapters but aligns them directly to the business perspective. We hope that this perspective will prove convincing enough for project managers of short, quick projects to recognize the need for using the principles.

The Glossary will serve as a ready reference for any terms that need further explanation. We have tried to make it as comprehensive as possible, and it is also included in both books.

■ The structure of the core chapters

Icon of project manager's responsibilities

In each book the core chapters begin with a résumé of the project manager's responsibilities. This will prepare you for the concepts that will be covered and will help focus your interpretation of them on the role outlined. During the books, the complete range of responsibilities builds up into the equivalent of a job description. If you are not an interactive project manager and

Icon of theory into practice

Icon of refer to companion website

Icon of summary

Icon of recommended reading

you are reading the books for a general purpose, then you can skip the résumés and read the chapters for salient information.

During the chapters you will find suggested tasks. These are to help you transfer the principles into practical activities of relevance to your own situation. Because there are so many types of multimedia projects we have tried to stick to principles that can be applied across the greatest variety of projects. But the principles will serve you for your own situation only if you take the time and effort to apply them. The 'theory into practice' tasks can help you build up project-specific sets of reference materials that suit the range and type of projects you develop.

Where appropriate during the chapters you will be referred to the companion website for information that is represented better in an electronic form, and for practical exercises on visual and audio examples. See www.booksites.net/england.

Each chapter has a summary. This reinforces the main points covered in the chapter, but can also be used as a quick reference when you are developing a project and reach the phase being discussed. Some people prefer to read the summary before reading a chapter to decide if it has direct relevance for them. Others read the summary first to preview the chapter, to prepare them for it.

Where possible we have included recommended reading or website references at the ends of chapters, but a few of the aspects covered here have relied on practical experience and represent the authors' interpretation of that experience rather than insights from defined theory.

■ Acknowledgements

Many thanks to all those who gave their time and expertise to comment on the drafts and helped shape the book through to this 3rd edition:

Judith Aston, Senior Lecturer in Time-based Media, Faculty of Art, Media and Design, University of the West of England, Bristol, UK.
Stewart Atkins, Development Director, Traffic, UK.
Jardine Barrington Cook, Logica, UK.
Birte Christensen-Dalsgaard, The Danish State Library, Aarhus, Denmark.
Mark Dillon, Director, On-Line Services, GTE Entertainment, USA.
Steve Hope, Technology Trials Manager, Orange Personal Communications Services.
Bob Hughes, Multimedia Author and Consultant, Bristol, UK.
Peter Looms, Danmarks Radio/Television/Online, Multimedia Strategist, Denmark.
Peter Marshall, Technical Director, The Digital Television Group, UK.
Mike Philips, MediaLab Arts Course, School of Computing, University of Plymouth, UK.

Malcolm Roberts, Senior Manager, Bank of Montreal Institute for Learning, Scarborough, Ontario, Canada.

Gisella Rosano, Designer/Developer, Bank of Montreal Institute for Learning, Scarborough, Ontario, Canada.

Claus Rosenstand, Head of Board, InterAct, Aalborg, Denmark.

Henry Steele, Associate Professor, International Business and Marketing, School of Management, The Open Polytechnic of New Zealand.

William S. Strong, Partner, Kotin Crabtree & Strong Attorneys at Law, Boston, USA.

Charles Walker, Partner, Walker Tomaszewski Solicitors, London, UK.

Jonathan Wilson, Account Director, BBC MediaArc, London, UK.

We both recognize that many of our past and present colleagues have contributed to the span of experience covered here, and we thank you all – too numerous to name individually.

Finally we also recognize the debt to all the pioneers who persevered against the odds and kept the faith that interactive media would be mainstream. You were right.

Elaine England
Andy Finney
April 2001

Trademark notice

The following are trademarks or registered trademarks of their respective companies:

■ Knowing the technical background

There is some debate about the amount of technical background and other kinds of detail that a manager needs to understand in order to manage the production of assets – and by assets we mean the content of a website or CD such as text, graphics, photographs, sound and video – and websites themselves. In conventional media areas, managers often come up 'through the ranks' and have done the job of the people they manage. In web design and multimedia this is less likely to happen simply because of the newness of this area and its multidisciplinary nature. A project manager might have worked as a television producer, a journalist, a trainer, a graphics artist or a computer programmer rather than as all of these; or the management of new media projects might be your first job on leaving school or university. So a detailed knowledge of one area under your control could be counterbalanced by complete ignorance of another. Multimedia production not only integrates these disciplines, it also has to balance them.

When you manage the production of assets, and of the web pages or computer software that make use of these assets, you could be working with people in the core team for your whole project, or you could be hiring in people or facilities for only a relatively small part of it. Your responsibility includes fitting their work into the whole project. This extended team will be less aware of your overall plan, and may be less involved and committed. In some cases, such as if you were to hire a photographer for a single day's shoot or book a sound studio for a few hours to do a voice recording, they may have very little knowledge of interactive media and its special requirements and idiosyncrasies. Because multimedia involves slightly different technologies from mainstream media there will be occasions when normal practices will not be exactly right, and a knowledge – or access to knowledge – of both will make it easier for you to explain your requirements and concerns.

If you, as project manager, know something of the processes involved in creating and manipulating the assets for your project, you are in a much better position to help the asset creator achieve the result you want. In some cases you might need to be able to unravel technical jargon to do this, and you will often find that the level of respect that specialists have for you, and their willingness to go that extra mile for you, is influenced by how well you communicate with them and how well they think you understand their point of view. Sometimes you will need simply to point people in the right direction, but in other cases you may need to direct them specifically to do what you want. It will depend on their abilities, how well you share ideas and how flexible your vision of the result can be. Experience will make this easier, but background knowledge will help you on your way.

In the course of the technically-oriented chapters of this volume of *Managing Multimedia* you will be introduced to some of the basic principles and terminologies so that you will be better equipped to achieve what you want. Although it is impossible to cover everything, the aim of these chapters includes pointers to those vital differences inherent in interactive media and, in some cases, to where assets for online projects differ from those for offline ones and where assets for display on a computer screen differ from those for a television. However, the production of assets for use on a website, interactive television or on a CD-ROM is very similar for all methods of distribution: it is at the final stages of preparation that the differences will become important.

This volume of *Managing Multimedia* also includes chapters outlining the way that the Internet, interactive television and mobile systems function. Even though, at the time of writing, there is often more talk about the opportunities convergent communications will offer than real examples, we will start with an overview of convergence.

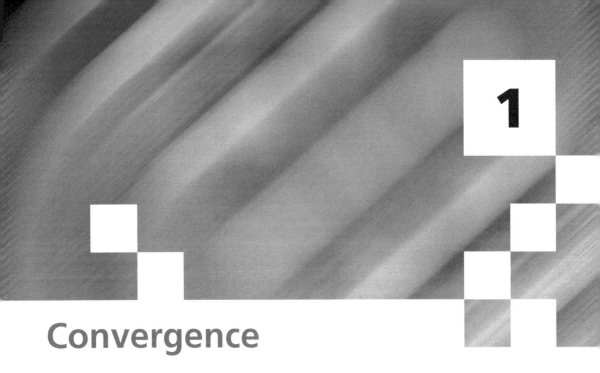

Convergence

Project manager's responsibilities

- To keep an open mind about which kinds of technology can be used to deliver whatever interactive application is under discussion
- To be aware of the emerging convergent platforms and their capabilities
- To take note of regulatory issues that emerge for the development of convergent applications
- To raise your own and others' awareness of the business challenges that converging media pose

■ What is convergence?

It has become increasingly difficult to find a single word or phrase to encapsulate new media as it stands now. The term 'new media' itself is problematic since 'new' redefines itself continuously. When the first edition of this book was published in 1996 it was quite clear that all this 'new stuff' we were doing on CD-ROMs, kiosks and the Internet was multimedia. However, to many people producing websites, and with no background in other media, multimedia is something you include in a web page like a video or an animation. Ironically, as the word was depreciating in one section of the industry it was being increasingly used by telecommunications companies (usually abbreviated to telcos) and broadcasters to describe the new kinds of computer-based services they were planning and delivering.

But while one buzzword was disappearing, a new one was emerging: convergence. When people talk about convergence in new media, they usually refer to the combining of personal computers, telecommunications and broadcast television. Including, or adding, the Web just about defines the key state of new media as we pursue it at the moment. In an alternative definition the essence of convergence is the ability to produce an interactive application once and be able to deliver it on all the media in the convergent group including the Web. I mention this definition in order to say that I believe this to be an element of convergence – something we sensibly aspire to – but not the core. More on this in a moment.

The most important part of this convergence is the role played by computers. Many devices now include microprocessors; ranging from vehicles to ticket machines, washing machines to microwave ovens, telephones to televisions. Once you realize how ubiquitous the microprocessor has become, you see how we no longer think of computers as being used to control things. They are now an integral and invisible part of the devices themselves. This is especially true where the devices themselves are digital: digital phones or digital televisions for example. Here the computer has as much access to the digital information as it has to the controls. To follow the McLuhan formula, the medium and the message become indistinguishable.

Convergence also recognizes that even though a sizeable minority of people have a computer in their homes, almost everyone (in the developed world) has a television and a telephone. It may be that by definition, convergent information technology spreads by stealth; disguised as something we already have and use every day.

There is the second use of the term in new media, and that is to refer to systems that are independent of the hardware or infrastructure they use. So a piece of convergent software would be equally at home on a mobile telephone or interactive television as on a computer. A good example of this point of view is Java. The Java computer language was designed so that a Java program would be able to run in many environments with little, if any, customization. In fact the original intention was for Java, or Oak as it was first called, to be a language specifically for convergence. The team at Sun who developed it tried to market it to makers of set-top boxes; but there was no interest at the time.

■ What does convergence mean to end-users?

One view, expressed in a PricewaterhouseCoopers analysis of convergence, is that the end-user – the consumer – is driving convergence. How might that happen?

Convenience is one factor. Why should we carry a telephone, a radio and a music player with us when we can carry a single device that does all three? You can already buy mobile phones that contain an FM radio or an MP3 audio player. It is significant that a radio-cassette player is not generally regarded as an example of convergence – perhaps because the two forms are 'old-fashioned' analogue and have been paired up since before the digital revolution – while adding a telephone into the mix now would be definitely convergent.

Another factor is expanded capabilities. A multichannel television with a powerful computer can not only record programmes for you to watch at another time but it could also learn your viewing habits and record programmes without the need for you to program it. The set would know what is available because it has access to the programme schedules, through the electronic programme guide, and because the programmes would be tagged with metadata which labels their content. This set could also respond to a request like 'What can I watch now?' or 'Are there any good movies on?'

A survey (published in 2001) in the USA and UK by Pace, who make set-top boxes, found that the two most annoying things about television programmes are that they are on while you are not at home to watch them and that you are interrupted while viewing. These would seem to be strong motivations for an intelligent approach to time-shifting of programmes. The American company TiVo were the first to market this kind of set-top box, called a personal video recorder (PVR). The boxes gather information about the viewing habits of users in order to predict and suggest programmes. There has been concern about the privacy implications of such kinds of information gathering. In essence, is the box working for you to help you with your viewing, or working to provide marketing information for the set-top box manufacturer?

Thirdly, convergence offers new opportunities and possibilities for markets and devices that currently do not exist and are sometimes difficult to imagine: which makes market research difficult.

Easy and/or automatic access to information can be achieved through devices that do not appear to be computers. An elevator in a building could give you a weather forecast if it detects that you are heading for the exit. Your shoes could give you directions when you go for a walk. Your refrigerator could check on the food inside and order replacements or warn you if some is out of date. It would be connected to the Internet in order to communicate. Actually this is not so futuristic. The web-fridge already exists and at least one US drinks company uses the Internet to monitor stocks in its vending machines.

End-users may be resistant to this. A UK car manufacturer added voice reminders for things like fastening seat belts and turning lights off. Owners were so annoyed with the reminders that most of them asked for the voice to be turned off. This suggests that the new capabilities will not necessarily be welcomed by everybody. However, it will always take time for new things to be accepted.

Other issues that bubble to the surface whenever convergence between consumer appliances like televisions and computers is discussed, are reliability and longevity. A crystal radio set constructed in the 1920s could still receive today's AM radio stations. A suitable television set from the 1940s could receive transmissions today (in black and white). There is nothing in computing that even approaches such a longevity and the computer market seems to thrive on its built-in obsolescence. The consumer market moves much more slowly than the computer world. It isn't unusual for people to use television sets that date back to the 1980s. The computer I used then has long since been thrown away. This attitude is partly because a 'machine' that is made out of software, like a word processor, is easily changed. Within some limits you can keep your hardware the same and change the software but eventually even that tactic will fail to keep up with the relentless march

of computer progress as new applications need new versions of the operating system and the new operating system needs new hardware.

We could debate for hours on whether convergence means a computer in your television (hence in your living room) or a TV receiver card in your computer (which would probably be in another room entirely). Later in this book we will also consider the differences in the ways the two devices work and how people use them. In time these issues may become meaningless. Twenty years ago, when you had a telephone installed, you probably had to decide where it would be. Would it be in the living room or perhaps the hallway? Now it is much easier to have more than one phone socket and move the phone about. More likely you will have a cordless phone in the house. By analogy, this suggests that in time we will not be concerned about where the convergent devices are since they will be moveable. They'll be small enough and/or light enough to go where we want them rather than make us go to them.

■ How do the convergent parts fit together?

Historically, the three parts of the convergence have been treated differently by governments: telecommunications, by now well over 150 years old, started out as an adjunct to postal services, offering increased speed of text messages. Most countries mandated their mail services to handle telegraphy and then telephony and the large investment needed to lay cables was seen as a role of central government or of large companies given monopolies to build infrastructure. In time, as the electronic services came of age, many split from the mail but often they are still controlled by government, directly or indirectly. In many cases, and certainly in Europe, the regulation of telephony now aims to prevent former monopolies from continuing to control the telephone infrastructure and so impeding competition and/or the growth of new services.

Similarly with broadcasting: here governments wished to exercise control over the sparse resources of the radio spectrum. With a general pattern of state broadcasting giving way to mixtures of state and independent broadcasters – some commercial and some not – governments have worked internationally to control access to the airwaves but locally their prime target has been content.

The computer industry, of which the Internet is a part, has been lightly regulated, if at all. The Internet is legendary as a frontier of freedom; its roots firmly in the freedom of speech enjoyed in America and the open exchange of ideas prevalent in academic circles. This background to the Internet has often clashed with its commercial use and, in the long term, another convergence will be between those two seeming opposites.

Converging the three – telecommunication, broadcasting and computers – leads to regulatory anomalies and curiosities. When, for example, is an Internet connection a simple transfer of files and when is it a cable transmission of content? How do you reconcile copyright laws based on the production of physical books or sound recordings with the instant transfer of digital files on the Internet? Nicholas Negroponte, head of the MIT Media Lab and a long-standing guru of the technological revolution, asserts, in his book *Being Digital*, that as copyright is a reactive process it will probably have to break down completely before it can come up to date.

Coincidentally, it was Negroponte who also pointed out that convergence is happening at the same time as a shift between wired and wireless technologies. Many of the things that we used to consider wireless, such as entertainment broadcasting, are becoming wired (i.e. cabled) while many traditionally wired domains, such as computer networking and telephones, are becoming increasingly wireless. This changes the way we think about things: for example a telephone number now increasingly represents a person rather than a place because we increasingly carry our phones with us and keep numbers when we move.

■ And the rest

Another aspect of convergence is that the convergent industries are going to beg, steal or borrow technologies and processes from each other. We are already seeing examples of this as wired and wireless technologies interchange and as multimedia – audiovisual content – gets onto web pages.

It will go further than this. Telcos are developing software applications called mobile agents which can be programmed to carry out autonomous tasks and sent off into computers in a network to carry them out. The telcos have a problem of a huge interconnected machine – the phone network, which is arguably the most complex machine built by mankind – and how to maintain it. Autonomous mobile agents can do this. For the rest of us an agent can carry out our instructions to do a wide range of tasks, just like a real life, say, travel agent might do. If we don't want to stay connected, or can't for some reason, then we can ask an agent to go off and do research for us and report back when we next log on. Greg Bear, in his science fiction novel *EON*, describes a future civilization where people often empower what are called 'partials' to do things for them. Since these people often travel in image rather than in person it can be difficult to know whether you are dealing with the partial (agent) or the real thing. You go on vacation and your agent carries on doing your job for you.

Another function for agents is in an area like video-on-demand and even broadcasting, where as more and more choice is available it will become increasingly difficult to follow all the possible programmes. This might lead us to stick with a small number of channels, as we might do in buying one newspaper over another. Alternatively we might allow our set-top box to learn our preferences and select programming for us. This is already being done with personal video recorders (as described earlier) which make use of your viewing habits and can match this against the programme guide to record and offer you things to watch. (See also the chapter on types of interactive TV: Chapter 3 in this book.) It is but a small step from that to empowering the agent to negotiate and pay for movies and other pay-per-view programmes we might want to watch. You might be able to buy personality scheduling agents so that your viewing choice gets off to a good start. Ironically, once you do this, you are coming back to the idea of selecting one television station and watching it, but again the agent will continue to learn and evolve following rules it learns.

■ How will convergence affect businesses?

Changes in technology usually lead to new business opportunities, and often entire new businesses. These will go through several stages in the way they operate. Thirty years ago there were no video shops and no mobile telephone shops and records were usually sold in electrical stores. In a further twenty years you might imagine what new retail outlets there may be.

Despite initial reluctance, and fear of fraud, the Internet has become a popular place to shop. The Pace report found that 41% of those surveyed in the USA had purchased goods or services using either a computer or television. In the UK the figure was 23%.

The PricewaterhouseCoopers report points out that consolidation, where like players worked together, was the phenomenon of the 1980s and early 1990s. In the early 2000s the trend is for complementary players to converge.

Business will find new opportunities as a result of new activities and new ways to do old activities. New supply chains and channels to customers will emerge, and increasingly consumers will trade with other consumers on a worldwide basis.

Of course consumer to consumer trading (C2C) has existed for many years in the form of jumble sales, car boot sales, rummage sales, yard sales and so on, and small ads in shop windows and local newspapers, but this has mainly been a trade in used goods. Everyone can have the opportunity to create something and it is especially easy to trade if your goods and your channel are both electronic. One example of C2C trading is the Internet auction website (of which the best known is the American eBay) but many people have their own website to promote and often sell their wares as if

they were operating a craft stall at a local market. Of course it is difficult to draw a line between B2C (business to consumer trading) and C2C with something like a small craft website, but the key point here is that the operation can be very small and ad hoc in a way that a bricks and mortar business cannot. Online businesses are sometimes referred to as clicks and mortar. The biggest barrier to doing business online is probably collecting the money. Fortunately as consumers have come to accept buying online, so have banks. It gets continually easier to get a merchant account to take credit cards on your website and many ISPs offer packages for setting up shops which include links to merchant services. Credit card companies are also going out of their way to reassure card-holders that the Internet is not such a risky place to shop and remind their customers that, in the case of fraud, the card company will bear the risk, not the individual customer. This presumably is a recognition that an online shop is no more likely to be a source of fraud than a restaurant in the high street or local mall.

The PayPal service, set up in the USA, takes the merchant account idea and strips away most of the formality. Anyone can register their credit card with PayPal and then not only pay money but also receive it. In this way someone without a merchant account can receive payments online and this has become one popular way to pay for auction wins. On a small scale PayPal has no charges for the transactions. In general, receiving money costs money and this ranges from 1% for a standard merchant account with a large turnover to as much as 8% or more for a bureau account.

One risk of all this convergence is the danger of reinventing the wheel and designing it to be square. An example of what might be inappropriate convergence would be streaming radio into a mobile telephone and forgetting that radio already exists. The obvious answer to this is to ask what features audio streaming has that radio does not: interactivity, extra information and a wide international choice of sources are three possibilities.

In this book we will explore some of the technologies in the convergent media and the basic techniques with which you produce programs for them. Much of this is new and so we will not be going into specific detail about how to produce, say, an interactive TV programme or a location-aware mobile application. But we can show you the directions that these things may take. The next few chapters explore the main features of the technologies and how you might work with them, then we go on to look at the key asset types you will use in convergent media, and in new media as a whole.

In producing an interactive project you may have the challenge of producing it for more than one of the convergent platforms, or you might have to choose which is most appropriate, either as the client or as the developer. Ideally, each converging technology is enhanced by the convergence and so there will be new business opportunities in that technology. In some cases a completely new opportunity will arise as a result of the convergence. The impact of the convergence can be greater than the sum of its parts.

THEORY INTO PRACTICE 1

Think of a profession – dentistry for example.

1. Try to predict a use of convergent technology that would be beneficial for the professionals.

2. Try to predict a fun but probably implausible piece of convergence for the same set of professionals.

■ Summary

- Convergence = the combining of PCs, telecommunications and broadcast TV.
- Convergent software is designed to work across the converging delivery platforms.
- Convergence offers convenience, expanded capabilities and new opportunities.
- Consumers take time to adjust to innovation.
- Converging technologies throw up regulatory anomalies.
- Convergent industries will use techniques and processes from each other.
- Convergent technologies will affect business supply chains and all that this implies.

■ Recommended reading

Sun Microsystems website for Java is at
http://java.sun.com and a brief history of the project is at
http://java.sun.com/nav/whatis/storyofjava.html
(there are other accounts on the same website and links elsewhere as well)

The Pace Report 2001 – Consumer attitudes towards digital television – is published by Pace Micro Technology plc, Victoria Road, Saltaire, Shipley, West Yorkshire, BD18 3LF, United Kingdom. A summary is available on the Web at
http://www.pace.co.uk/documents/PR/pacereport01.pdf

PricewaterhouseCoopers report on the six forces affecting business, including convergence at number one, is at
http://www.pwcglobal.com/sixforces/PwC_html/index.html

Negroponte, N. (1995) *Being Digital*. Westminster, MD: Knopf

The Internet

Project manager's responsibilities

- When setting up a website make sure the domain name has been chosen and registered correctly

- Confirm that the server can serve the types of assets (graphics, audio, etc.) included in the web pages

- If you are non-technical, know enough about the mechanics of the Internet to help communicate with the technical members of your team and your clients

- Act as intermediary representing any concerns and issues of the technical personnel to the client

- Be aware of the trends and risks to help guide your decisions

■ The Internet: Why? What? When? Who?

Networks are almost as old as computing itself. Before personal computers became widespread, most computers were operated using remote terminals connected to mainframe or mini-computers. A typical mainframe, occupying a whole room and typified by the huge machines beloved of movie makers in the 1960s, featured numerous cabinets, each with a different function: processors, memory, disk units, tape drives and so on. These parts of the computer had to be networked together.

A mainframe from the 1960s also featured a number of terminals which could be used simultaneously. Initially they were teletypes – basically electric typewriters – and then they became screens and keyboards. This combination became known as a terminal. In some cases the terminals were in different buildings to the computer, although the connection was always on a one-to-one basis with a long wire linking each terminal to the computer.

J.C.R Licklider at MIT is credited with first envisaging what he called the 'Galactic Network' concept – interconnected computers through which anyone could quickly access data and programs from anywhere in the world – in a series of memos written in August 1962. Within three months of writing up his concept, Licklider became the first head of the computer research program at DARPA (Defense Advanced Research Projects Agency) and his vision undoubtedly influenced his colleagues and successors in the organization. By the early 1970s, DARPA's predecessor, ARPA, had been behind a program to link together research computers around the USA, in order to make better use of what was then a scarce and expensive resource. This network was also designed to be connected up in such a way that losing a single connection (or even several connections) would not close things down because another route could be found between any two machines. This coincidentally made the network less vulnerable to deliberate sabotage or attack.

ARPANET – now wound down – was the result of this initiative and it was an internet: an *inter*connected *net*work. The protocols that were eventually used for traffic on the network, allowing files to move around the network intertwined with each other and to control how a file was routed from one machine to another, were the basis of the TCP/IP (Transmission Control Protocol/Internet Protocol) system used today. ARPANET's ghost lingers however, and occasionally Internet log files will show visits from the .arpa top level domain. These machines are used to map IP (Internet Protocol) addresses back to domain names, which you might want to do to identify visitors to your website in log files.

The National Science Foundation took over funding of the Internet backbone in 1988 and replaced the ARPANET with NSFNET. In the mid-1990s the backbone changed again, and is now a commercial operation run by commercial telecommunications companies (telcos) spreading into most of the countries of the world.

So who owns and controls this Internet? Undoubtedly different organizations 'own' the infrastructure on which the Internet exists. But if one of them disappeared the traffic would find another way to travel because the Internet is multi-connected. The Internet is not even like the world's telephone network, because the users don't even need to know which country their target is in. The domain name is all you need and the Internet systems do the rest. So although some organizations have responsibility for the numbers and names used on the Internet, the Internet itself has no centre, no administration and no owner.

■ Connecting a computer to the Internet

The Internet is 'out there' just like the worldwide telephone network. To make use of it you connect to it and use your computer to 'talk' (using the TCP/IP protocol) to other computers on the network. You have to have a unique IP address, which is the Internet's equivalent of the phone number. But how do you connect? Before we look at the role of the Internet service provider (ISP) and the use of domain names and other such paraphernalia we should look at the physical practicalities. Basically there are two kinds of Internet connection: dial-up and 'always-on'.

A dial-up connection means just that: you connect to the Internet by dialling into it using a telephone or ISDN line – Integrated Services Digital Network. If it's a phone line, a modem is used at both ends of the connection, and this translates the digital computer data into an analogue signal so it can go through the telephone system. Modem stands for modulate-demodulate. A fax machine works in the same way. But modems have limits on speed and even though ingenuity has lifted modem speeds up to around 50 kilobits per second we are probably getting to the limits of such methods. Modems are very susceptible to 'noise' and other imperfections on the line. In addition to this, telephone companies are usually using sophisticated techniques to maximize their bandwidth and this may conflict with what the modem (or indeed a fax) may need to work at its best. A digital ISDN dial-up connection will be more reliable and the process of establishing the Internet connection will be faster, but per channel you still only get 56 or 64 kilobits. It is possible to link channels together to increase speed but this usually counts as more than one call and is charged accordingly.

Increasingly people are connected to the Internet through a continuous link, rather than dialling up. Most companies with networks of their own will have a link over a private data connection. But cable modems, satellite and DSL (digital subscriber line or loop) are more recent options. Now we are getting into broadband territory with data rates in megabits available at – and this is the important part – quite low cost. We are talking about tens of dollars or pounds a month for this kind of connection and, because it is always on, there are no call charges. Unfortunately the lower costs mean that the telcos could see themselves losing money as a result of people moving away from dial-up and, when you add regulatory restrictions into the mix, you can see that the rollout of consumer-oriented broadband at low cost is not going to have a smooth ride everywhere.

Satellite broadband works by having a connection from the Internet to you through a direct satellite link to your computer via your satellite receiver dish. You would use a phone call or something similar to provide the connection from you to the Internet so then you'd receive the data back from the Internet via the fast satellite link. This can work virtually any-where and it will eventually be possible to dispense with the non-satellite part of the loop.

Cable modems are provided along with television and telephony services by many cable operators. Of course the cable has to go past your door, but in many parts of the world it does. Even though the potential bandwidth is high you will be sharing that with everyone else on your cable.

The most common form of DSL is ADSL (A for asymmetrical) and works by piggybacking the broadband data channel onto an ordinary copper tele-phone line. Within a few kilometres of the exchange you can get data rates up to two megabits from the Internet and half a megabit back. This doesn't interfere with the telephone so you can still make calls. Your ADSL operator, who may either be your telco or an intermediary buying in bulk from your telco, may share each connection between several people. This is what is called the contention ratio and if the ratio is 10 then there are up to nine other users competing with you for the two megabits.

There are other ways of connecting, for example you might pay for a permanent wired connection (known as a leased line), especially if you are a medium or large company in an urban area. There are wireless connec-tions using the services of a mobile phone operator (see Chapter 4) or even neighbourhood wireless networks using wireless LAN (local area network) cards and base stations. One important thing to remember about all of these systems (except the neighbourhood wireless one) is that they will be pro-vided commercially by an operator. This means that whatever is technically possible will always be filtered through business and marketing decisions and the service offering will change on a regular basis. So if you have an Internet connection you need to continuously review it. Neighbourhood wireless LAN can work by neighbours informally grouping together to share a single broadband connection, but this is actually illegal in some parts of the world since it can be interpreted as setting up a telecommunications network and therefore needs to be licensed.

Now we're wired up, let's look at the Internet connection from a systems viewpoint.

Connecting a computer to the Internet requires that the machine has a unique identifying number which 'places' it on the Internet, called its IP address. These addresses, which are numbers made up of four one-byte numbers separated by dots (such as 172.32.23.1), are allocated by a small group of organizations of which the main three are the American Registry of Internet Numbers (ARIN), The Asia-Pacific Network Information Center (APNIC) and Réseaux IP Européens (RIPE) who 'carve up' the world's IP addresses between them and sometimes delegate for individual countries. So you get the numbers from ARIN, APNIC or RIPE as appropriate. The possible number combinations used at present for IP addresses are large but finite and the system will eventually have to be updated.

You will probably connect to the Internet through an Internet service provider (ISP) who will themselves have a fast connection (fat pipe) to the Internet at large – known as the Internet Backbone – and they will give you a set of IP addresses for use on your network. In an organization which is already on the Internet, the IT manager will probably allocate IP addresses to individual machines from the list that the company has been given.

If you were Imaginaryco's IT manager and you wanted to put Imaginaryco on the Internet – and the .com domain was where you wanted to put it – then you'd contact a Domain Name Registrar for the .com domain (or one of their resellers on the many websites offering domain name services), see if the domain imaginaryco.com was available and, if it was, pay to register it. If you were in the UK you might prefer to go for the domain imaginaryco.co.uk or perhaps imaginaryco.fr if you were in France, because there are top level domains (TLDs) for countries as well. Historically US organizations have used the generic top level domains such as .com, .org and .net. This reflects the start of the Internet in the USA. The TLDs .edu, .mil and .gov are reserved for the US education, military and government although non-US organizations can register names in the others, and often do if they want to appear to be international. Incidentally, there is a .int TLD, but this is reserved for bodies set up by international treaty such as the European Union.

Different top level domains have different registrars. The .com domain actually has several registrars. Once the domain imaginaryco.com has been registered the computers on the Imaginaryco network can be named.

When you register a domain name you need to check that you are recorded as owner of the domain. For .com domains a check on www.whois.net will tell you. It has been known for some domain name registration resellers to leave their names as owners instead of changing it to the buyer's. This can cause a problem if you want to move the domain between ISPs because it appears that you are not the real owner.

All the allocation of IP addresses, domain names and Internet protocols is carried out under the auspices of the Internet Corporation for Assigned Names and Numbers (ICANN). This is a non-profit corporation that was formed to assume responsibility for the IP address space allocation and domain names, among other things. ICANN have an ultimate authority over certain aspects of the Internet and it is they, for example, who are responsible for creating new top level domain names to go along with the current ones. This process started in 2001 with the addition of the .biz and .info domains, and more will follow.

To sort out the domain name for a particular computer you look 'outwards' towards the Internet. If you work for Imaginaryco and their Internet domain is called imaginaryco.com and you want to add a machine called 'Bilbo' to their network you would ask Imaginaryco's IT manager to arrange this. The IT manager would set up the DNS (domain name server – of which more later) that effectively told the world at which IP address the machine bilbo.imaginaryco.com lived.

As long as your machine is the only one in imaginaryco.com to have the name then you can call it what you like. A computer used as a web server is usually called www for World Wide Web (which makes sense) but it doesn't have to be. You will sometimes see websites which have domain names that don't begin www. The World Wide Web uses a system called a Uniform Resource Locator (URL) which (in an absolute URL) consists of the domain name for the relevant machine together with the protocol being used. In our example this would be http:// which defines the protocol used (others might be ftp:// or mailto:) and www.imaginaryco.com which is our machine name. The URL can include more information like a path down to an actual web page, the file extension and occasionally there is an extra number which denotes which computer software 'port' is requested. The default port for a web server is 80 but others could be used. So the full URL might look like http://www.imaginaryco.com/sales/prices.html:8080 which says that this web server is on a different port to the normal 80. Unless you want to run more than one web server on a particular machine (or you are an IT specialist) you shouldn't need to worry about port numbers.

As an aside, you find interesting names on computers on the Internet. The IT people at ebay.com seem to be Star Trek: Deep Space Nine fans since they have machines named Garak, Kira and Keiko on their network. I know this because I looked at the route e-mails took from them to me and they passed through those machines. You need to remember that any Internet machine name might be seen by other people. (I am not really a Hobbit freak: Bilbo was just an example.)

So now you have your machine set up, connected to the Internet and ready to roll at its brand new domain name. If it's a web server you will have tried to find a domain name that best represents the website. This could be the company name as in the Imaginaryco example but you might have a more generic website name. You can probably guess what you'll see when you go to www.carp.org without me telling you.

■ Setting up a website

Let's look at what is involved in setting up the website itself. This chapter won't discuss how to produce the pages but it will cover the basics of getting a server and setting up the files to make up the site.

There are three choices for setting up the site. You can use a computer of your own on your own premises (as outlined above), you can co-locate your own computer at the premises of an ISP (or someone else with a good Internet connection) or you can rent space on an ISP's server. As far as your visitors are concerned these options can look exactly the same so the decisions about where to put the site are managerial and technical issues you, as project manager, have to address.

A web server is actually a computer program which accepts requests for web pages from the Internet (using a protocol called Hypertext Transfer Protocol or HTTP) and serves pages, graphics, Flash animations, videos and so on back as a result. It will also deal with requests to run other programs on the server for more specialized tasks. A web server can run on almost any computer but many of the world's websites are hosted on computers using the Unix operating system and many of those use a web server called Apache. One reason for this is that Apache is free, but it is still a very reliable and powerful web server. A common server for PCs is Microsoft's IIS (Internet Information Server) and the best-known server for Macs is WebStar.

There are others. Internet Product Watch listed 96 different servers and server-related software at the time of writing.

Web Site Construction Kit.

A static website – one which consists basically of linked HTML (Hypertext Markup Language) pages – sits on the server like a bit of a hard disk directory structure. That's because that is exactly how it is set up. The server will define which directory is the root of the website and everything on the site sits below that. The server also defines the default filename. This is the one you get if you don't type an actual filename (ending in .html for example) in the URL. This is usually index.html or default.html (or .htm) but some web servers will allow you to specify any filename as the default.

Bear in mind that if you don't have a file in a directory with the default name then visitors may see a complete listing of files in that directory instead. Visitors will also see the directory structure and file path when they select a page so you shouldn't name directories and files in a way that might cause embarrassment to you or your client.

The filenames on the website can be the same as the ones on your computer but you should consider a couple of issues.

If you have a PC or Mac then your filing system will treat upper or lower case in the file path, directory and filenames as being identical. PCs and Macs are case-insensitive and treat ABC as being identical to abc. The Unix filing system used on many web servers is case-sensitive (ABC is different to abc) and you will risk broken links if you don't take great care about this because if the filing system is case-sensitive then the URLs on that server will be case-sensitive as well. It is a good idea to always use lower case in the paths on a website and you can do this on your hard disk version as well. The case of filenames used in links is one of the easiest ways to break a site when moving it from your own machine to its final home on a server.

Some characters are not 'legal' in web requests and the most commonly used one is a space. The Internet should translate spaces into the characters %20 (because 20 is the ASCII code for a space) but it is better to avoid spaces altogether. To be safe stick to a–z, 0–9 and an underscore character '_' which you can use to simulate a space if you want a filename to be easier to read. Don't put an underscore in a URL you publish in print as most users will make a mistake with it. Other characters like hyphens are also legitimate and you will find many domain names with hyphens in them. However, some characters like =, +, $ and ? are used in passing variables to other programs running on the server, / and : are file path delimiters and the tilde '~' is used to refer to home page space in Unix so these can cause trouble. If in doubt stick to the basics.

A small website can be built using static HTML but as the site grows it will become increasingly difficult to manage. A large dynamic site (like a news one for instance) uses a database to build pages on-the-fly for visitors. The database holds the text, images and other resources. The journalists use a form in which they enter the text of a story. They might choose a page layout from a number of templates and they might specify an image or video that goes with the story. The database program would then build the page for the story each time the story was requested by the server and send it to the viewer. This is one aspect of a content management system. To the visitor this looks exactly the same as if the page was created statically with HTML.

The standard which connects the web server to an external program is called the Common Gateway Interface and so these programs are sometimes called CGIs. The language Perl is a popular mechanism for programming CGIs and is freely supported on most computer platforms. Since it is closely linked with Unix, Perl had a head start on many servers but its popularity has waned.

Server Side Includes (SSI) and systems like PHP, JSP and Microsoft's Active Server Pages (ASP) are now more commonly used to generate dynamic pages because they are more tightly integrated in the server software. This avoids an overhead where a program like Perl has to start up before being able to work. (The monthly Security Space survey of web servers, which looks at three million servers on the World Wide Web, determined in mid-2001 that the Apache web server was in use on about half of the sites and in those PHP was the most popular extension.) In these cases the page template appears to be an HTML file but with special tags. As the server-side scripting language parses the page, it replaces the tags with dynamic content as required. This can be as simple as calling up commonly used sub-pages of static HTML, like a menu bar, so that this code doesn't have to be included in every page. At this level, dynamic pages make site maintenance and updating easier. If necessary they can still link to another program, such as a relational database, to call up content. While web pages made of static HTML will end in extensions .htm or .html you can get a clue as to what other systems are being used from other file extensions in URLs, such as asp, dll, php, jsp and so on.

If the pages include JavaScript or some other client-side (browser) code together with HTML and server-side inclusions then what seems to be a single web page can be dynamically built from three or more sources simultaneously. We'll look at the client–server relationship in websites more closely in Chapter 5 of this book, *Platform parameters*.

When a website is being built, pages will need to link to each other. This can be done by including the full URL as the link address but it is usually better to show URLs relative to the page with the link. This means that when the site is moved elsewhere (as it inevitably will be) the internal links will still work. Obviously links outside the site still need the full (or absolute) URL. Less obviously, links in pages built by CGI programs might also need absolute rather than relative links. This is because the browser works out the whole path for a relative link based on where it thinks the current page is. If it thinks the current page is in a CGI directory then the links are unlikely to work correctly. From time to time it is possible for a browser to make mistakes with its paths, especially if it is running out of memory. This issue is dealt with more fully in Chapter 9, *Integration*, in this book.

There is also a more generic term URI which stands for Uniform Resource Identifier. A URL is a special case of a URI and since the difference between the two is rather esoteric, for most of us the term will be URL.

The web server needs to be configured to serve different kinds of content in the appropriate way. A browser doesn't necessarily use the file extension to determine how to handle something: it should also look at the Multipurpose Internet Mail Extension (MIME) type which is included in the header of the file the server sends back. Browsers are notoriously inconsistent in this and to be safe the extension and the MIME type must match. Incorrect MIME types can result in pages that won't display properly and are especially problematic with database-driven sites where the database has to specify the MIME types as it builds the page.

When a new kind of file is added to a web page it is important that the web server knows how to describe it in this header. This is part of the configuration of the server. If not, the file will probably be treated as text and if the file is actually an MP3 music file then you can see that it just won't work and the browser will display a page of gibberish.

MIME was originally specified to handle encoding of attachments to e-mails, as you might guess from the name. Some MIME examples: image/gif, video/quicktime, and text/html.

Other server configurations can be basic ones like the default file name described above or it can be setting different pages to be displayed depending on the language the browser wants to use. This in turn would have been set in the user's preferences for the browser and, by default, is usually set for English. Finally, the server logging will need to be configured so that the information you want will be recorded for later analysis.

■ Scalability

Websites can be victims of their own success and if your site is going to receive thousands of hits it needs a different technical design approach to that of a simple server. This extends to every aspect of the system: the link to the Internet backbone, the number of computers used, the amount of disk storage, the server software and the middleware or gateway (CGI) techniques.

This goes beyond 'mere' load balancing between machines, where a number of separate computers work together sharing the load on the website. The system will need to take into account the overhead involved in serving pages and executing the searches (or whatever) required to build a dynamic page. Server software will need to be able to execute many transactions simultaneously, ideally as threads of the one server process rather than by spawning many processes – because it's faster and more responsive. The links to any commercial transaction system need to be efficient and the programs may need to be written using optimized fast code using, say, Java rather than interpreted Perl scripts. At a much simpler level, image download times can contribute to scaling difficulties.

The difficulty with scalability is that you can get swamped by a sudden wave of traffic to a website. New media developers coming into the world of

Stress Testing.

television can find the speed of response and sheer numbers involved very surprising. But if you think about it, if millions of people are seeing a plug for a web URL at the end of a top-rated show then a significant number of them will attempt to go to the site within a very short period of time and this can make many web servers fall over.

If there's any risk of this then the server should be stress tested. This can be done by writing a suitable program which impersonates one or more web browsers and users doing things like looking at pages, entering passwords, clicking on links and doing their online shopping. Run many of these on many machines and you can give the site a hard test. There are companies who will stress test websites with prices into hundreds of thousands of dollars: but they would argue that this is better value than seeing your mission-critical shopping site go down under a heavy load. For smaller solutions, vendors like Microsoft (who have a free Microsoft Web Application Stress Tool for IIS) provide software so you can do it yourself and there is a Java-based tester called Jmeter provided by the Apache web server project. Clearly this kind of testing should be done before the site goes live for real.

These issues of site size, type of page and scalability affect all the decisions that your programmers need to make about how to organize and develop the applications for a client. It is questions around these issues that your technical analyst or equivalent would need to raise as an extra part of the analysis for a scoping questionnaire when getting to grips with a new project for a new client (see Book 1 Chapter 3, *Scoping*).

■ DNS and other initials

Back in 1965, when researchers connected computers in Massachusetts and California together over a telephone line for the first time, identifying the machines was not an issue. But today we have millions of machines on the network. To recap, IP addresses are used to uniquely identify a machine and these take the form known as dotted-quads, like 123.231.12.23, and if the user of the machine wants to access another, the first machine has to know what the IP address of the other one is. IP addresses are the telephone numbers of the network.

Clearly these IP address numbers are not very friendly and so machines are named instead. A distributed database called the Domain Name System (DNS) holds a lookup table that maps IP addresses to domain names so you can find the IP address when you start from the domain name. A complete machine domain name – one that uniquely identifies it – is known as the fully qualified domain name (FQDN). So, .com is a domain but mailhost.imaginaryco.com, which identifies a mail server computer at the imaginary company Imaginaryco, is an FQDN. But for simplicity let's just call it the domain name.

If you make a request for another machine you will either know its IP address or (more likely) you will know its domain name: you don't need to know where it is physically. (In fact, at the time of writing there is only one server on the whole Internet which will tell you where a domain name is physically/geographically.)

Each computer on the Internet (with its own IP address) will have a gateway to the Internet. It will also know another machine's IP address where domain names can be translated into IP addresses. This is the address of the domain name server (also sometimes known as the DNS). So if someone wants to connect to mailhost.imaginaryco.com what happens, in simplistic terms, is that their computer will first ask its local domain name server to supply the IP address that corresponds to mailhost.imaginaryco.com. The server will probably do this by first asking the name server that holds information for .com for the coordinates of the name server for imaginaryco. When it is told this it will ask imaginaryco's name server for the address of mailhost. The DNS then passes mailhost's IP address to the computer that made the request in the first place and it will be able to make its own connection to, in this case, send some mail. The Internet is so large that it is not practical for every DNS to know where everything is, and also ruggedness criteria mean that there is always more than one DNS available to each user and more than one server that has the data for each domain. In fact there will be a large number of servers which have information about the larger domains like .com and they will be synchronized and updated regularly. It is the time taken for this information to reach all the servers that limits the speed with which a domain can be set up or moved.

If you have a network connected to the Internet you can have your own DNS machine which will store information about the machines on your network and also about other computers that your network regularly contacts. You could also delegate your DNS to your ISP, and many smaller networks will do this.

■ We know where you live!

The 'fountain of all knowledge' about a domain is known as the Start of Authority (SOA) and this is the DNS computer which has the authoritative record of the IP addresses for the domain name. The authoritative record for a particular computer is called its A record. So in the case of our Imaginaryco example, the SOA might be called dns.imaginaryco.com and this computer would know about every machine on Imaginaryco's network connected to the Internet.

However, the A record that says where a domain name is can point outside the local network and this can be useful when a domain is moved and its IP has to change. This happens more often than you might think: servers move from one location to another or the management of a website changes. To move the domain from one network to another the relevant DNS records have to be changed for both networks. This can take time as the changed information is passed around the DNS computers. A useful shortcut is to modify the A record on the original SOA DNS machine to re-route the connections until the new SOA information works its way around the Internet. One other thing that the SOA record contains is the MX record. The MX identifies the computer that will accept mail for the domain. In the case of imaginaryco.com, the MX record would point to something like mailhost.imaginaryco.com.

There are special reserved blocks of numbers which are never allowed to be on the 'real' Internet: these can be used on your own internal network. They are:

10.0.0.0	to	10.255.255.255
172.16.0.0	to	172.31.255.255
192.168.0.0	to	192.168.255.255

and you can use numbers in these groups without reference to anyone else outside your own closed network. You don't have to use these numbers if you have been allocated enough IP addresses by ICANN but using them will give more flexibility. Incidentally, a closed network which uses all the protocols and programs of the Internet but is not necessarily connected to it is known as an intranet.

So can your closed network with these reserved IP addresses connect to the Internet? It can by going through a gateway router that uses Network Address Translation (NAT) and which will hide your network's addresses from the world outside. The Internet only sees the router, not the network behind it. One advantage of this technique is that whole networks can be hidden behind a single IP address, which saves using up numbers. (Another way this is done is by dynamically allocating IP addresses to machines when they connect to the network and this is usually done by dial-up ISPs and on many private networks.) Using NAT is one way of implementing a firewall, which is a computer which acts as a gatekeeper to keep intruders out of your network.

When one machine connects with another on the Internet it will usually be asking for a transaction using a particular protocol and/or at a particular port. In this case a port is an abstract software concept to help with the management of Internet traffic. The port number is one of a standard group including things like HTTP (for web pages) on Port 80 or a DNS enquiry on Port 53 and these are called 'Well Known Ports'. A firewall or NAT router can be programmed to route requests for specific ports to particular machines on the closed network. It could, for example, route requests for Port 80 to a machine that operates as a web server.

Every machine on the Internet has to have a unique IP address, although not every one has a name. Of course, if it has a name then you can pin it down to a company or at least an ISP. Most ISPs (but not all) allocate casual users an IP address when they log on, so it is not possible to pin down the individual machine in this case. If the surfer is routed through another computer then it is the IP of this machine that you will see.

You should note that this is not necessarily the case with all Internet transactions. My e-mailer, in common with many others, notes the IP address of the machine on which the mail was written, even if it is a reserved IP address on a private network.

As we've introduced the function of a firewall, you will find that a firewall can also decide whether to admit connections by checking for unusual use of ports or protocols and by blocking or allowing access depending on the IP address of the computer asking for the connection.

■ … or do we?

How much can the identity of an individual machine be pinned down – even what country it is in? This is a subject of more than passing interest since, increasingly, Web content is being subjected to boundaries. Some web pages may be 'illegal' to view in some places – such as Nazi memorabilia – and some organizations may wish to limit access to sites geographically.

If the web address is www.societeimaginaire.fr then that should be clear. If they are not in France then they want to be. Some countries are not so nationalistic about their top level domains. Italy's .it is used elsewhere because 'it' is a useful English word – consider a site called 'book.it' and you'll see the attraction, and the Tuvalu domain .tv is marketed at television companies. These top level domain names can be worth a lot of money and could be the next big thing for small countries since stamp collecting. But, of course, where is a .net or a .com?

You might think that the IP address would be traceable territorially, and this should be the case, although you would have to have a database relating IP to countries for it to work. In this case, if a proxy server in a different country was used, this would fool the system. Why would you need a database? This is because the allocation of number groups to countries is not simple.

Let's use, as an example, a set of what are called Class B numbers. Here we are looking at a grouping of IP addresses representing medium-sized networks. My own ISP is Demon Internet in the UK and they have a Class B allocation starting at 158.152.0.0 which, by going up to 158.152.255.255 allows them about 65 thousand addresses. You might think that the other Class B networks starting with 158 would be geographically similar. No, they're not. They are probably allocated in the order they were asked for. So you find such geographically diverse networks as Moscow State University, Hong Kong Baptist College, the Australian Prime Minister and Cabinet and the USAMC Logistics Support all sharing IP addresses starting 158.

To add to the problem, it is possible that different subgroups of IP addresses allocated to an international organization may be in different countries. Where are the networks of the European Commission, for example: in Brussels, in Luxembourg, in Strasbourg?

You can follow the path from your machine to a distant one by using a utility called TraceRoute. This is a standard part of Unix but for other machines you will need to get a small program which does it. When you run TraceRoute you see all the hops that the connection makes as it makes its way around the world.

Information on where a Domain Name or IP address is can be found by querying what are called WHOIS servers and the registries who allocate the IP addresses. This is probably not totally foolproof since it is technically possible for a machine to come into the Internet via an anonymous mirror or even using internal connections in a multinational organization, but the chances are that if you really need to know where your web visitor is, you can find out with a high level of confidence.

Even though many people browse the Web through proxies or firewalls and these machines' IP addresses are the one you will see, they are probably in the same country as the real user's machine.

■ There's more to the Internet than the World Wide Web

The Web has been described as the 'killer application' for the Internet, but there are other things you can do with it, of course.

■ E-mail

The biggest use of the Internet is for e-mail. There was e-mail before the Internet but the Internet has forced a standard so that anyone can exchange mails with anyone else. Some transactions on the Internet, like file transfer and web browsing need a full point-to-point connection between the machines at either end so that a dialogue can take place. Mail, which works using a relay system, does not need this.

Any e-mail you send will initially be a transfer between your machine and your mail server. You will send the mail to the server and the server will work out what to do next. It will look at the e-mail address – of the form user@machine.subdomain.domain – and will find out from the domain name server which machine handles mail for the domain in question. The mail will then be sent to that machine as a point-to-point transfer. In some cases the mail will be relayed more than once but eventually it should reach the mail server for the destination. The recipient will then either download the mail when they log on to the server (known as Post Office Protocol or POP mail) or the final point-to-point destination will be the recipient's machine (using Simple Mail Transfer Protocol or SMTP). A recent alternative to POP is IMAP (Internet Message Access Protocol) which allows users to use their electronic mailboxes seamlessly from any location and some mail clients can be configured to work with either standard.

An e-mail address can be an alias, which means that any mail received for that address is automatically routed to another address (or addresses). In this way mail to sales@imaginaryco.com can be routed to whichever person is handling sales at that time. The alias can be any e-mail address and doesn't have to be a local one.

There is no set way of tracking a mail. Usually, as it is relayed along, each server will store it briefly until the next scheduled time for a transfer and will then send it. If, for some reason, it can't be transferred the server will wait until the next transfer time. Sometimes the server will send a message to the sender of the mail saying that the mail is being held. Rarely, the system will 'time out'. I have found a particular problem with some university mail servers being turned off during vacations!

Because of this relaying of mail, the system is not instant, although it can work within minutes if the mail servers being used relay mail frequently. Some are set up to relay on demand, but not all. Another mail relay issue is the relaying of mail for unauthorized users. In the golden age a mail server would relay mail for anyone who asked, but this was so abused for spam (bulk unsolicited e-mailing) that now mail servers will usually only relay mail for people in the same domain.

If you set up a mail server you have to take care that it cannot be used for spam. If you do not do this it is likely to contravene the agreement you have for Internet connection through your ISP. If you only set up websites then you might think this doesn't apply to you but don't forget that a form on a web page can generate an e-mail. You will need to check to make sure that someone impersonating your form cannot send spam. (If you didn't know, the use of the word spam is in homage to a Monty Python comedy sketch about a restaurant whose speciality was the said tinned meat product that was part of every dish.)

In theory, e-mails can only contain text and, on almost all computers, text is represented by a standard called ASCII (American Standard Code for Information Interchange) which maps alphabetical and other characters to numbers. Strictly speaking e-mails can only be 7-bit ASCII (numbers up to 127) and although 8-bit ASCII (numbers up to 255) can be transferred, some servers may lose that eighth (top) bit which can change some of the more unusual (as far as English is concerned) characters. It is possible to attach a binary file to an e-mail but in order for it to pass through the mail system the mail client will encode the file into ACSII using one of a number of standard formats such as Base64, BinHex or UU-encoding. MIME types were specified to help this process. If this seems archaic then it is sobering to think that there was something of a battle to get ASCII to include lower-case characters, never mind anything 'foreign'! It is increasingly popular to produce an e-mail message as if it were a web page, in which case graphics and other assets are referenced using links in HTML and the HTML itself is, of course, text.

■ FTP – file transfer

A file transfer uses File Transfer Protocol (FTP) and, like mail, the computers at each end need to be able to handle the protocol, usually with special programs. FTP is important for websites because their files will probably be loaded onto the web server using FTP.

Unlike mail, a file transfer has to be between two machines connected point-to-point via the Internet. The sender makes the FTP connection and the recipient says 'OK send me something'. The file is then transferred, with checking done continuously to make sure the transfer is correct. (This is similar to the x-modem protocols used before the Internet.) Along with this function is the ability to do simple file system work such as view directories and even delete files.

A file can be transferred as a text file or as a binary file. If the file is binary then it is transferred without changes, but text files are usually checked to make sure that the carriage returns (CR) and/or line feeds (LF) are appropriate for the machines involved and, if necessary, changed because they can cause problems. If a binary file is incorrectly sent as a text file then there is a strong risk that it will become corrupted. If in doubt, transfer as binary. (End of paragraph/line is CR+LF on a PC, CR only on a Mac and LF only on a Unix box.)

If you have a Windows or Unix machine then FTP is built in. On Windows it is available from the Run dialogue box. On the Mac, Fetch is a common FTP client with, as you would expect, a mouse-driven interface.

■ Remote control – TelNet

Working with a remote computer can be done using a protocol called TelNet. There are WYSIWYG visual systems for remote control such as Timbuktu from Netopia (originally from Farallon) and Virtual Network Computer from AT&T Labs in Cambridge (UK). With TelNet your machine operates the distant machine as a text terminal and this is often used to allow website 'owners' to work with their websites on a remote Unix or NT box. You can't TelNet into a Mac web server (unless it is System X, which is Unix-based) in order to control it because the Mac has no command line interface, so Timbuktu or VNC would be more appropriate if you wanted to remotely control a Mac. Depending on how the remote computer is configured, a TelNet connection can do anything a local user can do. This is, of course, a throwback to the 'bad old days' of teletype terminals and mainframes.

If you have a Windows or Unix machine then a TelNet client is built in. On Windows it is available from the Run dialog box. For the Mac there is a free client from NCSA called NCSA TelNet, now produced under the name 'Better TelNet' and MacTelNet.

■ Chat

There is an Internet standard for chat, called the Internet Relay Chat protocol or IRC, but some other standards have caught on including ICQ, AOL Instant Messenger (AIM), Yahoo! Messenger and MSN Messenger. All these systems use servers through which chat messages are routed and on which users are registered. IRC can also work between two machines as long as each has an IRC client.

In some respects more sophisticated Internet messaging (AIM for example) is like the SMS text messaging system used on mobile phones (see Chapter 4) and can be used as a 'push' system as long as users are logged on. It can be used to send status messages telling you your stocks have moved or send you news headlines. Since the client is likely to be on many machines and since the chat systems generally don't leave files lying around you can log on wherever you find yourself. The linking of chat and mobile phones seems inevitable.

Videoconferencing is also possible over the Net. Depending on software and bandwidth you may get stills and text or full motion video with sound. CU-SeeMe was one of the earliest such systems but iVisit is an alternative (written by the same person) and Microsoft's ubiquitous NetMeeting can videoconference as well. Just as with ISDN-based videoconferencing, some of these allow you to share whiteboards and documents as well.

◼ Newsgroups

One area of the Internet that has existed since long before the Web is the Newsgroups (also known as UseNet groups). These are bulletin boards on which users can hold threaded discussions and, in some cases, post files. The threading of a discussion is very useful and can be applied to bulletin boards or forums on websites as well. Basically anyone who posts a message to a newsgroup can either do it in isolation, as a new subject starting its own thread, or the message can be a comment to a previous message, so continuing the thread. This method allows for a discussion in a way e-mails don't do so well.

There are two kinds of newsgroups. The main groups are set up under a formal system where someone from an existing group posts a suggestion that another group be set up to cover such and such a subject or subdivision and other people then vote on it. If it gets enough votes then the group can be set up. The group will need to be placed within the hierarchical structure of newsgroups so that a group on multimedia authoring might go in the comp area (for computing) and thence in the multimedia area. So its name (and path) would be comp.multimedia.authoring. Physically the files for the group need to be put into the news system, of which more in a moment. Alternatively it is possible to set up a newsgroup without a vote in the alt (for alternative) hierarchy. This is one place where the Internet has its 'wrong side of the tracks' with postings of extreme politics, sexual content and pirate software alongside the legitimate stuff.

ISPs will usually offer newsgroups to their customers. This means that they have a server which has access to the newsgroup files in their various hierarchies. A user then needs a newsreader, a client that supports the news protocol NNTP (similar to the mail protocol SMTP). This may be a stand-alone piece of software or it may be built into the web browser or e-mail client. News postings, like mail, can only include ASCII text so any posting of binary files (to the often-notorious alt.binaries groups) needs a trans-coding program to turn the binary into text. We shouldn't give the impression that the alt newsgroups are all 'dodgy', many are just as good/useful as the 'legitimate' ones, perhaps just a bit more quirky.

ISPs and other Internet hosts share news groups with each other. In this way a message posted to a group in one part of the Internet will soon migrate around the whole Internet as the various news servers swap files. This assumes that the whole news group file-set is made available. Some ISPs, and even some countries, censor the news groups for reasons of taste or, sometimes, for practical business reasons. Some ISPs do not give access to the alt hierarchy. Not all news groups are available free so sometimes a set will not be available simply because the ISP doesn't want to pay for them.

Recent legal precedents (including one in the UK) mean that an ISP has a responsibility for newsgroup content even if the content originates else-where. This means that if, as in the UK case, potentially libellous material is posted then the ISP should remove it once they are notified or find it. Sad to say, the use of Nicks (nicknames) by chat, forum and discussion group users seems to occasionally encourage aggressive and even obscene and offensive verbal behaviour (particularly from young males). An article on chat rooms in the UK's *Guardian* newspaper commented that postings on sites dominated by male posters 'often tend to read like Monty Python's famous "Argument" sketch, only less funny'. If you have the equivalent of a chat room, discussion group or forum on a website you are responsible for then you should monitor it. An ISP with thousands of news groups is faced with a formidable task. Some ISPs are now removing potentially trouble-some groups rather than risk repercussions.

It is possible to use news servers elsewhere than with your own ISP and some news content is available on the web – through www.dejanews.com for example (now acquired by Google) or at newsone.net.

■ The Web – HTTP

I've left the web protocol, Hypertext Transfer Protocol (HTTP), until last because it is a very sophisticated and complex protocol. You will be familiar with the letters because a web URL always starts by defining the protocol – you can see file://, ftp:// and even gopher:// but usually it is http:// – followed by the domain name or IP of the machine. The domain usually starts www but it doesn't have to.

To access a web page, the web client (usually a browser but not neces-sarily, it could be a robot indexing the web pages) sends an HTTP request to the web server and this request is in the form of a string of letters and numbers. Although we often refer to a machine as being a server, the server is really a program running on that machine. This request to the server has several sections to it including information about the requesting machine, the web page containing the link clicked on to generate the request (if any – known as the referrer), which language is expected (sent as a two-letter code such as 'en' for English) and the version of HTTP being used (sent as a number). A language request can be used by the server to customize the response by sending a web page in the appropriate language.

It is possible for the HTTP request to contain extra information generated by the browser based on a form that the user fills in. This information might be hidden (a form of message called POST) or it might appear in the URL sent back to the server as a string following a question mark in the URL (a form called GET). The server will have to respond appropriately to the POST or GET, usually by passing the information to a CGI program running on the server.

Any file sent by the server to the browser will have a header which will identify the type of file it is. Not all browsers react to this information and may take more notice of the suffix (file-type) of the file to see whether it is a GIF or JPEG, text or HTML. But it is possible for a header to be wrong and in that case the browser may not display the file or may display it incorrectly. This is one cause of a web page which displays correctly in one browser but not in another. Servers need to know how to deal with different types of files. There are standard MIME types – such as image/gif and text/html – and if new types of file are used the server needs to be told. Otherwise it might send the file labelled as text. Similarly the browser needs to know what to do with MIME types it is sent. Unknown ones will usually be downloaded as files.

Each HTTP request in a web page is independent. If you have a page containing five graphic files and a video then the server will receive seven separate HTTP requests, including the page's HTML file. Those parts of a web page don't have to be on the same server and banner ads in web pages are usually served from elsewhere. A browser has a limit to the number of simultaneous HTTP requests it can handle, usually eight. If a page requires more than this number than the browser has to wait for individual files to finish transferring before it can ask for another. If you have a web page with more than eight components the visitor will usually see parts arriving at different times. You basically have no control over the order in which things arrive at the browser although in principle the browser starts at the top of the web page and works its way down. Unfortunately, network delays may frustrate that and things held in a table will often remain invisible until the whole table is displayed.

The HTTP protocol has been extended in order to make transfer of files more efficient. If both browser and server support it there is now the concept of a visitor's session where the link is kept open. It is known as 'persistent'. This will reduce the overhead in accessing the web pages.

■ Security

When the protocol is HTTPS this means that a secure server is requested. If one exists at the domain then the server sends a certificate string to the browser which can then decide whether to set up a secure link or to ask the user if they want to take a chance. Other than encrypting the messages passed back and forth, HTTPS does not do anything else and any web pages can be served using HTTPS instead of HTTP. But the encryption and decryption add an overhead to the process and slow down the serving.

To set up a secure server requires two things. First is HTTPS server software, which probably comes built-in to your web server and will then allow you to run HTTPS as well as HTTP on the same website.

Second, you need a certificate from one of the recognized issuing companies like Verisign. They will check your bona fides before issuing the certificate. (This will include verifying the existence of your company, so be sure you have the form of the company name correct.) Without a certificate your secure server will not work: you may not even be able to run the software. As you might expect, the process of issuing the certificate can take some time, although the application can be done online. There is a mechanism for using temporary certificates for testing, but they have limitations, the most significant being that they will only allow a connection to the server from a known machine address. This stops temporary certificates being used for real transactions.

The public face of e-commerce is the ability to take orders online. This usually involves taking people's credit card details. With a secure server you can transfer the credit card information from the customer to your server. But what do you do with it then?

In a sophisticated e-commerce set-up your website will be linked to a banking system that will verify the card information and give you an author-

ization. Based on that authorization you can send the goods and the bank will send you the money.

A simpler set-up can involve the server taking the information and then either saving it locally – somewhere safe from prying Internet eyes – or re-encrypting it and e-mailing the order details to you. A server-side program can easily be written to do this, possibly in Perl. You can then process the transaction as a standard 'Customer not Present' transaction as if they had telephoned you. This will only work if you have a merchant account and can take cards but your merchant will want to know if you intend taking cards over the Internet and may impose conditions even if you already have a standard merchant account.

There is another aspect of security and that is the risk of your website being damaged by an unauthorized person changing files on the server. This is hacking. It has become common for hackers to change the home pages of well-known sites, sometimes to make a political point. Your access to the web server to change pages will probably involve logging on remotely and sending files over by FTP. As in any access to a remote computer, care must be taken with the user names and passwords that you need when you log on. Passwords should not be easy to guess and should not be words from a dictionary – it is possible to reverse-engineer passwords by reference to a dictionary – and should not be written on a sticky note on the computer monitor. The higher the profile of the website the greater the risk of a hacking attack. This risk is not limited to websites, if your own computer is not protected by a firewall then you may find someone will try to hack into it. Although public websites have to be accessible to the outside world they can still be placed behind a firewall and this firewall can be configured to allow only web requests. That will reduce the hacking risk but it will also mean that you have to be on the same side of the firewall as the server to update files on it.

Most web servers are vulnerable to hacking but servers running on Apple Macintosh computers (prior to system X) are reputed to be hacker-proof and that is why the US Army uses a Mac web server. But you should never say 'hacker-proof' – it just makes the challenge greater. Cliff Stoll's book *The Cuckoo's Egg* documents his battle to track down a hacker who was breaking into US military computers back in the early days of the Internet.

■ XML – separating style from content

When the Web started, HTML (hypertext mark-up language) was a mark-up language which specified the structure of a document by means of 'tags' – codes which define what was the title, what the main headings were, what kind of lists there were and so on. In a simple way, the look of the page was down to the reader and the way the browser was configured. Before long, designers wanted to be able to control the layout of pages so that the page as seen could be defined and everyone would see the same thing. To achieve this, tags could define fonts and typeface sizes and colours. Tables, or positioning of layers using DHTML (D for Dynamic) could be used to say where things should be. A large website would be difficult to define if you had to put style tags in every paragraph. Cascading Style Sheets were introduced to allow sections of a document, or individual HTML tags, to be given their specifications. All this was defining the appearance of the document often at the expense of its structure since it became increasingly easy to dispense with structural tags like headers completely.

The structure struck back with XML – eXtensible Markup Language. The author of a document can define any XML tags to define the document structure and a style sheet is used to say how the page will then be laid out. Since the latest browsers will render XML as well as HTML it is likely that you have seen XML web pages without realizing it. As you might expect, the file extension is .xml but there is a half-way house. XHTML is a strict version of HTML written in XML.

You can define a completely new mark-up language in XML if you want to. A Document Type Definition (DTD) can be written to specify what you have devised and there are many XML languages around including SMIL (pronounced 'smile'), the Synchronized Multimedia Integration Language.

In the long term, XML is a very important development for the Web because it provides a way of marking a document which can then be served in appropriate formats for the various delivery media such as iTV, mobile and the Web. Since elements within the document can be tagged with meaningful names such as <author> it will be possible to carry out much more sophisticated searches than can be done at present. Currently we are only searching 'blindly' on the text itself without being able to specify the actual meaning of the word.

◼ Network architecture

The Web can function quite simply with a connection between a server and a browser (the client in the client–server architecture). But the Internet can get clogged up, speeds can vary and some websites might attract more hits than a single server can happily handle.

You can insert a proxy server between the client and the server. In its most usual form this proxy server will receive all requests for web pages and will pass on those requests to the real server, keeping a copy of the web page as it goes through. The next time the page is requested then the page is served from the proxy rather than the real server, and this is usually a faster process although it runs the risk of the proxy holding an out-of-date copy of the page. This will also, incidentally, disguise the identity of the client machine, since the distant server will see the proxy as making the request.

To handle large numbers of requests for data, a load balancing arrangement might be used in conjunction with a number of servers, each with identical contents. The load balancer is another computer which monitors the traffic coming to the site and also monitors how busy the servers are. Since each request for an item on a website is independent of all the others, it doesn't actually matter that the component parts might be served by different machines. To the client, the load balanced system looks like a single server.

You might wish to hide your computers from the Internet, and make it difficult (hopefully impossible) for someone to hack their way in. Here you would use a firewall. This is a computer that monitors the traffic coming in from the Internet and controls the access. It might be configured to allow only certain kinds of requests, for certain ports on the computer: port 80 for web pages or port 53 for DNS requests and so on. It might only allow access from certain other computers. It might make the whole network appear on the Internet as if it were a single 'virtual' computer. This is known as Network Address Translation (NAT) and would be done by having a router provide the bridge between the local network and the Internet at large. The router/firewall could be a computer running a program but is more likely to be a dedicated box which is remotely configured using TelNet or a web browser.

■ Who am I?

While we're on the subject of security, let's consider what the server knows about you when you access a web page (or, from the point of view of the management, just what can you find out about your visitors?).

As we saw earlier in this chapter, when a browser makes a request for a page it sends a string to the server which tells it such things as: the computer platform and operating system, the language preference, what browser it is, the web page which contains the link (if any) that was clicked to get here, and the requesting computer's IP address. This IP address can be mapped back to its domain name by what is called a reverse DNS look-up.

Actually, you may not really see the IP address of the requesting computer, because if there's a proxy server or firewall or router in the way that is what you will see instead. It is not straightforward to identify exactly who is making a request of the server. Since each request is completely separate, it was necessary to invent another method to keep track of visitors: cookies. A cookie is a short string of text that the server sends to the browser and which it can check on later. A visitor can be identified from a cookie to track such things as user preferences, identity of a shopping basket or validity of a password. (More recently, the extension to HTTP allowing a user session doesn't require cookies to keep track and incidentally also provides for a more secure login where the user's name and password are not actually sent over the Internet to the server at all and so cannot be intercepted.) However, browsers have limited memory in which to store cookies so you need to be a bit careful in sending them. Some users don't trust them and many check to see what is being sent. If your website is sending cookies, don't forget that the user has certainly visited other sites with cookies recently and you might also get cookies sent by embedded content on your page such as advertisements and counters. The user might also refuse to accept the cookie or might delete it later.

Cookies can be tracked across more than one site. If they are attached to banner ads then it is possible to pick them up as you move from page to page with these ads on the pages. The banner ads are possibly provided by a central advertising agency and the cookies associated with these ads can be used to track which sites you have visited. In turn, this information can be used to target the advertising you are shown by the server. While this customer information is used to target advertising it seems pretty innocuous but if it gets associated with personal data then you could be heading for a data protection problem at worst or, at least, dissatisfied customers who don't want their online habits tracked like this.

However, you may often find that your client wants to track customers as part of their customer relations management (CRM) so that the relationship can be made more personal. With this a customer's experience when visiting the website can be more tailored and targeted. This might involve a log-in process or it might involve tracking using cookies or both. A full CRM system builds a database with a record for each customer or even site visitor but it is possible to do some simple CRM without actually storing anything on the web server. A cookie can be used to store visit parameters on the visitor's machine. These could be preferences such as what style sheet the customer wants for the site. The cookie could even store information about parts of the site visited so that you can offer to show a visitor something new. By doing this in cookies you don't actually need to have a database on the site although you rely on the user keeping the cookies and coming in from the same browser each time. If you do have a database-driven CRM system on the server then you might find there are data protection implications. (Data protection is discussed more fully in the rights chapter in Book 1 Chapter 15.)

When surfers leave one site by following a link and arrive somewhere else, on this surfing journey of theirs, one bit of their baggage is the URL of the page that they just left. This information ends up in the log of the next website, assuming that the referring page information is logged. This information tells you who is linking to your site and, if the visitor has come from a search engine, there will probably be a list of the search terms as well.

There may be a downside to this. If you check your logs to find that a referring page has the URL www.biggestrival.com/takeover/prospects.html then you might be in line for a surprise. You should check your website to make sure that referrers don't carry any unwelcome message from you. (Web consultant Russ Haynal has a website at http://navigators.com/cgi-bin/navigators/persona.pl where he discusses this question of your 'persona'.)

Logs

The information in the browser's request is the basis of logging and the analysis of logs is one way to see how successful a website is. The logs are generated by the server and, as mentioned earlier, one of the things to set up when configuring a server is exactly what is wanted in the logs.

Besides the things such as IP address, browser and operating system – which tells you about the surfer's computer – and referrer information – which tells you where the surfer came from – the logs will record information about the visit to your site. The URL requested will be recorded and this will be every page and every graphic and every other kind of file.

Here's a line from one of my logs:

Let's look at the information in this line bit by bit.

hse-ottawa-ppp158445.sympatico.ca
This is the fully qualified domain name of the machine making the request. In this case the log file is not configured to give an IP address if it can resolve a domain name but sometimes you see an IP address here, not a name. This is not necessarily the user's machine of course since there could be a firewall or proxy in the way. We can guess that this is a dial-up user in Ottawa and the ppp suggests a dial-up connection being allocated an IP and domain name on the fly by the ISP which is Sympatico who describe themselves as Canada's national Internet service. PPP – Point to Point Protocol – is commonly used in dial-up connections.

10/Mar/2001:03:43:59 +0000
The date and time are next, as determined from the server clock at my ISP, not the user's. The +0000 at the end tells me that the clock is set to GMT.

GET /ilight/images/ioffice.gif HTTP/1.1

A GET request is one for the whole file, not just its header information (which would be HEAD) and in this case the file path is shown relative to the root of the website. The version of HTTP being used is 1.1 which means that my server should respond using the same version, which allows persistent connections. If my server only supported HTTP 1.0 then it could use this since the system is backwards compatible.

200 5494

Finally the server records a transaction code of 200 which means the file was sent correctly with a transfer of 5494 bytes. The notorious 404 transaction code means the web page requested was not found and the user would have seen an error. If the code had been 304 and no data had been transferred then this would mean that the file was already held locally in the browser or proxy cache and had not been updated, so it was not sent again. You would not usually expect 304 responses while a visitor moved around the site during a single visit, revisiting menu pages, because the browser would normally not request any particular page from the server more than once in a session unless the cache filled up. If you saw a lot of 304 codes this might indicate frequent visitors returning in different surfing sessions who are not seeing new content. Time to update your website!

The particular log line above is a pared-down one from an ISP. Since adding user agent and referrer information can significantly increase the size of the log file many ISPs are reluctant to include them. Unfortunately this information is very useful to you since it tells you what hardware and software your visitors have, which helps you design your site's features to suit the visitors. It also tells you who is linking to you, which is an indication of peer review since people tend to link to sites which they think are good or useful. Of course a link to your site from 'Web Pages that Suck' needs to be taken with a sense of humour and possibly a review of your design.

In general, people don't look at individual lines of log files, they run the whole file through a log analysis tool. This is a piece of software that reads the lines of the log and produces an analysis based on criteria you set up.

There are the basics such as how many times a page was viewed (called 'page impressions') but with a little more sophisticated analysis you can see how visitors move through the site and how long they stay (called 'stickiness'). Finding where they go when they leave is more difficult. One tactic is to pass every link out of your site through a CGI routine that logs the event since the standard server logging can't do this.

There are many log analysis tools, ranging in price from free upwards. Some of them work by reading log files downloaded from the site onto a local machine and others can be run on the server so that the resulting analyses can be viewed as web pages.

■ Search engines and spiders

When a website has been set up and is running, it needs to be promoted. Unfortunately, the best way of promoting a web URL seems to be putting it onto the end of a television advertisement (or some other conventional method) but for the rest of us a more realistic option is needed.

The usual mechanisms for promoting websites apply whether the site is a commercial one or a hobby home page: search engines, cross-linking and portals. For those of us with money, listings can be bought.

Search engines work by following links through the Web and indexing what they find along the way. They will often start from links submitted by site-builders and surfers, and work outwards. Since the average website links to many others this can be a fruitful process. Getting a search engine spider (as its roving agent is known) is not the difficult bit. What the spider finds and how it indexes your site is crucial to where in a particular search you will end up. Near, or at, the top of the list is best. But what search terms will people be using?

If you are the only supplier of thermoincabulators in the world (or at least on the Web) then a search on thermoincabulators will find you. But if you are a supplier of CDs you will have more competition.

Spiders will show up in your logs, and there are well-known ones associated with the well-known search engines. A file called robots.txt should be placed in the root of the website, where the home page is. This can be used to configure the spiders' searches and to tell them where they are not allowed to go to index. You can even turn away particular spiders by name, or turn them all away. This assumes the spiders obey robots.txt, but they usually do.

Different search engines use different criteria to rank websites but as a general rule you can improve your chances by following a few sensible guidelines. Firstly make use of the meta tags in the web page header to set up a description of the page and its keywords. If you have a keyword or phrase that you want to hit high in searches then use this in the page title, description, keyword list and in the first paragraph of your text on the page. Ideally include it in an <H1> header tag as the main title. Don't use the phrase a large number of times in a particular way because this can be counterproductive and if done to excess is usually discounted by the indexing.

Not every search engine will index based on all these places. Some will not go further than the <HEAD> section. If the engine only reads the <BODY> then you will have a problem if your page consists solely of a Flash animation and no HTML. Spiders can't read Flash. Framed home pages might similarly fool some spiders – in which case the <NOFRAMES> content can be useful.

Search engine sites usually have a page explaining how they index pages so you can fine-tune pages to suit, and there is a useful website at www.searchenginewatch.com as well. If you want to be extra clever then one possible tactic is to use the server to detect the spider as it arrives and direct it to a special version of a home page especially structured to milk the sympathy of the indexing in question. You can identify the spider because it should identify itself by name either in its domain name or from what is called the User Agent string and this can be read by your program from the incoming HTTP request. You'd do this differently for each spider based on its indexing criteria.

■ The dot.com bubble

The business perspective on the Internet is bound to be coloured by the rises and falls in the fortunes of so-called dot.com companies. The boom in Internet shares will probably be remembered by historians in the same way as the so-called South Sea Bubble scandal of 1720 (when the South Seas Company also saw its share value rocket without ever making a profit, and took lots of money from British investors until the bubble burst) and the Wall Street Crash. This all risks missing the point about what the Internet means to business as a whole, rather than just to companies who exist only in cyberspace. The Internet may itself change and evolve, but the genie has been let out of the bottle and the way we all do business and communicate is changed forever.

For those of us working at the coal face, producing the web pages, e-databases and e-everything that modern companies need, the changes in cyber-fortunes change our business too. Website makeovers may become less frequent. Design of websites will be governed less by the laws of cool and more by the sensibilities of usability and communication. We will work with structured information across a huge variety of devices. Perhaps more important is the international growth of the Internet. It may be reaching saturation in the USA and other English-speaking western markets but there are still millions of people speaking hundreds of other languages who have yet to be reached.

Technically the Internet changes over time. New IP numbering is under discussion, new top level domains are being introduced, protocols are re-defined and updated. A parallel educational high-speed network, known as Internet2, has been set up. End-users of the Internet may be surfing over telephone lines, broadband connections, televisions, mobile telephones and satellites. The only constant factor is that the Internet has changed the way we make use of information for ever.

THEORY INTO PRACTICE 2

Assuming you are non-technical and you work for a company, tap into the expertise of your technical expert. It should be evident from this chapter that many difficulties can arise from Internet related issues.

1. Ask about any e-mail or FTP problems that has given your company problems.
2. How is your own system set up? Where are the A records kept? What domain names and IP numbers does the company have? What security measures are in place?
3. What are the worst web page problems that they have encountered – what caused them and how were they resolved?
4. What log analysis is kept on your own site? If applicable, what extras have been needed for client sites?
5. Ask them to describe the more major incidents that they have had to deal with on clients' projects, what caused them and how they might be avoided in the future.

Assess whether you feel more confident about discussions of this type now you have a grasp of the background issues.

■ Summary

- Dial-up and always-on are the two common connection methods to the Internet.
- To set up a website you need to have a domain name and a computer with an IP address.
- Web pages can be static or dynamic. Dynamic pages – or pieces of pages – are built on-the-fly from one or more sources.
- Scalability of websites needs to be planned and tested.
- E-mails are relayed – FTP file transfers and web page requests are sent point-to-point in real time.
- Websites can be managed remotely using FTP.
- Security issues concern credit cards, personal data and hacker protection.
- XML allows document authors flexibility in delivery media by separating style from content.
- Log analysis provides a range of information about the use and users of a website.
- Site recognition by search engine indexing spiders can be enhanced to your advantage.

■ Recommended reading

Stoll C. (2000). *The Cuckoo's Egg*, New York, NY: Pocket Books.
For a view of life in the 'dark ages' of the Internet, you should read Cliff Stoll's book. It tells of his detective work in tracking down a hacker who was trying to get into US military computers. Along with a ripping good yarn, Cliff explains how the Internet was connected up.

Wallace P. (1999). *The Psychology of the Internet*. Cambridge: Cambridge University Press

Sebesta R.W. (2001). *Programming the World Wide Web*. Reading, MA: Addison-Wesley

Tittel E., Mikula N. and Chandak R. (1998). *XML for Dummies*. Foster City: IDG Books

Albitz P. and Liu C. (1998) *DNS and Bind*, 3rd edn. Sebastopol, CA: O'Reilly & Associates
This book is aimed at system administrators and network techies, but it gives detailed information on how DNS works.

Spainhour S. and Echstein R. (1999). *Webmaster in a Nutshell*, 2nd edn. Sebastopol, CA: O'Reilly & Associates

Niederst J. (1999). *Web Design in a Nutshell*, Sebastopol, CA: O'Reilly
O'Reilly publishes a wide range of useful reference books on all aspects of programming. The author makes extensive use of their HTML, Perl and JavaScript books.

The Internet Society has a page of links to various historic documents at the logically named:
http://www.isoc.org/internet/history

The NetGeo server (http://www.caida.org/tools/utilities/netgeo) maps IP addresses to latitude and longitude or to country. The system queries WHOIS servers and parses the information there in order to obtain its data. A more detailed abstract is at
http://www.caida.org/outreach/papers/inet_netgeo.html

The IP Network Index (http://www.ipindex.net) can be used to see to whom a particular IP address is registered. This will usually resolve to an ISP if the end-user is a person or small company.

The Internet Assigned Numbers Authority has a list of country top-level domains and information about who adminsters them at
http://www.iana.org.cctld-whois.htm
Usually this is logically geographic but sometimes, as in the .tv domain, it has become vertically commercial.

Information from IANA on the generic TLDs such as .com and .edu is at
http://www.iana.org/gtld/gtld.htm

The All Whois website (htttp://www.allwhois.com) enables you to look up information on domains to see who registered them and (sometimes) who owns them.

Anonymizer (http://www.anonymizer.com) claims to allow anonymous web browsing and will presumably make non-Americans seem to be in the USA since the domain name or IP will be for anonymizer.com rather than the actual user.

Internet Product Watch (http://ipw.internet.com) provides news, specifications, information and announcements about the latest Internet hardware and software. (Note there is no www in the URL.)
http:///www.internetproductwatch.com also gets you there.

Russ Haynall's 'Check your Persona' web page is at
http://navigators.com/cgi-bin/navigators/persona.pl – again, no www.

Vincent Flanders' site on web page design that doesn't work is at
http://www.webpagesthatsuck.com

Security Space Network Monitor is at
http://www.securityspace.com/s_survey/data

One freely-available stress tester is a Java-based project from Apache called Jakarta at
http://jakarta.apache.org/jmeter

Guardian newspaper (http://www.guardianunlimited.co.uk) – online supplement appears
each Thursday. The article on forums was written by David Rowley and appeared on
19 April 2001.

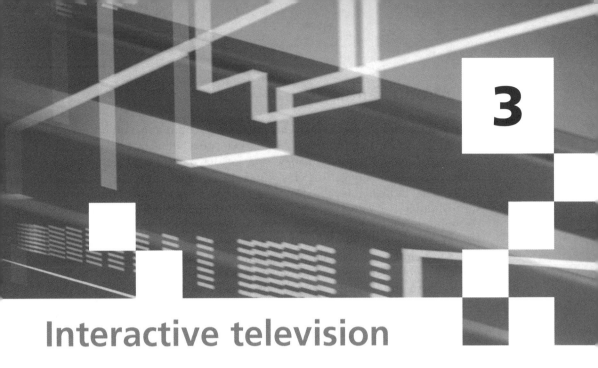

3

Interactive television

Project manager's responsibilities

- To know the potential problems of transferring assets between the mediums of computing and TV

- To recognize that there are many ways to introduce interaction into the viewer's TV experience

- To keep an eye on the emerging iTV market

- To build up an understanding of which interactive formats work with the public and why they appeal more than others

■ Introduction

Even if their numbers worldwide are increasing, computers still have a long way to go before they achieve the market penetration of television. The convergent model for technology sees media, computing and telecommunications gradually getting closer and closer together and perhaps eventually being indistinguishable from one another. So eventually there will be no real difference between a PC with a TV tuner and a TV with a built-in computer or they may blend into a single device. (This ignores the psychological differences whereby people might want to differentiate the two in order to help keep work and play separate. To follow this train of thought you could consider in what ways a truck is different from a family car.)

Of course, interactivity is heavily dependent on digits and so digital TV is often seen as a path leading to interactive television. This is particularly true in Europe, since at the time of writing the American and Australian routes to digital TV are geared more towards high-definition pictures than interactivity. A heavy early take-up of digital TV in the UK was further fuelled by subsidized hardware from the major players, Sky and ITV Digital. The result was that the curve of user take-up for digital TV was an order of magnitude steeper than for comparable technologies such as compact disk and VCRs.

But there are philosophical differences between how we view a computer and how we view television. Arguably there is a fundamental incompatibility between the lean forward, 'nose touching the screen' philosophy of a computer user and the lean back, 'couch potato' environment of a television viewer. It is still debatable whether the average television viewer wants to interact anyway but it does tend to be older people who raise this point. If you were raised on computer games your take on this would probably be different.

This chapter will explore the technical issues dividing television and computing and explain how those influence the development of interactive applications that use television as their medium. Along the way we'll consider the thorny issue of the return path, web-on-television and the influence of interlace ... amongst other things that make up Interactive Television: iTV.

There are two other important areas that relate to iTV: Video-on-demand and DVD. Although they have technical differences in the way they are distributed as compared to each other and to iTV, people usually watch them on a television so I include them in this chapter.

Linguistic note: in British English, there is a computer program and there is a television programme. I unashamedly retain these different spellings partly to help distinguish between the two.

■ What defines an interactive TV system?

It helps to consider the key elements that define an iTV system; define but also limit. One is the remote control and the other is the characteristics of the display.

A computer user will normally interact by moving a pointer around the screen with a mouse and then clicking on one or more mouse buttons. The iTV or DVD viewer has a remote control handset to control the system. Individual options on screen may be marked to correspond with some of these handset buttons. Some handset buttons allow the viewer to move a 'selection point' around the screen in simple 'up, down, left, right' movements, usually between graphic screen buttons, and some handset buttons control features (such as 'play' and 'stop') without having a specific screen button. Some handset buttons may be used only to control the TV itself and play no part in the interaction. They may not even be accessible to interactive applications.

When a user is interacting with an iTV application, that application may have some control over the TV receiver so that, for example, a TV channel can be previewed in a box on the screen. This is different to actually changing channel on the receiver: the user may press the handset button to select an option that says 'Show me the movie' and the channel may change; but it is the interactive application that changes the channel. The sophistication of interaction will be limited by the remote control. It may be possible to

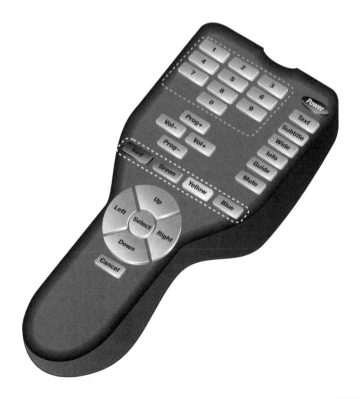

Idealized Interactive TV Handset
(with thanks to the Digital Television Group).

play games but the kind of smooth cursor movement familiar on a computer is traditionally not a feature of TV interaction.

A television screen is inherently different to a computer screen. We have gone into more detail about this in the chapter on video assets (Chapter 7) but essentially a television screen has a much lower effective resolution than a computer and the viewer is almost certainly sitting much further away so the screen appears smaller to the eye.

VGA computer screens and standard televisions have a similar resolution in pixels (TV is 720 pixels by either 480 or 576) but you cannot just move an image from a computer across to TV without taking some care. A sharp computer image will shimmer and flicker when you view it on a TV. The interlace of the television screen means lines of the picture that are next to each other on screen are not actually displayed next to each other in time because an interlaced display writes half of a screen's worth of lines all the way down the screen and then goes back and writes the rest in between the first half. So interlaced pictures have information arranged along a frag-mented time-line because adjacent lines show times a 60th of a second apart in NTSC and a 50th in PAL and SECAM. (Assume SECAM timings are the same as PAL in this discussion.) To compensate for this the TV image is much softer (out-of-focus to some extent) than its computer equivalent since a computer display writes all the lines in order from top to bottom of the screen. This is known as non-interlaced or progressive scan. So any text on the television screen must be larger than you might use on a computer and 24 or 26 point text is considered as 'small' in this context.

Moving video footage between a television display and a computer can leave visible artefacts. (A fuller discussion of the effects can be found in Chapter 7.) A moving object will appear to fragment and vertical edges of horizontally moving objects will show this worst. Moving in the reverse direction from a computer to a television, instead of the vertical edges breaking up, you'll see double images.

You can get around this inherent difference between a computer's pro-gressive display and a television's interlace in four ways:

- shoot on film (in which all parts of the frame show the same moment in time),
- using a progressive scan video camera which shoots like film,
- calculating a frame from the two fields, and
- when moving from TV to computer, reduce the size of the image to a quarter frame or smaller and drop one of the fields. This is a special case of calculating a new frame, of course.

With any of these methods you can produce movie files that will play satis-factorily on both television and a computer.

Television always has a fixed frame rate of 30 (NTSC) or 25 (PAL) frames per second. Since a computer screen can have a wide range of frame rates the two might not fit together very well. This might occasionally show up as a slight juddering in what should be smooth motion.

The television might have a standard aspect ratio of 4 by 3 but it also might increasingly be wide-screen and so have a ratio of 16 by 9 (for comparison, 4 by 3 is equivalent to 12 by 9). Television is often now treated as if it has an aspect ratio of 14 by 9 which is a reasonable half-way house between standard and wide-screen and so an interactive application might be distorted slightly for both normal and wide screen, but by only a smaller amount and being horizontally squashed for the former and stretched for the latter. If the application is being made to work on both NTSC and PAL sets (rather than being specially produced for each) then a similar distortion will occur since the 480 visible horizontal lines in an NTSC picture would not fill a PAL screen which expects 576 so the picture would be squashed vertically. In all cases the same number of pixels is seen across the screen – 720 – but the shape of those pixels changes. On a computer you can assume that pixels are square.

So the displays are different, and that affects the way the application on iTV looks. But what kind of applications might you find as either enhanced TV or fully interactive TV?

■ The carousel

The carousel is the most venerable element in iTV. The term refers to a sequence of data that is repeatedly transmitted, ad infinitum. A viewer pre-selects a portion of this data as it passes 'on the carousel' and the television set displays it or runs it as a program in an interactive system.

Teletext, introduced by the BBC in September 1974 and still going strong, is a carousel digital information system. Hundreds of digital pages are cycled continuously including news, sport, weather, programme information and features. Each page is exactly one kilobyte – 25 rows of 40 characters, each character defined by an 8-bit code. They correspond to ASCII but with additional codes allowing crude graphics, colour and effects such as 'reveal' and 'flash'.

Although teletext is a digital system it is actually transmitted as pulses in part of the analogue TV picture, in the lines 'above' the picture known as blanking or vertical interval. Most countries outside the US have teletext systems. The most common is the so-called World System devised by the BBC but other systems exist, notably in France and Japan (and bearing names like Captain and Antiope).

The viewer chooses what to see by selecting a page number, from 100 to 899 on the remote control. The TV will default to 100, the Index page. There are other 'reserved' page numbers: for example 888 which is used in the UK and elsewhere for closed caption subtitles. These subtitles are displayed in a box cut into the picture and are synchronized to the programme. They are usually intended for people with hearing difficulties but they can also be used for translations, opera libretti and commentary. Since teletext signals can be recorded on professional videotape, television programmes offered for sale to broadcasters often include subtitles built-in. This became especially common when the Australian government insisted on a certain percentage of programmes, including imports, being subtitled. (World System teletext signals are too complex to be recorded on VHS videocassettes, although they can be stored on analogue LaserDisks, many of which have subtitles. The Closed Caption Line 21 system used for hard-of-hearing subtitles in the USA is more rugged than teletext and can be included on videocassettes.)

The television set needs a kilobyte of memory to store the page of data so that it can be captured as it passes on the carousel and is displayed. The average delay between a viewer pre-selecting a page and it being shown is called the latency and it depends on the number of pages in the carousel and the number of TV lines on which the data is transmitted.

The apparent latency of a teletext system (as with any carousel) can be reduced by caching pages. As the carousel goes round, pages can be cached so that when the user selects a new page it will appear instantly. Unfortunately set manufacturers seem unwilling to put memory in a TV for this and the nearest most teletext sets get is to have a few pre-selected 'next' pages attached to the currently viewed one. This is the Fastext system and the broadcasters implemented it by invisibly tagging each teletext page with the page numbers of four related pages. Sadly, many manufacturers gave their sets four kilobytes of memory to implement Fastext, forgetting the kilobyte required to display the current page which resulted in one of the four Fastext buttons not working instantly.

Teletext suffers from its limited graphics capabilities, although some non-World System systems offered more sophisticated graphics and a level of World System was defined (but not used) that even allowed RGB colour photos. But the available bandwidth in the vertical interval from the top to the bottom of the TV screen would be the limiting factor since it would always coexist with a television frame.

World System was also the basis for other early network interfaces, the best example being the British Prestel system which was a telephone-based digital information system and which even allowed e-commerce (as it is now understood). Prestel is still used extensively in the UK by the travel industry but it offers little more than a VT100 terminal would.

Of itself, a carousel is arguably not really iTV but more a progenitor of it, often referred to as 'enhanced TV': but it certainly gives a lie to the adage that changing channel is the most interactive thing people did with their TV since, in Europe at least, the majority of TV viewers use teletext.

With the advent of digital television, a new and more sophisticated form of teletext magazine with better design and photographic quality has become available, using the high-quality display and interactive capability of the set-top box. This has enabled the humble text and block graphic pages to take on all the sophisticated features available to web pages. It is also important to remember that many iTV applications will be delivered to the receiver from a carousel since they cannot be requested on demand. One key task of the programmers will be to fine-tune the carousel so that the latency of the system is not apparent to users.

▦ Multi-channel

Back in the 1980s, British commercial television ran an advertisement – the product was financial services – which was made in two different versions: one used a sober 'man-in-a-suit' approach and the other featured a song and dance routine. Since the two commercial channels available at the time were synchronizing their commercial breaks, these two versions were run simultaneously. The viewer was even asked, at the start of the commercial, which style of exposition they wanted and was told to switch channels to make the choice. If you watched the commercials carefully you could catch a glimpse of the other version passing in the distance, emphasising the co-incident nature of the different ads.

This was an early example of the simplest form of interactive television, where the viewer chooses a particular channel to watch in order to see a different 'view' of the same event. This is, of course, a very wasteful form of interactivity since each option takes up a whole channel of its own, but choosing a camera angle is a feature of many iTV programmes, especially in sport.

Unintentional iTV had existed before this. As soon as television stations were in competition, there were instances of double coverage of a notable event being done using different resources. The inauguration of a President, key space launches of the 1960s, some sporting events, were covered by two (or sometimes more) stations. The viewer would be making an interactive choice between the options.

Where a broadcaster has sufficient capacity (the digital satellite channels available to BSkyB in the UK provide a good example) it can offer viewers a choice of views of, say, a football match. The match is already being covered using a number of cameras and the programme's director will be selecting which one the viewer sees from moment to moment. At an event like a football match, every camera is likely to see something of the game. Altern-atively, at a golf tournament, different cameras would be covering different holes.

As well as these simultaneous views, the broadcaster could provide related material such as a camera showing the trainer's bench, following the game from the point of view of one or more players, or a time-delay feed so the viewer can choose their own 'action replays'. A continuously updated feed of statistics and possibly some highlights from other matches or sports could be added to this mix. The viewer might be able to view two or more images on screen at once by using picture-in-picture.

This combination of features provides a pretty rich set of material for what is probably the simplest true iTV structure. For the broadcaster it also makes use of existing resources.

Multi-channel iTV, like the carousel, illustrates a basic premise of iTV: all the options will be distributed and the viewer catches them as they flash by or stashes them away for later consumption. This is distinct from inter-activity on the Web, where the material is only really made available if it is requested.

Near video-on-demand (NVOD) is another multi-channel form of en-hanced television. With genuine video-on-demand (VOD) the viewer has a broadband connection to a video server and receives a unique stream of data which allows control over the video providing the same functionality as a VCR. NVOD uses a number of channels to transmit the same movie but with staggered timings. The movie might start every ten minutes which means that someone wanting to watch the movie can do so with a wait of no longer than ten minutes. To do this with a two-hour movie would need 12 channels.

Interactive television needs to be distinguished from interactive video (IV). IV was essentially the result of hooking an analogue videodisk player up to a computer and, after having a brief popularity in the 1980s, has been largely forgotten. (A variation of IV, which used DVD instead of a videodisk player, has been promoted by Pioneer, basically as a way of leveraging exist-ing IV programs in the digital age. The videodisk is transferred, frame by frame, to the DVD so that a simple conversion of the original controlling program can be used. Cheap and very cheerful. At its simplest the system makes use of bar codes. To view a sequence the viewer swipes a bar code which programmes the player and shows the sequence. This method proved very popular in education since it didn't require a separate computer and the controlling 'software' could be copied by photocopying. A splendid example of lateral thinking.)

■ Associated material

One format for iTV allows a standard linear programme to be enhanced by the transmission of related and possibly synchronized material which can be viewed along with the programme. A website which contains extra information on the subject of the programme is one example; and so you can watch the programme at the same time the video might be windowed into the page. But such things can be much more sophisticated.

One popular format is the quiz show where the audience can take part along with the contestants on-air. If you ever felt that you could answer the questions better than the person on the TV then this gives you the chance. The interactive program running in your television or set-top box provides you with a user interface, possibly shows you the questions in written form and keeps track of your score. This program could be fed from the Internet or a telephone, but it is more likely to use signals transmitted with the TV programme or even from another on-air source, such as the data channel of a local FM radio station.

The extra incentive that iTV can bring is allowing you to compete against not only the contestants but everyone else watching the interactive quiz. Here you need a return path going back to the broadcaster, probably using a telephone line. If the set-top box determines that the viewer has beaten the contestants on-air it might dial up the studio and inform the programme team. The viewer with the best result could then be declared a winner during the programme, if it is live, or announced during the following week's edition.

A similar concept, if simpler, is voting. Quite often TV programmes will ask viewers to telephone certain numbers to choose the winner of, for example, a talent show. All the viewer does is choose whether to dial one number or another, each representing a choice. It's the dialling of the number and connection of the call that registers the choice: this is much more efficient than making a call to a single number and then saying your choice to an operator or pressing a number on your phone key pad. This voting can be so efficient that the feedback takes only a few minutes and there are specialist companies who will provide the facilities for this. (A bonus is that the calls usually cost the viewer a little more than ordinary calls and so the programme can actually earn some income from its voting and help offset the production costs.)

■ *The Golden Shot*

Once upon a time there was a very popular television programme in which viewers gave instructions over the telephone to a blindfolded camera operator who pointed the camera, and a crossbow attached to it, at a target in the studio. This was *The Golden Shot* and listening to callers saying 'left a bit, up a bit, shoot!' was a common part of 1960s viewing.

Touch-tone telephones have revolutionized this concept and it is possible to configure an aspect of the television studio so that a viewer can control it this way: perhaps to select a camera view.

Of course, this is interactivity only in a special sense since only one viewer can interact at any time. But it is still counted as interactivity and by a broad definition so might a phone-in radio show. These are not really what we would consider a part of iTV now.

■ TRANSIT and the backwards news bulletin

Back in the late 1980s, when the BBC first had an Interactive Television Unit – who actually made videodisks rather than real iTV – the Unit's head presented a paper to the Royal Television Society which outlined an interactive approach to broadcasting which still has merit.

Peter Armstrong called his modest proposal TRANSIT, for Transmitted Interactive Television. He envisaged a viewer having a receiver which could receive and store television and which would have sufficient computer capability to run a program which used the recorded material as a resource. The broadcaster would transmit component parts of a TV programme together with the controlling software, and the viewer would then interact with this on their TV using the remote control.

There are now set-top boxes which contain hard disk storage which allows the viewer to time-shift, or even pause, programmes received. This is known as a Personal Video Recorder (PVR). Although at the time of writing there is no sign of additional controlling software, this shouldn't be too difficult to envisage. So what kind of facilities would this provide?

If one side to iTV is giving viewers the opportunity to interact with a TV programme as if they were at their computers, the opposing philosophy looks at the current linear experience and asks how it could be logically enhanced. With this latter model in mind, imagine a viewer tuning in to the evening news programme: *60 minutes, TeleJournal, News at Ten* or whatever.

The viewer selects the iTV version of the evening news and watches the headlines at the start of the programme. She might have selected to see a headline version of the bulletin or to see a full half-hour programme with all the news reports included. If she sits back and does nothing then the programme proceeds as usual. If, however, the viewer wants to take control of the programme then she can go back over the menu of items and start to pick and choose which to watch and in what order. Or she can watch through the programme and 'click out' of any item she doesn't want to see any more of and skip on to the next item. Another scenario would have the news weighted depending on the viewer's known preferences.

The key to News is topicality. But the items in a news broadcast are not created simultaneously. The most topical breaking stories are created last, but they usually go at the beginning of the programme. The light-hearted 'and finally' story may have been 'in the can' all day. So the programme can be broadcast to the viewer's set-top box in reverse order. The breaking story may even be viewed live.

So here is another iTV model. The broadcaster transmits the component parts of the programme and the viewer sees a tailor-made compendium of them. You could envisage a continuously re-built news programme which would store stories and update stories and even delete stories, waiting for the viewer to grace it with her presence.

A key to this kind of iTV is indexing. A template program to construct a news programme running in the set-top box needs to know how to treat the news reports that come its way. The program works using templates and the news reports need to fit into templates.

◼ Trimedia production

It has become common for broadcasters to work with radio and television simultaneously and bi-media working has become commonplace, especially in news.

The next step is to produce programming which can be used on radio, television and the Internet. The requirements and preferences of each are different. Radio has a relaxed intimacy rather like a companion person who hangs around chatting, while the Internet is responsive and can be directed like a servant. Television, on the other hand, rather takes over and sits you down and force-feeds you short extracts from the world outside.

In trimedia the relationship has another dimension. Radio can provide the community of interest and this community can then interact socially via the Internet. Television can pick up the community and present a distillation to a wider audience still. In 2000, the German broadcaster ORB, based near Berlin, produced an audience participation trimedia 'reality' show called *Waldländer* which means Foresters. This featured a group of three young men and three young women dropped blindfolded in the middle of a forest and having to fend for themselves for 72 hours with only broadcasters for company: described as having 'beds made from leaves, nettle tea and worm soup'.

The local youth radio station, Radio Fritz (yes really!), carried news of their exploits and listeners could also follow it on the Internet and contribute help using SMS, e-mail, telephone or fax and providing advice about edibility of mushrooms and the calorific value of earthworms … amongst other things. Local television broadcast occasional visits to show highlights and significant events. Satellite ISDN was used to provide occasional streamed video coverage from the forest which was then left on the website for further viewing. Unlike *Big Brother* this had to be a collaborative effort and you won by working together.

Material was produced by the ORB team for all three media using specially designed equipment, workflow models and techniques. Web and radio audiences were significant although a late night slot for TV coverage took viewing

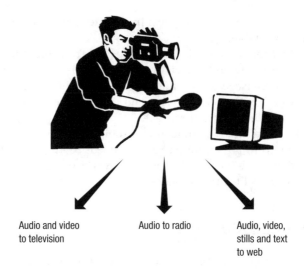

Audio and video
to television

Audio to radio

Audio, video,
stills and text
to web

In Trimedia Production a reporter (or team) produces
material for all media at the same time.

figures down too low to be measured. However, one approach to interactivity
in broadcasting is to harness disparate technologies and let them work
together. Audiences seem willing to play this game and so will broadcasters,
once they achieve trimedia thinking to go along with the programming.

■ An object-oriented future

There is a way in which issues of differences between computer screens and
television screens become irrelevant. If a broadcast programme is made up
of a set of distinct objects then artefacts of interlace or resolution (and
more) can be avoided by tailoring the format of the object specifically for
the display medium. This approach is a key part of the MPEG-4 standard.

A future television receiver will build up the image seen by the viewer
based on the objects in a scene and the rules by which they operate: for
'rules' read 'script'. The virtual studios seen in broadcasts work this way,
but the image is built in the studio rather than in the viewer's home. The
principle is the same.

The objects could be broadcast along with the rest of the programme, or
the viewers could define elements of the programme for themselves. The
programme presenter will be defined as an object: imagine being able to give
a child a gift which allows their own persona to be used as the presenter of
a favourite programme. A viewer might feel inclined to use a clown 'object'
to present the parliamentary report or the legendary broadcasters like Ed
Murrow, Richard Dimbleby or Walter Cronkite might return to present the

news once more. Viewers could in any case choose presenters with whom they could identify.

With this technology, viewers will be able to take a much greater level of interactive control without losing the seemingly essential linear narrative aspects that make television (like all linear entertainment) so compulsive. Let's face it, the best stories take the narrative through twists that the audience could not have imagined. This appears to contradict the approach to interactive narrative adopted in Book 1 Chapter 16, *Multimedia narrative*, but the strengths of linear narrative need not be discarded even after the new strengths of multimedia narrative are established.

The object-oriented nature of MPEG-4 will work alongside wider adoption of XML and MPEG-7. XML allows authors to embed structural and descriptive information in a document (and that document could be an audiovisual programme) while MPEG-7 aims to provide a standardized way of describing audiovisual material for indexing. The combination of these three technologies has the potential to allow programme producers to present audiences with a kit of structured parts from which a programme can be built in a number of ways, depending on a viewer's preferences. (In case you're wondering, the MPEG numbering isn't continuous. It currently goes 1, 2, 4, 7 and 21.)

■ The return path

The connection back from the viewer to the television station is known as the return path or the back channel. As we have seen, it is possible to broadcast interactive television without a return path, but it limits the kinds of interaction that are possible. Significantly, having a return path makes the individual viewer part of a community, just as Internet users are.

The most obvious return path is part of a cable television system. If each individual end-user has a clearly defined connection back to the cable-head-end then this can be used for interactivity. This requires a configuration called a 'Star'. The alternative configuration, called a 'Tree and Branch' only identifies the end-user back to a local node and so is not automatically set up for a return path. Such a configuration is not necessarily physical in a digital system, since digital markers can identify separate packets of information sent along a single path.

Cable operators have long been aware of the importance of the return path. The most sophisticated analogue cable experiments back in the 1970s allocated a return path, but in this case it was for analogue video and audio. The viewer could contribute to the programme back down the cable. This needed a complex distribution mechanism and was never really a commercial proposition: partly because the trial users who had access to the interactivity just didn't want to communicate with the broadcaster.

The return path today is a data path. It could be used for video, but there is usually just not enough bandwidth to allow this.

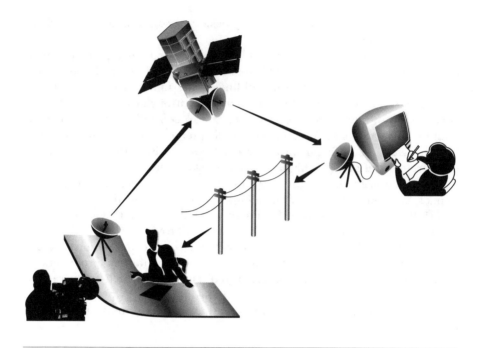

Interactive TV via satellite currently needs a telephone to
provide the return path.

Satellite and terrestrial television seem to be set up so that providing a
return path would be impossible. Thousands of receiver antennae point at
a single transmitter whether it is at the top of a nearby hill or high in the
sky on a satellite. Certainly currently available implementations of iTV
using satellites or broadcast use the humble telephone line to provide a
return path. Despite this it has been proved possible to provide a return
path to both kinds of transmitter without resorting to using a telephone line,
even when the viewer is on a communal aerial system. At the time of
writing, this is a proof of concept rather than a full-blown service.

■ DVD

Since this chapter is basically dealing with interactivity using a television
it seems sensible to briefly describe DVD. Although DVD Video is primarily
a format used for distributing movies and similar audiovisual programmes it
has some built-in interactive capability. Strictly speaking DVD is a family of
formats but for simplicity we will follow consumer convention here and use
the term DVD to refer to the videodisk format used to distribute movies.

Digital video disk (now retro-renamed digital versatile disk) was first
designed to be a replacement for compact disk. It had become apparent that

there was not enough data on a CD to hold a full movie at a quality high enough to satisfy the movie companies and the movie fans. The CD-based movie format (Video-CD) used MPEG-1 video and almost always needed two disks for each movie. DVD had data space to spare for the higher-quality MPEG-2 and, with two layers of data on each of two sides of the disk, sometimes room for more than one movie. Although DVD swept the board in Europe and America, Video-CD remains a popular format in the Far East and, surprisingly, DVD-icon movies like *The Matrix* can be found on CDs in places like Singapore. The new format did not have an easy start, since the major movie companies insisted on strong copyright protection and also a system of region codes to restrict where in the world disks could be played. (See also Book 1 Chapter 15, *Rights, copyright and other intellectual property*.) Region coding is not mandatory however, and you can make disks that will play anywhere.

A DVD-ROM disk is just like a high-capacity CD-ROM and DVD videodisks and audio disks are just DVD-ROM disks with a special standardized set of directories and files. DVD players look for certain files in these directories. Since a DVD player has to be a simple device sold at consumer prices the interactive facilities available are tightly specified and limited compared to those available using a computer. The functions, and how to access them, are contained in the DVD video specification and allow you to produce menus, buttons, video segments that can seamlessly jump around and, of course, play sounds and movies.

DVD production will almost certainly use a dedicated authoring software package which will give you a choice of the options available. This used to be a relatively expensive proposition but in mid-2001, with the price of a DVD-R writer coming down, Apple and Dell launched desktop computers that came fully fitted out to produce home DVDs that would play in real DVD players. This distinction is important because the DVD-RAM format, available alongside DVD-R, produces disks that do not generally work in DVD players.

Producing a DVD involves three stages: encoding of the video and audio, authoring of the menus and other interactive features, and pre-mastering to make the (usually) digital tape to send off to be replicated. More information on encoding (which in practice means compression) can be found in the audio and video production chapters of this book: Chapters 6 and 7.

Navigation around a DVD uses menus with up to 36 hot-spots. Since DVD players are operated using hand-held remote controls the user-interaction is deliberately kept simple. Usually a remote's left-right-up-down buttons will move the selected hot-spot around the buttons, highlighting as it goes. When the highlighted button is the wanted one the user presses a 'select' button and initiates the required action.

Besides commands to control the content playback and select from menus there are simple programming functions. These allow a DVD interaction to read timers and registers, do simple maths (including random numbers and comparisons), and numerical operations such as AND, OR and eXclusiveOR. (If you have never used XOR, it is extremely useful for flipping the value of individual bits without needing to know their original state). In an environment with limited memory and power, such as a consumer player, working with bits at such a level is advantageous.) To continue the similarity with old-fashioned computer programming you also get system and user registers to play with: these are places in memory where you can store and read flags. The system register, for example, will tell you things like language preference or parental control level set.

Seamless branching is built into the DVD specification. It can be used to instantaneously change camera angle on a scene for sports or concerts. It works by laying down interleaved chunks of the various streams in the data. Seamless branching can also be used to allow variation of storyline or to allow different versions of a movie to be played without having to encode each version in its entirety separately. In these cases the branching is done under program control rather than user control.

Subtitles (alternatively known as subpictures) are held as bitmaps so sub-title text is bitmapped text. This neatly avoids any font problems, especially with languages like Chinese, and since the subpictures are the same size as the video the information can be overlaid anywhere on screen. This image-based format is also compatible with the way subtitles are generated for movies. Closed caption subtitles (for the deaf and hard of hearing) are held as data and can be put onto line 21 by the player for decoding and display by the television set.

It has to be said that the plethora of CD and DVD formats available in the last few years are not easy to keep track of.

The replication formats are DVD-ROM, DVD-Video, DVD-Audio and SACD. The last two are discussed in more detail in the chapter on audio (Chapter 6). But, unlike CD formats, all DVD formats are essentially DVD-ROMs. Consumer DVD movie players (and software players for computers) look on a DVD disk to see if they can find information in specified direct-ories. DVD Video disks use a directory called VIDEO_TS while the audio disks look for AUDIO_TS. Open the disks using a computer and you will find one or more of these directories. You might also find directories of accom-panying material for use on a computer as well, such as screen savers to help promote the movie.

So a replicated ('pressed' if you prefer) DVD disk is always going to be, at heart, a DVD-ROM. The basic unit of any such DVD is a layer and a layer can contain 4.7 gigabytes of error-corrected data. A particular DVD disk can be single- or double-sided – most disks are single-sided – and a side can have two layers. The DVD player can select a layer by changing the focus of the laser pickup so you can have up to 9.4 gigabytes in two layers. Such a disk is called a DVD9.

These are the main 12 cm (5-inch) formats for DVD. The duration of video assumes an MPEG-2 capacity of two gigabytes (2^{30} bytes in a gigabyte) per hour.

DVD-5	Single-sided, single layer	4.37 gigabytes
DVD-9	Single-sided, double layer	7.95 gigabytes
DVD-10	Double-sided, single layer	8.74 gigabytes
DVD-14	Double-sided, double on one side	12.32 gigabytes
DVD-18	Double-sided, double layer	15.9 gigabytes

A DVD-18 would allow 18 hours of MPEG-2 video. The usual bit rate for DVD encoding averages around 3.5 megabits for video (5 to 6 megabits is regarded as 'transparent', meaning you shouldn't see any difference from the master) with just over a megabit used for audio on top of that. The audio can be up to six-channel (5.1 surround) and in several languages. The audio format on the disks is most likely to be Dolby Digital format but some may be multichannel MPEG or DTS. These sound formats are mutually incompatible but some players can handle more than one and some disks contain more than one.

Although the level of interactivity provided in the DVD Video specification is limited, with some resourcefulness very sophisticated interactive scenarios can be developed: particularly since menus can be made from movies as well as stills. As more and more homes have DVD players you can expect more resourceful use of the medium.

■ Web on TV

In many homes (and especially in the living room) the only display device is the television. This is an opportunity to marry the Internet with television. At its simplest this means using the television, possibly with a keypad, as if it were the display of a computer. Several manufacturers have produced set-top boxes, and even complete TVs, which can be hooked up to the Internet.

Microsoft's WebTV is the best known of these, but not the only one. It can offer three levels of service: an Internet connection with Web and e-mail (WebTV being the Internet Service Provider); enhancements to regular television viewing; and, at the highest option, a satellite connection which gives the user video-on-demand with individual control over the videos.

The Web and television make strange bedfellows. I mentioned the 'lean forward' and 'lean back' issue at the beginning of this chapter. Until Web content is divorced completely from the display device, there will always be incompatibilities which hinder use of the Web on televisions and mobile hand-held devices. If we assume, as a starting point, a web page as designed for a computer, then displaying this on a TV has some, all or even more of the following problems.

■ TV resolution is much lower than a computer screen. This is because of the smaller number of pixels (comparable with a 640 by 480 computer screen) whereas most websites are designed for 800 by 600 pixels or more.

- Television displays are interlaced (as was mentioned at the beginning of this chapter and as is explained more fully in Chapter 7) while computer displays are not. Television pictures are usually a little softer than computer images. The combination of these two effects results in shimmering and flickering when a sharp computer image is displayed on a television.

- Television programmes don't have scroll bars or windows. What you see is all there is.

- Televisions don't have mice so selecting a link on a web page can be difficult, especially if the link is in a group on the screen and small. The TV user is probably trying to do this using a remote control handset.

- Televisions have different gamma (brightness curve) settings to computers and even the colour phosphors are different.

And this is before we consider the psychological implications of watching TV from the couch on the other side of the room.

Of course the solution to this is specially-designed web pages with larger text and plenty of space to help couch-navigation. This could be achieved by careful use of cascading style sheets and XML. The set-top box can also filter the text and picture information to help readability but currently the provision of special pages is the best option. For this reason many web-on-TV ISPs offer a 'walled garden' of web pages which are designed, selected and vetted for the service.

The link between the web and interactive TV is an important one. There is a mass of information being produced for the web and many iTV features, like electronic programme guides and enhanced teletext, are so similar to web pages that it makes sense to provide XML or even HTML-based systems to program them.

You can see from this chapter that there are many ways of providing interactivity on a television set. Which of them are genuine interactive television, as opposed to being just, say, enhanced TV, is unclear. Certainly, to many long-standing multimedia developers and web designers the features available are not yet sufficient for real interactivity. Whatever the level of interactivity available, the key to iTV will be its role in our lives. Our friendly television set could be a more popular channel for interactivity than the business-like computer after all.

THEORY INTO PRACTICE 3

Either
Choose a DVD and use its 'extra features' section if it has one.
Assess your reaction to the interaction allowed.

1. How easy is it to use the remote control with the menu system	Easy						Difficult
	1	2	3	4	5		
2. How readable are the menu options	Readable						Hard to read
	1	2	3	4	5		
3. How easy is it to navigate between options	Easy						Difficult
	1	2	3	4	5		

4. Write a paragraph about your experience.
   Are you positive/negative? Why?

Or
If you haven't tried iTV, perhaps you can get a demo of it from a salesman in one of the larger consumer electronics shops. What are the pros and cons? How do you assess the potential?

■ Summary

- The role of the remote control is vital in iTV.
- If producing video for joint use on both the computer and TV, the production needs to take account of the difference in displays.
- Different models of interactivity are emerging for iTV – carousel, multi-channel, 'return path', and tailored are a few.
- It is possible to combine the strengths of radio, computing and TV into one programme appealing to different audiences.
- Object-oriented approaches to TV component parts may allow far more interactivity for a viewer in the future.
- DVDs allow limited standardized interaction in a consumer environment.
- Web on TV has production problems to take into account but these can be overcome.

■ Recommended reading

ITV Insider (http://www.itvinsider.com) has news information, news and links to resources for the iTV market and developer community.

The UK Digital Television Group (http://www.dtg.org.uk) provides information on digital television, including iTV.

http://www.opentv.com and
http://www.liberate.com – proprietary iTV software platforms.

http://www.mhp.org – website for the Digital Video Broadcasting consortium's
Multimedia Home Platform interactive platform.

TiVo, who produce a PVR (personal video recorder), have a section of their website at
www.tivo.com that uses Flash to demonstrate the system.

The Pace Report 2001 ('Consumer attitudes towards digital television in the UK and US')
is published by Pace Micro Technology plc, Victoria Road, Saltaire, Shipley, West
Yorkshire, BD18 3LF, United Kingdom. www.pace.co.uk. Summary report is available at
http://www.pace.co.uk/documents/PR/pacereport01.pdf.

Everything you needed to know about DVD can be found in the DVD FAQ at
http://www.dvddemystified.com/dvdfaq.html

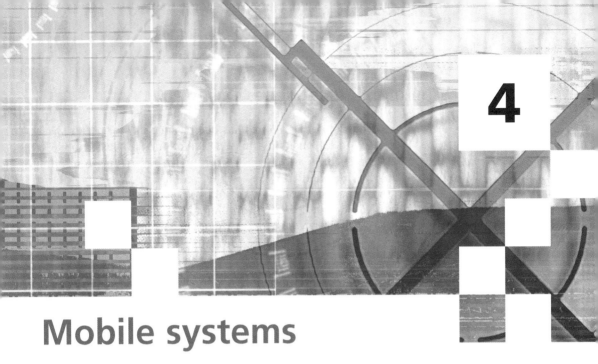

Mobile systems

Project manager's responsibilities

- To understand the potential, limitations and rapid change of mobile technologies
- To recognize the place of mobile technology in convergent technologies
- To understand the capabilities of the mobile services currently available and how best to fit these to particular user requirements

■ Why mobile telephones?

The growth in use of mobile telephones has been a success story of the past few years. We are close to considering mobile telephones (or just 'mobiles') as appliances like refrigerators, televisions and video recorders. You know when something has reached this stage when people ask 'What mobile do you have?' rather than 'Do you have a mobile?' A 2001 survey of consumers' attitudes to new technology in the home (carried out by Gallup on behalf of Pace) indicated that hand-held mobile devices for messaging were top of most people's gadget lists and in 2001 50% of all calls in Scandinavia were being made using mobiles.

Telephony and radio grew up at the same time: the start of the twentieth century. Initially you needed something like a ship, or at least a motor vehicle, to carry the sheer weight of equipment needed for what was then called wireless, and until the 1920s the radio spectrum carried telegraphy, like Morse code, rather than speech. With the 1920s came speech and the birth of radio as a means of communication and entertainment.

Part of the issue over size had to do with the use of valves (or vacuum tubes) and although valiant efforts were made at producing portable radio-telephony units (known to the military as R/T) it wasn't until transistors and then integrated circuits came into existence in the 1950s to 1970s that telephones could really get mobile. Power was also an issue and mobile telephones need small effective batteries coupled with low power consumption, and low heat generation as well. Longer wavelengths needed bigger antennae, so early mobile systems needed whip antennae of several feet in length because at the time it wasn't practical to work at the ultra-short wavelengths (high frequencies) we do today. And then there was the cost.

So the developments in electronics made it possible to produce a telephone small enough to be practical on the move. Initially it might have been the size of a small suitcase but that was no problem: we put them in motor cars and called them car telephones.

A smaller phone wasn't the only issue. Early car telephone systems worked with a single transmitter working to each telephone. This was very wasteful of radio spectrum and certainly didn't encourage volume usage and production. It wasn't until the idea of using small cells of transmitter/receiver coverage and letting the phones move between the cells that the infrastructure was able to handle high volumes of use. Instead of a single transmitter on the top of a hill – the broadcasting model – mobile phones used lots of small, low-powered transmitters on nearby buildings and on small masts.

The infrastructure problem was solved by using a cellular structure – hence cellular telephones or cell-phones. The idea of using many small cells each covered by its own low-powered transmitter (called base stations) was suggested in 1947 by AT&T in the USA, but it took until 1968 before the regulatory body in the USA (the FCC) allocated sufficient frequencies for trials. By the late 1970s cellular telephony was a reality and the first such network started in 1979 in Tokyo. The first US system started in Chicago in 1983 followed by the UK in 1985. The networks and telephones were analogue. The next step was to make the system digital and this helped make the telephones themselves smaller and cheaper: eventually. There were early fears that the extra cost of digital handsets would stop the take-up of mobiles. In fact mobile telephony has a history of exceeding predictions with a mid-1980s report suggesting that the UK usage would be 20,000 in 1990 when in fact it reached a million. Such underestimations seriously affect the radio spectrum allocated by governments, so they are not a trivial matter.

Digital brought a world standard (but not used in Japan or in some of North and South America) called GSM. Competing operators started to bring the prices down, users could buy a cheap phone and pay for calls as they went using pre-pay cards. This resulted in mass use of mobiles in most of the world with places like Finland and Japan showing the way. Mobile phones were no longer the preserve of business. (Unfortunately the Pay-as-you-go phone pricing was based on the assumption that users would actually make calls. A significant number of them did not, only using the phone in 'emergencies'.)

The situation in the USA was not as strong. This was partly because of a charging structure that made people pay to receive mobile calls rather than to originate them and also because of a more fragmented and patchy coverage. But the USA is a big and sprawling country. Ironically, mobile phones proved very practical in emerging nations. Putting in base stations for a mobile network is often more cost-effective than laying cables. And guarding a few base stations is easier than trying to stop theft of copper cables from a wired network in remote locations.

Eventually the mobile telephone became a disposable item. A facility called 'chat and chuck' became possible where the phone itself was so cheap that it could be discarded when the airtime ran out. No keypad was needed because voice recognition could be used, putting the computing power in the network rather than in the handset and also making it cheaper. The phone could even become small enough to be contained in the phonecard. In these cases, unlike Pay-as-you-go, users could make calls but not receive them because the phones did not need to have a telephone number at all.

Incidentally, you will sometimes hear the developments in telecommunications – fixed as well as mobile – referred to as POTS and PANS: POTS are the Plain Old Telephone System and PANS are Positively Amazing New Stuff (or similar).

■ There's more to mobiles than telephony

Mobiles started out as telephones. In some parts of the world that is their main use. But the growth areas in mobile communications are not necessarily for speech. The Small Message System (SMS) designed for use with pagers is available on most mobiles. On some networks of the world messaging is free and many times sending a quick message is better than making a voice call. The result is that SMS has taken off in a big way. The 'billion messages a month' mark was passed in Europe in April 1999. You may be limited to only 160 characters (70 if you are using multi-byte languages such as Japanese) and your recipient must have an SMS-capable device but it has led to schoolchildren in Scandinavia repeatedly messaging each other across the playground and bullying by SMS has become a twenty-first century problem in some schools. You don't pass notes in school any more, you message. But don't forget to turn off the warning 'BLEEP!'.

Much of the SMS traffic consists of service messages such as a notification of a voice mail message. It is possible to gateway between e-mail and SMS with the user's telephone number becoming part of their address and another common use of SMS is notification of arriving e-mails and faxes. Downloading of new ring tones for mobiles is also done using SMS. Vehicle tracking systems taking status input from the vehicle and combining it with global positioning information can then send the resulting data over SMS. SMS is asynchronous (meaning that it is not a 'real-time' activity) and does not need a continuous connection to the network other than for the times of sending and receiving. It can fit in around synchronous network traffic such as speech and it is a 'push' technology. Unfortunately, being a push technology means that you can be sent unsolicited messages. So SMS is vulnerable to spam.

After SMS came icon-messaging and it was possible to connect up your laptop and surf the Internet using your mobile telephone, but at a snail-pace 9600 bits per second. (Slow for people who never had to use a modem at 300 bits per second or telex!)

At the time of writing the mobile industry is looking towards so-called third generation systems (called 3G) which are just starting to be rolled out. If the original analogue cell-phones were 1G then digital cell-phones were 2G and the next big step was a broadband (by wireless standards) infrastructure which was to be called the Universal Mobile Telecommunications System – UMTS.

Part of the plan for UMTS is to allow seamless movement of telephone calls between different types of cell. You might have a pico-cell in your home or office (a very low-powered mobile phone cell working like a cordless telephone and possibly connecting to your land-line telephone line) with more familiar cells working at an urban, rural and district level. In theory you could even reach the coverage of last resort using satellites.

The mobile telephone user will, in theory, have access to more bandwidth which makes it possible for several services to be used simultaneously, or for a few broadband services such as video-telephony or media-rich Web surfing to be possible. This could be in situations we now recognize as typical for mobile telephone use or it could extend this, for example by making

special arrangements to provide Internet access to airline passengers. At the opposite end of the scale, a UMTS phone handset might be able to move seamlessly between being a cordless phone in your home to working as a cell-phone away from home.

In between 2G and 3G is 2.5G. This takes existing mobile telephone systems and stretches their capabilities to provide more bandwidth. Using GSM for a data call makes what is called a circuit switched data connection since for the duration of the call the user has use of a circuit. High Speed Circuit Switched Data (HSCSD), General Packet Radio Service (GPRS) and Enhanced Data Rate for GSM Evolution (EDGE) are three 2.5G steps on the road to 3G.

HSCSD allocates more of the radio spectrum between the user's telephone and the base station to give higher data rates. It otherwise works like a normal mobile call but for data it can give a theoretical maximum speed of 28.8 kilobits/sec. For mobile operators it is mainly a software upgrade (and users need new phones) so is easy to implement and is already out there on some networks. All calls are discrete dial-up calls and you pay for the duration of the call as usual.

GPRS goes a stage further than HSCSD and provides an always-on connection for data which can handle 172.2 kilobits/sec although since data is sent in packets the connection is not necessarily continuously in use.

A third evolution, called EDGE, builds on GPRS and changes the way the mobile cell is used to make it more efficient. In theory EDGE will give 384 kilobits/sec, but this will only be possible under certain conditions such as close proximity to the base station. Always-on connections also have to vie with each other for use of the 'space' available in the mobile cell so it is possible for many users to slow each other down. Any switched calls, such as for voice, will deny space to the always-on connections. In practice, space may need to be reserved for each form of communication. This is similar to the concept of a contention ratio in ADSL where a number of users, typically ten or twenty, share the bandwidth.

These 2.5G technologies may well coexist. It is particularly likely that circuit switched data calls and always-on data calls will coexist because certain applications are suited to one or the other. A video-telephone call would best be served by circuit-switched while web browsing or e-mail is best served by always-on. It is also worth noting that 'always-on' data is not the preserve of 2.5G systems. The Japanese (and some American) 2G mobile telephone systems are using a method of transmission that also allows for this kind of connection.

The i-mode system, provided in Japan by NTT DoCoMo, gives mobile telephone users access to web-like services on their mobiles. Apart from a service fee, users pay for their data calls by the amount of data transferred, not by time. This is different to the Wireless Application Protocol (WAP) technology used in GSM.

Unfortunately mobile systems will rarely achieve a throughput of data as fast as the maximum claimed. For example, UMTS/3G in theory offers over two megabits of data transfer, but typical mobile rates were predicted to be as low as 500 kilobits. This is partly because of transfer overheads but also because working truly mobile – while moving – introduces errors in the raw transfer which slow down the user's data rate. Being stationary close to a base station would give much better performance. Also in the real world there will be interference and congestion. In the early stages, technological difficulties in producing the handsets could reduce the practical rates as well.

We should also mention that wireless LAN cards and Bluetooth technologies are also mobile communication methods. Wireless LAN systems like IEEE 802.11 (Wi-Fi) which is marketed as, among others, Lucent's Orinoco or Apple's AirPort enable users to achieve basic Ethernet speeds (11 megabits being the current state of this particular art) without needing wires. This is revolutionizing the networking of schools and open-plan offices. Wireless LAN itself is not giving rise to many applications; rather it is enabling a freer use of things we normally can do over our fixed networks. Bluetooth, on the other hand, is aimed fair and square at linking devices together at high speeds across very short distances, such as from hand to mouth or mouth to belt, or phone to laptop. In this it has similarities with the application of infrared communications such as IrDA but it is not restricted to line-of-sight. The aim here is to let us carry on doing much of what we currently do with these small devices, but without having to keep plugging them into each other. Again it possibly means more for freedom of movement than the generation of new applications.

■ Web on mobiles

Mobile access to the Internet, for web browsing and e-mail, is available using some mobile telephone handsets. Some of these combine a cell-phone with a Personal Digital Assistant (PDA) and have a small but reasonable screen size of the order of 160 by 100 pixels, sometimes in colour. Arguably, the future of mobile Internet lies more with PDAs than with phones but, despite the small size of display available on a phone, mobile Internet exists.

The primary limitation is the display on the telephone handset. This is usually only a small number of lines of as few as eight or ten characters. This does not give much room for manoeuvre in web design. Both i-mode (the system marketed by NTT DoCoMo in Japan) and WAP provide Web access on handsets but they operate in different ways. i-mode handsets include browsers that recognize a subset of HTML whereas WAP browsers use WML, which is a derivative of XML. The difference means that an i-mode phone can display any website, although ones not designed for the system may, as DoCoMo put it, 'not display properly': an understatement perhaps. An i-mode user will automatically be given an e-mail address on the handset, initially based on the phone number but changeable. A telephone number can be an i-mode URL so that clicking on the link dials the call.

A WAP site is inherently different to an ordinary website and this is because of the limitations of a handset display. The website becomes a WAP deck and the individual screens (pages) that are displayed are called cards. Moving from one card to another involves moving between small sections of the deck to display a different card. A deck is (at least in early WAP implementations) limited to 1400 bytes in size. Since the WML is based on XML it follows much stricter syntactical rules than HTML, which is rather loose. The result of this is that websites cannot be displayed on a WAP browser even if they fitted the small screen on a handset, and need to be specially coded with WML and its scripting extensions in WMLScript. However, these WML decks can be held on ordinary websites with ordinary-looking URLs (but with .wml at the end). If you open a WML deck in a standard HTML browser it will either show the WML as plain text or ask you to save it to disk if the WML MIME type is not one your browser recognizes. There are also several WAP emulators available on the Web and these allow you to browse WAP sites using a web browser.

Whether a WAP phone can access the Internet at large, in search of WML, depends on the service provider. A walled garden might be provided (a self-contained subset of the Internet ready 'wapped') or a gateway to the Internet itself. Since WAP is designed to put as little load on the phone as possible – the WAP micro browser is a very 'thin' client in this client–server relationship – the gateway has to do a significant amount of processing.

From the mobile operator's perspective, WAP provides a mechanism for sending data to the user much like SMS. Indeed, WAP sits on top of what is called a bearer, and SMS can be one of these bearers although the 160-character limit is restrictive. But whereas SMS can push messages to the user, WAP as it presently stands cannot. Since SMS is free-of-charge to receive (and WAP using dial-up air time is definitely not so) system messages using SMS will not inconvenience the user.

At the time of writing, WAP is a new development and has suffered from being sold as a means of surfing the Web on your mobile telephone – a task for which it is not ideal. It can be argued that with broadband data available through 3G mobile systems WAP is a very short-lived possibility. But it can be used very effectively to retrieve short items of information such as train timetables, news headlines or where the public toilets are.

■ Location-based services

A mobile telephone, by definition, has no fixed abode. However, once you know where it is at 'this' moment you can feed it with information pertinent to its location. This can range from very localized information along the lines of 'when will the next tram arrive?' to more general 'what movies are showing in town and starting within the next half hour?'

A mobile telephone network always knows which cell a cell-phone occupies since this is the way the system works (ignoring ambiguities when the phone is at the edge of more than one cell). But a cell can range in size from a few hundred metres in a city to several kilometres in the open countryside. The FCC in the USA has recognized this as a problem when alerting emergency services to respond to cell-phone calls. Whereas a fixed line such as a road-side phone booth has a known position, a cell-phone does not. The FCC's approach has been to ask for positioning systems to be built into the cell-phone system so that 67% of the time an emergency call can be positioned within 125 metres. This needs to be accurate enough to pinpoint whether an accident is on one carriageway of a highway or the other and was cited as one reason why the US-run GPS satellite system increased its civilian resolution recently. Even if the telephone does not have GPS built-in, it is possible that the motor car soon will.

But GPS is not the only way. If the cell-phone has sufficient processing ability then it can triangulate its position from the base stations in range. This can be done by GSM phones with what is called the SIM Application

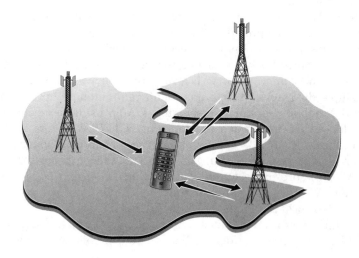

Tool Kit. Since the phone will usually be receiving more than one base station at any time and since accurate timing information is available from these base stations, or since signal attenuation can be measured or since sometimes the angle at which the phone signal is detected at the base stations can be determined (by detecting which of a circle of directional aerials is receiving the signal), the system can pinpoint the phone's location. Some of these systems require modifications to the handset or to the base station or to the network infrastructure.

Even though the mechanisms described above may not, at this point, be ones that are available to programmers of WAP sites, it is still possible to provide location-based services. The interim solution is a simple one: you ask the phone's user to tell you where they are. This probably involves asking for a post or ZIP code since the databases containing the information will usually rely on these codes to geographically pinpoint the data. Alternatively you can ask the user to choose from a list of place names. This, at least, enables you to try the services out without having to wait.

Location-based services are considered a key opportunity for mobile service operators and so should have similar potential for application and content developers. The link will best work where there is data which is resolved by location and which people want to access while on the move. The handset (or PDA) needs to be able to display sufficient information for it to work. A small WAP phone handset display is not likely to show sufficient detail for a good map, but a PDA will. You will no longer ask a passing stranger how to get to your hotel, you will call up a map on your PDA which will show where you are and what route to take.

There is an irony in this situation. The telephone was originally a device to enable us to communicate at a distance. Location-based services on our mobiles will bring us more information about what we are close to.

◼ A broadband future

Simon Buckingham, Managing Director of Mobile Lifestreams Limited, listed a number of key applications for mobile data in a paper published on the GSM World website. He listed:

- access to Internet chat rooms;
- textual and visual information such as news and sports results;
- live transfer of digital stills from camera to website;
- videoconferencing, surveillance and other video applications;
- web browsing;
- collaborative working;
- high-quality audio for broadcast or law-enforcement purposes;
- job allocation and briefing for repair workers and general dispatch work such as for taxis;

- corporate e-mail and intranet;
- Internet e-mail;
- asset tracking and vehicle positioning;
- home automation.

There are two different aspects to mobile broadband: better connection at a distance and doing away with wires. Simon's list covers the former. If we have access to faster connections in a device as small as a telephone, or at least something we can put in our pocket, then we can make information come to us, wherever we are. This can be location-based but it can just as easily be web surfing, listening to Internet radio or videoconferencing. In fact, it could be anything that you could do at your desktop.

The dilemma with mobile broadband comes more from the mobility than from the data, since whatever services can make use of the increased amount of data the equipment still needs to be carried around. Of course we might go back to the notion of the car phone and the luggable rather than portable telephone. But this assumes that key elements of desktop systems cannot be made more compact and lighter. We can replace the keyboard with speech recognition or have a keyboard that we can fold up like a handkerchief and put in our pocket. We could have a folding display, or wear eye-phone glasses to see whatever we needed to see.

More realistically in the short term we could use a broadband mobile phone to access two linked services simultaneously. This might involve booking a hotel by talking to the travel agent and simultaneously looking at room plans and maps via the Web. Collaborative working between colleagues already happens using desktop videoconferencing systems but it could easily extend to a business-to-consumer transaction. Making it work with a mobile telephone can greatly enhance things like tourism and travel as well as telemedicine. If you have an always-on connection in place then telemedicine can extend to include continuous remote monitoring of a patient. People can be sent home for observation remotely in circumstances where today they would have to stay in hospital.

This promise of mobile technology has to be tempered with concerns about safety and health when radio transmitters are used so close to the body and the head in particular. Mobile telephones are regarded as a safety hazard in aeroplanes and in hospitals, many local authorities will not let cell-phone masts be put near schools and there are an increasing number of objections being raised by local residents when new masts are planned almost anywhere. These concerns cannot be ignored, especially since 3G mobile networks, working at higher frequencies, will need more masts. Only time will tell if the health and safety issues come to dominate the use of the technology – it is sobering to remember the optimism about the 'power of the atom'.

The second part of broadband mobile is less to do with telephones and more to do with computer networks. We've already mentioned standards like IEEE 802.11 (Wi-Fi) and Bluetooth, which are enabling people to do away with wires in their offices, schools and homes. There are even publicly-accessible wireless networks in places like airports. Currently these systems are limited to 11 kilobits per second but in time the speed of the links will get faster although the very fast speeds may well only be available over very short distances. The limitations of many current systems are compounded by them using radio frequencies that are shared with many other devices including microwave ovens. This is an obstacle that can be overcome in time and there is a vision of 'holistic communications', where every device would be able to talk to every other device and, sitting in the centre of this, would be a very mobile portable computer.

Olivetti's famous active badge experiment, which equipped identity badges in an office with infrared sensors, allowed the office 'system' to know where people were. Telephone calls would be routed to the telephone next to them and when they walked up to a computer workstation it would immediately come to life with their own personalized desktop. (If they wanted privacy they just put the badge face down to obscure the infrared sensor.) Extend this concept to a museum or art gallery and make it work with a visitor's own mobile phone or PDA. Without necessarily invading visitors' privacy it would be possible for a museum to provide individually tailored information and in a broadband world this could include video to show objects in action.

It may be that mobile systems will always lag behind their wired counterparts when it comes to speed of access but in many ways the opportunities that mobile systems offer are greater than for any other part of the emerging convergent technologies. It is even possible that, before long, all our personal communication will be wireless.

THEORY INTO PRACTICE 4

Set a challenge for you and your colleagues to come up with three clearly-defined location-based services that would be useful for a person to access by a PDA.

Perhaps you could pitch your ideas to a mobile service operator as a funded research project.

■ Summary

- The introduction of a cell-based infrastructure established mobile communications for the masses.
- Digital technology allowed smaller, lighter, standardized and ultimately cheaper mobile phones.
- SMS text messaging has proved a highly successful extra facility.
- 3G systems look towards the use of broadband via UMTS and seamless movement between different types of cells.
- Broadband will allow more services including richer media services.
- Different types of connection – switched-circuit or always-on – serve different purposes.
- Wireless LAN and Bluetooth technologies are revolutionizing networking by linking devices at high speeds across short distances.
- Mobile access to the Web via WAP and i-mode have strong limitations partially overcome by the larger display of a PDA.
- Location-based services can reach people with information tailored to their roving position and are proving of interest to mobile operators.
- Wireless services offer great potential and, eventually, all our personal communication may be done this way.

■ Recommended reading

www.phonewarehouse.com/History.htm
  Phone Warehouse in Houston, Texas have an interesting set of mildly technical articles about the history of the telephone: wireless and wired. The history of the telephone itself includes the incredible but true stories of the man who was a few hours too late to patent the telephone, the measles epidemic that led to the invention of telephone numbers and the undertaker who invented automatic dialling to frustrate the attempts of rivals to steal his business.

http://www.gsmworld.com is the website of the GSM Association and includes background information on the technology.

Simon Buckingham, Managing Director of Mobile Lifestreams Limited has written a number of briefing documents on mobile telephone technology which can be found at http://www.mobilepositioning.com

Another comprehensive site is Mobilecomms Technology at http://www.mobilecomms-technology.com/

The Pace Report 2001 ('Consumer attitudes towards digital television in the UK and US') is published by Pace Micro Technology plc, Victoria Road, Saltaire, Shipley, West Yorkshire, BD18 3LF, United Kingdom. www.pace.co.uk. A summary report is available at http://www.pace.co.uk/documents/PR/pacereport01.pdf.

Akass C. (2001). *Smart Machine in a Smart World* (Holistic comms), London: *PCW*, June 2001 issue

Dornam A. (2000). *The Essential Guide to Wireless Communications Applications: From Cellular Systems to WAP and M-Commerce*, Upper Saddle River, NJ: Prentice Hall

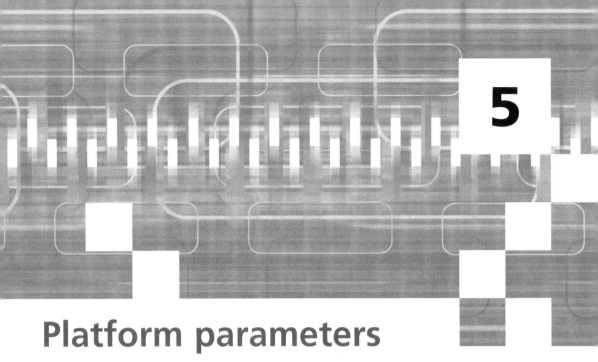

Platform parameters

Project manager's responsibilities

- To understand the implications of platform choice
- To discuss the chosen delivery and development environment with the client and advise on the best choice for the particular application
- To similarly advise on delivery medium

■ Introduction

The word 'platform' was traditionally associated with hardware: the computer platform. But a platform can also describe software as well as hardware, and it is increasingly used in this way. On the Web, the platform is made up of the browser plus computer, operating system and even a particular plug-in. For an offline application the operating system and computer is generally enough but sometimes more detail, such as the capabilities of the graphics card, may be important. A useful definition might be that the platform is whatever you have to specify in order to run the application. Often the specification will be extended to say what kind of display is needed, or

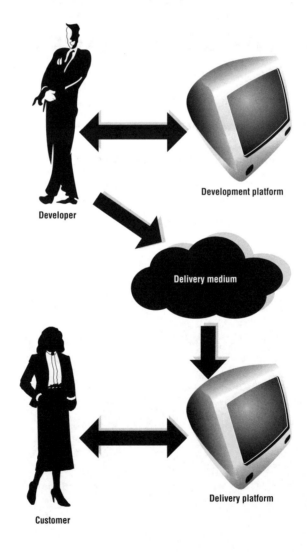

Development platform

Developer

Delivery medium

Customer

Delivery platform

how big a hard disk, or how fast an Internet connection. This chapter will use the word 'platform' in this broad sense.

There are three options that will be discussed in relation to platforms. The first is the most obvious, and is the delivery platform: what does your user have to use in order to see your website (or application)? Then we come to the delivery medium: how do you get the application to the user? Finally we shall discuss the development and testing platform: what do you need to use in order to make the application in the first place?

■ Delivery platforms

Sometimes a client will come to you with a project and they will know exactly what platform they want to use. This may be because they use a certain machine or browser in their business, or because the target market for the application has mostly machines of a particular type. They may have other websites and have a set specification for those. Sometimes they will be a little more vague, and often they will ask for your advice. This chapter will not offer any advice for your particular project but it will help you to ask the right questions about the requirements, and to work out how to identify the positive and negative factors influencing the choice. The basic question we are asking here is 'Which platforms are useful for what purpose?'

☐ Online delivery

Delivery on the World Wide Web usually sidesteps many issues of the delivery platform because web browsers all take the HTML (and more) that makes up a web page and display it on the user's computer. The Web is the multimedia delivery system that works on most computers because the browser takes care of the underlying operating system and hardware. It is an example of document-based programming, because the web page is a document made to certain standards, which is displayed by any browser that adheres to those standards. Despite the vagaries of differing interpretations of JavaScript (particularly between major browsers) and whether or not the browser understands ActiveX, the web page is the most cross-platform format.

There are several main issues affecting the delivery of a website over the Internet: speed of access, updating, security/payment, and the 'unlimited' size of the data space that can be provided online. You can restrict access, charge your users for access, and even keep track of who has accessed your information and when. (Some of these techniques spread themselves to CD-ROM, with software and fonts being sold by giving away encrypted versions on CDs and then charging for decryption.)

The speed with which your potential users can access your application is unpredictable. You may have users sitting at the end of fast permanent connections such as ADSL where download speeds are measured in megabits (not many megabits admittedly, but megabits nonetheless) and you may have users with 28.8 kilobit modems or even slower mobile connections. Unfortunately, speeding up the local link between the user and the network does not necessarily resolve the overall problem, because other links in the system will in themselves be unpredictable. Speed will depend on the bandwidth of the link itself (colloquially 'how fat is the pipe') and on how much other traffic there is on it. Also, the fatter the pipes become, the more data people want to pass down them.

Having a fast server, as well as a fast Internet connection, will help but at the end of the day your web page will be at the mercy of every possible bottleneck as the data flows between your site and its visitor; perhaps across opposite sides of the world.

On the Web, problems of download times for audio and video have been addressed by streaming the data for audio and video rather than copying it and playing it later. Streaming is the method whereby a steady stream of data is expected from the data source, and it is processed and displayed as it arrives (on-the-fly). The classic example of this is digital audio from a compact disk. The 16-bit digital audio data arrives at the decoder chips and is converted into analogue audio immediately. There is no storage of the data. If for some reason the stream of data is disturbed then you hear either clicks, where a single sample is misplaced, or pauses and hiccuping. A DVD player will be receiving a stream of MPEG-2 movie while it plays a disk.

A way around the problem of disturbances in the data stream is buffering and/or caching. For buffering, the data from the source is read into memory at the rate at which it arrives, and is read out of memory at the rate at which it is needed, hoping that you don't run out. In this way small discontinuities can be removed. To continue the CD example, some portable players have buffers so you can cope with knocks to the disk while jogging. With a cache the data is read completely into the cache memory and, once it has all arrived, the application accesses it. (In this case it's more like an MP3 player reading a song out of its RAM.) The disadvantage of a cache is that the application has to wait for all the data to arrive, although once the data is in the cache it can be accessed many times. The program or the data format can be designed to allow the data to be both streamed and cached, of course, but that is practical only if the data stream is fast enough.

So what are the pros and cons of using the Web as a platform? On the plus side you have a low cost of entry but with sophisticated possibilities. The application itself, the website, can be changed at any time either to update it or to fix errors and there is potentially an infinite amount of space to hold information for the website. The Web's reach is global and instant. On the minus side you have a heterogeneous user base and you need to decide how much you can cater for the differences in the users' systems. There are security implications which may or may not be important for your client, although unless you are carrying out online transactions this shouldn't be a real issue. Many of your users will be on relatively slow connections, which means you need to think carefully about the use of bandwidth-hungry media such as video.

☐ Mobile multimedia

Mobile multimedia is likely to polarize into applications delivered onto a handset, with limited display size and keypad but great mobility, and 'bigger' devices such as PDAs where you might even get handwriting recognition or even a 'real' keyboard. Working mobile onto a laptop, while being bandwidth-dependent, doesn't really imply many other differences from conventional computer delivery. The services might be different and location based for example. As a delivery platform, mobile systems have many similarities with the Web but have the issues of bandwidth taken to an extreme since even though the stated aim of third generation systems is two megabits this will be slow in coming and may be very dependent on your distance from a base station. One potential benefit of mobile over the Web is the delivery medium through a telephone network because such a network will be set up to keep track of the user, for billing purposes if nothing else. The variation of performance of handsets might also be relatively small compared to the variety of platform parameters on the Web. Chapter 4 of this book has looked at mobile systems in some detail.

☐ Interactive television and DVD

The arrival of digital television brings with it the possibility of interactive services. Initially the broadcasters are greatly concerned about the stability of the whole transmission system and take great pains to ensure that nothing could crash the set-top box or, in extreme circumstances, more crucial parts of the system. One result of this was the use of tightly-controlled proprietary software environments such as OpenTV and Liberate used on satellite and cable systems. An open environment based on MHEG (an open standard for multimedia) and Java is specified for terrestrial digital television.

Video-on-demand (VOD) may provide another market for interactive services on the TV or via ADSL to a PC, and if so it will provide a potential market for multimedia developers for the navigation (more so than content which is probably pre-existing). The way in which VOD develops as a platform will depend on which of the two proposed models for it is used, and where. You can say that in one model the VOD server pushes the application for display in the home on a television linked to the service by a set-top box. In the other model the set-top box itself pulls the application from the server.

The 'push' model works like this: the set-top box functions as an audio-visual version of the dumb terminal and basically passes user commands down the line to the server, takes the data the server sends, and displays it. This means that the application itself, usually something to run a movie, is actually being run in the server and not in the set-top box. This can be a crucial situation for the developer because the servers are often going to be very powerful processors running real-time operating systems totally unlike those you would usually find in multimedia. This is unless the servers are set up to run virtual machines that emulate other platforms. Since the set-top boxes are operating only as dumb terminals, including MPEG decoders, there is relatively free rein for potential manufacturers as only the display and communications need to be standardized, not the application environment because that is in the server.

The 'pull' model has the server operating as a data source, whether for downloaded data or for streamed data, and the downloaded application runs in the set-top box, which therefore has to be more than a dumb terminal. This raises a different problem both for the developer of applications and for the service provider. Since the set-top boxes are likely to be from more than one manufacturer, compatibility between the boxes and the applications is in question. In practice this can be overcome by offering only applications that the server knows the set-top box can support or that the set-top box itself knows it can support.

The biggest difficulty in producing interactive television is currently the high entry cost. The tools may cost money and/or need skilled but hard-to-find programmers and the service operator may charge a significant sum for access to their system. The positive aspects of iTV are that in the long term this is likely to be the interactive delivery medium with the highest reach among the general population. For some purposes, such as entertainment or public services, this is a very strong incentive.

DVD is easier since it is possible to produce DVDs on the desktop. But with both iTV and DVDs you are likely to have a particular kind of client, one with access to and experience of those kinds of distribution channels.

☐ Computers and operating systems

When it comes to computers, the platform is not just the microprocessor or operating system. For a mathematical calculation program it may be sufficient to name the operating system, but for multimedia there are issues of screen resolutions and bit depth, sound parameters, the speed of the CD or DVD-ROM drive, the way that video is handled, the amount of RAM and the size of the hard disk ... at least. There may be issues of whether the system is capable of multitasking (doing more than one thing at once) and whether you should take account of this.

In an ideal world every computer program would run on every kind of computer hardware. However, there are serious differences even between the way the basic microprocessors work, let alone differences between operating systems. Fortunately there are also similarities.

The 'standard' computer for many years has been the PC. Although 'personal computer' is a generic term, the initials PC have come to refer to Intel-based machines with the Windows operating system. Originally it was a disk operating system produced by Microsoft called DOS (for Disk Operating System) which defined the basic platform. The kind of screen available has been the subject of separate 'standardization' starting with screens designed for use with American television sets. Ironically, a screen resolution of 640 by 480 pixels (this is the active size of an NTSC television picture, of which more is said in Chapter 7) used to be one of the most standard things about computing systems, although this is now changing as higher screen resolutions have become commonplace.

PCs are made by a large number of companies, and it is this range of competing manufacturers that has led to the PCs becoming so inexpensive and widespread. Only Unix (especially its freely-available variant Linux) is as successful, but it remains successful in a niche in education, science and technology rather than on the business desktop. In multimedia, Unix variants such as Linux have most impact in web servers because many of the machines that run servers on wide area networks run one of these, and if you are producing CGI (Common Gateway Interface) programs for websites, then you might come across them.

With the introduction of Microsoft's Windows the PC found itself a more friendly face, and Windows itself became the defining factor for the platform, which was vital, as the underlying microprocessors became more powerful and part of the Multimedia PC (MPC) standard.

Competition for Windows came from the Apple Macintosh, which had adopted a friendly windows (with a small w) approach from its inception. Only programmers drove a Mac from a command line; the users moved a pointer about and pressed virtual buttons on the screen. In some other niche areas there were companies such as Commodore (with the Amiga) and Acorn (whose Archimedes machine was firmly lodged in British education, but boasted the most bangs for the buck of any desktop machine of its day and was the world's first RISC workstation).

Besides general-purpose computers there were games machines (from the likes of Sega, Nintendo, and Sony), short-lived home entertainment machines like CD-TV, 3-DO and CD-i, and set-top boxes for video-on-demand, Web-television and interactive television. As a multimedia developer your choice of offline platforms, for CD-ROMs and kiosks, encompasses these and more.

☐ Criteria for offline choice

It would be nice to be able to say that, as a developer, you have the freedom to choose the platform best suited to deliver your multimedia vision. In fact the market is more likely to drive your choice, and often that points to whichever machine is prevalent in your target sector. Businesses have business machines, often not suited to entertainment techniques even if those techniques are appropriate.

You will have to research your sector and find a lowest common denominator for the machinery your customers have. This relates to factors such as:

- manufacturer and machine type;
- type and speed of processor (and therefore performance);
- amount of memory (RAM);
- size of hard disk (speed is less important but should not be forgotten);
- operating system (don't forget which version);
- CD-ROM/DVD-ROM drive (speed and capacity);
- access to online systems (local networks, Internet, World Wide Web, and so on);
- speed of network connection;
- resolution of the screen;
- number of colours on the screen;
- ability to handle moving video, and the multimedia architecture;
- sound handling (8- or 16-bit, mono or stereo, what compression?).

In some cases you may need to find out how often your users actually make use of their machine. This could be especially true in a business or training situation, where machines may be shared between people. It would be awkward for your users to spend half a day using your training package if someone else needed to use it every two hours to read the electronic mail.

☐ Cross-platform chameleons

An alternative to choosing a single platform for an offline project is to produce the application for a number of platforms. This can be done by using an authoring system that produces versions of the application for several platforms. Macromedia Director is such a package, which will produce files that will run on Windows and on Apple from the same 'source'. At a lower level, there are libraries for graphical user interfaces, which can be used with C or C++ to run on different platforms with separate compilation. Director can also produce applications that will run with the Shockwave/Flash plug-in with a web browser.

It is possible for one computer platform to emulate another. A fast processor can run a program that appears, to the application, to be another platform entirely. The more powerful the platform, the more easily it can do this. There are Mac emulators for the Sun and Windows emulators for the Mac, where one machine pretends to be the other. It can even be possible (if rather strange) to run a program under emulation where the emulator is itself running under emulation.

A further refinement of this technique is the virtual machine. Here the application code runs in a specified environment. That environment is provided by a program, the virtual machine itself, that runs on the host machine. To run the application on a new platform you need only a new virtual machine. The ancestor of C, BCPL, ran in this way, and used a compiled intermediate code (called CINT code), which then ran on the virtual machine. This technique has a new lease of life through Java.

This technique needs fast processors, otherwise it is best suited to low-interactivity applications. This is because interpreted software (interpreted by the virtual machine) is likely to run more slowly than software compiled to run directly on the target machine. There is also the problem of the abilities and drawbacks of particular machines. A virtual machine has to have an audiovisual capability (since it is, to all intents and purposes, a platform in itself), and this will be the same as or less than the capabilities of its host.

If there is an incompatibility between the different platforms that can run the software then the software might have to run differently. A lesser platform may run the software in a less than optimum way. The way that the application (and possibly the virtual machine if there is one) copes with this is by degrading the performance of the application. Pictures may have fewer colours; movies may run more sluggishly. If this is done well, and possibly even invisibly to the user, it is called graceful degradation. Graceful degradation was inherent in the Web as it existed in the early days, and is relatively

Graceful degradation.

easily achieved today by providing versions of web pages for browsers with or without frames, with or without plug-ins, and so on. You add plug-ins, JavaScript or Java if you think that your Web pages need them and your viewers have the motivation, but you can be sure they will see something even without them. Offline multimedia has no such guarantee, and graceful degradation has to be programmed specifically rather than assumed.

A classic example of graceful degradation is illustrated in basic HTML. The browsers that display HTML documents have differing abilities, and it is recommended that any graphics used in documents are supplemented by words that will be displayed on browsers that cannot display pictures: although these are rare they are still around. In this way the document display gracefully degrades from graphics down to text only. If you are designing interactive applications that will run on networks you might have to account for extreme cases like this.

■ Delivery medium

We have already defined the delivery medium as the means by which you get your application to the user. If it is a Web page then the World Wide Web is that medium, and we shall come to that in a moment. Let's start by considering offline delivery.

Besides deciding on what computer platform the end-user will actually use to view your production, there is the question of how you will actually distribute the end result. To a certain extent this will depend on the size of the application, and might even have been specified up front. It is not unknown for small applications to be delivered on floppy disks, with a little help from compression.

Here are some of the options.

☐ Floppy disk

Using a floppy has the advantage of using a standard medium, as you can assume most of your potential market has access to a floppy disk drive. However, the downsides are the capacity, the slow access times, and the relative difficulty of replicating in large numbers. Compressing the material on the disk means that it has to be decompressed onto the user's hard disk to run, but this also overcomes the slow speed of the floppy. It is, however, very easy to copy floppies to order if the quantities are small enough. Alternatively, small applications can be distributed easily using e-mail or the Web.

☐ Compact disk and DVD

This medium has become so universal that it seems unlikely that it may ever lose its supremacy as a carrier. Currently it is splitting into an increasing number of different incarnations (Video CD, multi-session, CD-Plus, Photo-CD and the various formats of DVD). Back in 1984, when CD-ROM first appeared, it was touted as the data carrier to exceed all our requirements; but that was before digital video. DVD is a higher-density format than CDs; it makes use of a smaller physical structure on the disk and more layers of data to increase capacity, but otherwise it is effectively a 'turbo-charged' CD. Replication of CDs in quantity is very cheap (almost down to pennies), and the disks are very robust. Since a blank recordable CD now costs about a dollar (or less than a pound) each you can even consider 'burning to order' in small quantities and you can get self-contained machines which will copy CDs onto blanks in semi-bulk.

CD-ROMs usually adhere to ISO 9660, which specifies file structures. This is based on DOS but has extensions to cover other filing systems. Importantly, an ISO 9660 CD-ROM can be read on a large number of computers. Extensions to ISO 9660 have allowed longer file names and the ability to handle multi-session recordable CDs. Using ISO 9660 means that the computers can access the data on the CD: they cannot necessarily do anything with that data unless they have the appropriate application. DVD-ROM uses a system called universal disk format (UDF) to give multi-platform compatibility in the same way.

DVD-ROM disks (as distinct from DVD movie disks) are still relative newcomers and have been mostly used for large games and encyclopaedias but DVDs have either one or two sides and each side can have either one or two layers. A disk side can have two layers because the laser beam that reads the data on the disk can be focused at different depths in the transparent surface of the disk and so read two different layers. It is theoretically possible to produce a disk that has a CD-ROM upper layer with a DVD-ROM lower layer and so be backwards compatible to what is still a substantial installed user base.

CDs can be cheaply produced on the desktop for less than a dollar a time and the disks can be sent to pressing plants for replication. This is more difficult with DVDs since the recordable format is not practical for anything other than small DVDs. For movies the DLT tape format is usually used just as, once upon a time, Exabytes were standard for CD-ROMs.

Disk-based multimedia has been overshadowed by online systems in recent years. Now we also have the influence of DVD and interactive broadcasting and cable to consider, and this makes it uncertain as to what delivery platform will dominate. In practice, it is likely that evolution will find favour over revolution, and on- and offline systems will coexist. DVD-ROM evolves from CD-ROM, and broadcasting and the Internet will find that they have much in common. Added to this are mobile systems. Within the individual formats there will be evolutionary developments.

■ Hybrid delivery

Sometimes you can make use of both on- and offline delivery. Web links can be part of DVDs. Updating a CD or DVD from the Web allows a publisher to keep a product up to date between editions. Many encyclopaedias do this. Sometimes the application will update the offline data so that the updates are seamless; sometimes the application displays the new data in its own right as an addendum. This kind of application becomes less necessary as more users of the application are able to read all the data from the Internet.

Splitting data provides a good way of holding big assets such as movies but also allowing volatile information to be available from the website. This is easily achieved because web browsers will happily read files from hard disks or DVD/CD-ROM as long as the web pages are written with relative file paths or addresses.

■ Websites and server/browser balance

On a network, where there is software running on the user's local computer (the client) and it is working closely with software running on a server, the platform issues can become more complex. For the purposes of our discussion here we shall be dealing only with the Web, but sometimes similar issues can develop in any client–server application.

There are four software components in the web page chain: the page itself, the browser, any software that dynamically generates the pages (probably using a server-side include system like PHP or alternatively a separate gateway (CGI) program), and the server itself. The web page runs on the browser, and the dynamic page generation software runs on the server. HTML, Java, JavaScript and plug-ins are part of the page/browser combination.

When a web page is requested by a browser a set of HTTP (hypertext transfer protocol) requests are sent to the server. Besides the information about the requested page or asset, the browser will also pass information to the server telling it such things as the type of browser and platform, the referring page (where you clicked), the network address of the browser's machine, and possibly a string called the environment variable. All this information is available to any programming running on the server.

Sometimes you will need to decide whether a particular task is best handled by HTML or a server program. On the author's infrared photography site, Invisible Light at http://www.atsf.co.uk/ilight, there are a number of photographs that are displayed in individual web pages. When a viewer clicks on a link to display one of these pages a CGI program (written in Perl) is executed, which takes as its input the picture name that is passed in the HTTP request as a parameter. You will see that the URL requested has the extension .pl at the end rather than .html. The Perl builds the necessary HTML for a web page to display the photograph, reading the image size from the picture's JPEG file itself, configuring GIFs to form a frame around the image and incorporating a caption from another file. The resulting HTML is sent back to the browser exactly as if it had been a static file. In this way there is no need to have a separate HTML document for each page: the page is generated on demand. So the programming removes the need to have a lot of HTML documents on the site, and this is the essence of dynamic web design and a very simple example of a content management system. The Invisible Light software happens to be written in Perl but the same thing could be achieved by other means. Sometimes you will have a free hand in choosing what software to use. In this case Perl was used because the web space rented for this particular site supports it.

As has already been mentioned, a very large site with hundreds of pages or more will almost certainly have to be generated by a database in order to be maintained and updated – in other words, dynamic.

You should not confuse the size of the design task with the number of pages on a website. Database-driven websites may have hundreds of pages, but those pages will have a small number of different layout templates into which the database 'pours' the content. For example, in the casting directory on the Internet for the UK company *The Spotlight* there are over 20,000 possible pages available – one for each actor – but there are actually only three different Web page layouts used for the database: one for the search card, one for the list of hits resulting from a search, and one for the individual actor's information and photograph. A relational database generates all the pages based on HTML templates.

Another decision is whether a particular task can be carried out at the client side or the server side. For example, if you want to modify the web page according to the browser being used you can do this either by using JavaScript in the web page to dynamically rewrite the web page itself or by using a CGI program on the server. The advantage of JavaScript is that the load on the server is lighter, but the disadvantage is that the HTML is larger because of the JavaScript embedded in it and support of JavaScript is inconsistent between browsers and operating systems. The advantage of doing this using a server-side application is that the results appear to be normal HTML to the browser, and so the solution is more reliable. However, running a lot of CGI programs can be a problem if the site is heavily visited in which case one option is to separate the dynamic generation of the pages from the requests to view them. The CGI can be used to generate HTML files and save them on the server where they are accessed in the usual way. The pages might be generated at regular intervals using a timer or they might be generated every time the content changes. The latter seems more sensible but it is possible for you to have no real idea of when some of the content is changed since it might be being pulled in from an external source.

Sometimes the choice of where to generate the dynamic content is made for you. If you want the web page to reflect the time of day where the user is situated – remember they could be anywhere in the world – then only the browser knows this, and so client-side is your only option. Conversely, if you want to show visitors what number visitor they are then this has to be done at the server because only the server can keep a count of all visitors. There are also many web surfers who do not enable JavaScript or Java, or who are prohibited from using them on a business network.

CGI programs can be written in any language that runs on the server, and databases are a common form of program run using CGI. In practice, server owners may restrict you to using server includes such as those written using PHP or using interpreted languages such as Perl rather than running compiled C code because this dramatically reduces the risk of accidental damage to their server by your code. On the other hand, a compiled C program could be less prone to hacking.

■ Platforms for development and testing

So far, this chapter has dealt with the delivery of your application to the end-user: your customer. You will also be making choices about the platform or platforms you use to design and build your application or your web pages and to test it.

You do not have to develop your application on the delivery platform. This is especially true for a cross-platform offline application, since the usual practice would be to develop the application on one of the group of delivery platforms and test it on them all. Even low-level code can be produced on a different computer using a cross-compiler.

It is more likely that you will use one consistent platform for your asset creation and manipulation for every application. Even though the IBM PC 'standard' has been the most common delivery platform for multimedia and the majority of web surfers use PCs, many multimedia developers have used Apple Macintoshes for their asset work and have moved the assets across to their delivery platform during integration. The reason for this approach is that the best tools tended to appear first on the Macintosh and that, for the graphically minded, the Mac was already the platform of choice. The wider availability of tools and the more 'corporate' policies of larger development agencies means that this is much less the case than it was but you still hear managers saying that they'd like to 'wean the designers off their Macs'.

Moving assets between platforms needs to be done with some care and attention to quality and parameters. For example, screen gamma is different on different platforms: the same image looks lighter on a Mac than on a PC. This and other asset formats will need to be checked and tested on both platforms. If you are producing an application for more than one platform, especially if you store your assets in a single common format, this will be even more important.

In fact, it does not matter whether you are a Mac fan or a PC fan or a Linux fan or whatever. The point is that you can retain your platform of choice for asset creation and manipulation even if your client or market wants a particular application delivered on something else. The only limiting factor is that the asset creation platform must have a display that matches or exceeds that of the delivery platform. It is clearly no use whatsoever to try to do colour graphics on a black and white machine, or to use an 8-bit audio system to produce sound for a system with CD quality 16-bit sound.

Similarly, you should create and manipulate your assets in the highest convenient standard and convert down, if necessary, at the last moment. This will not only give you the option of porting the assets to other delivery platforms if required, but will actually help you to keep the quality as high as possible.

For online authoring you can use almost any computer since an HTML page is simply a text file. But just as any browser should be able to read the web pages, so you have a choice of the ways you author them. Some people like to handcraft the HTML in a text editor or word processor, while others use one or more of the many WYSIWYG packages for web page layout. The production of web page assets is very much like offline work. The same packages can be used to produce the images, sounds and movies, and even animations and interactive mini-applications. Again, you can choose to produce your HTML and assets on whatever platform you can use.

An exception to this is production of websites with JavaScript. The vagaries of JavaScript implementation mean that you need to be able to test for both main browsers (plus others you want to support) on both platforms. This problem has been so acute that many developers are refusing to guarantee complete cross-platform compatibility of sites with JavaScript. The great thing about standards is that you have so many to choose from!

It is certainly true that your design platforms have to include your delivery platform so that you can, at the very least, test the performance and carry out debugging. This can mean that you have to have access to every possible configuration of platform that your customers will have. This is no trivial task. With a website you can test with a validator to check that your code is correct, but you should also look at the pages on as many combinations of browser and computer as you can. (There's more on this in the *Testing* chapter in Book 1 Chapter 11.)

With an offline application the problem can be significantly worse because you are likely to make more direct use of the computer's facilities. To show the magnitude of this problem, let's consider variations of a computer:

- different models
- different amounts of RAM
- different screen resolutions and numbers of screens
- different sizes of hard disk
- common extensions to the basic system
- different versions of the system software
- different CD-ROM drives
- different network configurations.

With that list, and assuming five possible options for each category, the number of possible configurations is $5 \times 5 \times 5 \times 5 \times 5 \times 5 \times 5 \times 5$, which is 390 625. This is not really practical, and you will test for the most likely problem areas such as system software versions and amounts of RAM.

■ Author once and deliver everywhere

There are delivery platforms for convergent media that seem as similar as the proverbial chalk and cheese. We either have to prepare to produce different applications or different formats of web pages for each of them or we need techniques that allow us to author once and deliver on many platforms. XML, which is discussed in Chapter 2, *The Internet*, is one part of the solution to this: it allows the content structure to be separated from the way it is laid out, so that the layout can be changed depending on the delivery platform.

Fortunately the range of platforms available to us is increasing just as techniques are developed to cope with them. Eventually content and display will be so separated that we won't even worry about the delivery platform, in the same way that a television programme maker does not need to worry about the type of receiver the audience is using.

THEORY INTO PRACTICE 5

Experience is the best teacher on moving applications from one delivery platform to another. You can learn a lot by talking to people you know who have direct experience of this and by discussing the detailed problems they may have encountered.

For online, set up as many computer/browser configurations as you can and look at some websites with them to compare the results. If you have PCs, Macs and Web-capable televisions you should also compare the brightness of the screen images.

For offline, look at a multimedia application that is available on more than one platform and compare the versions.

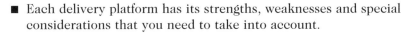 Summary

- The choice of delivery platform will usually be decided by either your client or your target market.

- You do not have to do all your development on the delivery platform, especially when it comes to working with your assets.

- Each delivery platform has its strengths, weaknesses and special considerations that you need to take into account.

- It is possible to develop an application that will work on more than one platform, but moving from one platform to another can lead to changes in performance, and you should be aware of what is likely to happen.

- When planning web gateway programs you should consider the balance between the browser and the server.

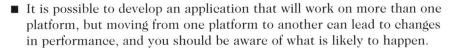 Recommended reading

Siegel D. (1997). *Creating Killer Web Sites*, 2nd edn. Indianapolis, IN: Hayden Books

Vaughan T. (2001). *Multimedia: Making it Work*, 5th edn, Berkeley, CA: Osborne McGraw-Hill

The Digital Television Group have reference material on use of MHEG in television in the reference section of their website at
http://www.dtg.org.uk/reference

6

Audio asset production

Project manager's responsibilities

- To book the studio and the artiste
- To make sure scripts are ready
- To make sure that the recording session is successful
- To ensure that the material is prepared to the correct specification and encoded with an appropriate codec
- To understand the processes involved in producing this kind of asset

Managing audio

During the course of making an offline multimedia production there will be, by definition, assets to be created or manipulated that make use of time-based media such as sound and video. Web pages are also incorporating such things as the bandwidth of Internet connections steadily goes up. Unlike text and graphics, you may make use of specialist facilities with personnel that you hire to work on your assets, but even if there is a studio in your office which you can use for the recording, the basic principles are the same. Video will be discussed in the next chapter; this chapter describes the processes involved in dealing with audio from a practical point of view.

The basic idea behind this chapter is to provide you, as a producer or project manager, with enough background on the technical processes to enable you to hold your own in discussions with experts. It will also make your use of specialized facilities more interesting and rewarding. Of course, depending on your background, you might already be an expert in one of these fields. It may also be the case that, in a small development company, you will have the opportunity to 'be' the expert and carry out some of the audiovisual manipulation yourself. So treat our use of the word 'you' lightly, since if you hire an external facility to record, mix or edit, it will be an engineer that actually carries out these tasks.

The aim in writing this chapter will be achieved if, next time you go into a sound suite and the engineer asks if you want the sound limited, or what sample rate you want, you can tell him or her, or even discuss it, with confidence. If you hire a facility and an engineer, make use of their knowledge and do not be self-conscious about asking advice.

One final point: working with sound on a video is much like working with sound by itself. The main extra difficulty is in keeping the sound in time with the video: in synch(ronism) with it.

Before the session

It is most likely that your first use of a sound studio will be to record a narration voice-over for your project. This might be for the soundtrack of a movie or to accompany an animation or group of stills. Music and drama are other possible kinds of material you might record, but this chapter will concentrate on recording a single voice. The basics are the same, but music and drama have the bells, the whistles and the fairy dust.

When you decide to record a voice you need three things: the script, the voice, and the studio. You will also have thought about how you want the voice to sound, and this will have influenced your choice of voice-over talent.

Incidentally, do you have to use a studio for this, or could you record in an ordinary office or at home? If you or a member of your team have a background in sound recording and have the equipment then of course you have that option. But it can become very frustrating when you begin to notice all the extraneous sounds, such as aircraft and motor cars and sometimes even birdsong, that are so much part of our background sounds that we often forget they are there. Being in a studio can actually be more relaxing since the voice-over artiste can concentrate on the performance rather than worry about yet another passing motorcycle.

When choosing a voice-over artiste you might have decided to use a famous actor or actress, and would like to include their name and photograph on the cover of the CD or on the home page of the website. Alternatively your voice-over artiste might be a person who specializes in being a voice. In some circumstances you might do it yourself, or use a friend or someone in your company who has experience, perhaps as a radio presenter. For the first stages of a project it is not unusual to make a guide voice track yourself, which will be replaced with a professional one later. You might even record this guide track at home or in the office.

Unless you know someone already, your route to your voice will be through an agency. There are many who specialize in providing voices, usually for radio advertising, and they will have both famous actors and professional voices on their books. Many of them now have websites or produce CDs where you can listen to their clients and make your choice.

The voice-over artiste will like to have a clean script, probably double-spaced so that changes can be made clearly. The artiste will often mark in the emphasis to be used when reading. You should send the script to them a few days before the recording if you can. The script should be printed out so as to avoid paragraphs going over a page boundary. The paper should be stiff so that it does not rustle. You should check pronunciations of any unusual words, especially proper names, and if you are producing the session you should be sure about every word in the script. Be prepared to make changes to make the script easier to read. Often the voice-over artiste will make very useful suggestions about this. Besides the possible direct benefit, you will be helping to create a good working atmosphere, and that will help the artiste to perform better.

With any luck you will find that your voice-over talent can read virtually anything you put before him or her. Many of these people spend the whole day reading one kind of script or another and can cope with most things. Interactive media may be so different from their usual work of advertising and corporate videos that telling them a little about the project will pay dividends or alternatively they may have worked on more websites than you have.

You can work out the timings for the speech yourself before you go into the studio. All you need to do is read it at about the right pace, and time yourself. A rough guide is about 200 words a minute.

You can find your studio either by asking a professional studio body (in the UK this is the Association of Professional Recording Studios) or from a yearbook or even the *Yellow Pages*. Word-of-mouth recommendation or a studio you saw credited on another product is also a useful guide. When you book the studio, as with any outside facility, you will need to agree the rate, how overruns (needing more time on the day) are charged, what happens if you underrun, and the arrangements for paying. You need to tell them the format that you want to take the recording away on (for example do you want to take away a DAT tape or a WAV file on a CD), and whether you will edit the recording yourself (if you have the technology to do so) or will ask the facility to do it.

■ The background

The processes for recording sound date back over a century. Sound is the result of fluctuations in air pressure, which cause our eardrums to vibrate. If the frequency is right these vibrations get passed to the brain and are heard as sounds. In the earliest kinds of recorders you spoke, or rather shouted, into a horn, and the power of your voice caused a diaphragm to vibrate. A stylus was connected to the diaphragm, and this distorted a metal or wax surface over which it moved. To play the sound back you reversed the process and listened to sound coming out of the horn.

The microphone (usually just called a mic or mike and always pronounced 'mike') and loudspeaker (usually just called speakers or monitors) are still the mechanical components of sound reproduction. They work by detecting or creating the movement of air.

■ In the studio

You will find that a recording studio will almost always be in two parts: the control room and the studio itself. The studio may be called the booth if it is small and used only for recording voices. There will usually be a glass window between the two rooms.

Recording studios are strange places. You might find that no two surfaces are parallel because this stops sounds bouncing between the walls and setting up resonances and standing waves (where the room acts like a big organ pipe). Legend has it that some enthusiastic builders once thought that the plans for a sound studio were wrong because the corners were not right angles. So they kindly corrected the error.

The windows, while not being parallel either, will have double or even triple glazing, and the walls, doors and even the furniture will look as if they are either carpeted or designed by someone who likes to hang carpets and boxes on the wall. This is to reduce the reflections (for which read echo or reverberation) in the room. The difference between echo and reverberation (reverb) is simply in the time between the echoes. Reverb sounds smooth and continuous because the echoes are too close together for us to distinguish them. Unless you want to remake 'Heartbreak Hotel' you are unlikely to use echo as such. If there is no reverberation around a sound then we say the recording (or the room) is 'dead' as opposed to 'live'. In fact a room with absolutely no reverberation (called an anechoic chamber) is very uncomfortable to talk in, because we need something of the sound of our own voice to help us speak and some room reverberation around a recording to make it seem natural. With music, especially popular music, this reverb is normally added afterwards using reverb units (the modern electronic version of the echo chamber – which was simply a room with hard walls like a bathroom). Sometime a short delay is added before the reverberation starts, to mimic the sound getting to the walls, and this can help make reverb sound more natural and less obtrusive. This reverb should not favour some frequencies of sound over others. Reverb that does is called coloured and sounds unnatural. The natural small amount of reverberation in a room, together with any other background sounds, is sometimes called ambience or ambient noise.

To record a voice the microphone is usually placed about 18 inches to 2 feet (45–60 cm) in front of the speaker's mouth in a reasonably dead room. If the mic is too close it will pick up lip smacks and other bodily noises. If the mic is too far away the sound will be too 'live', which means there will be too much reverberation.

When you get close to some kinds of mic you suffer from a phenomenon called bass tip-up or proximity effect. This is, as the name suggests, an increase in the bass sounds in the voice, and it is caused by cancellation of high frequencies when the source of the sound (your mouth) is too close to the diaphragm of the microphone.

In general, the positioning of the mic in front of the speaker is crucial in getting a good sound, and an experienced engineer will know where to move the mic to avoid popping, breath noises and sibilance, which is an unnatural whistle in any S sounds. Popping, as the name suggests, is the effect caused by blasts of air from the mouth hitting the microphone. In fact it is sometimes also called blasting. This is at its worst with the letter P, and a good test is the old tongue twister 'Peter Piper'. If the mic is very close, just breathing out may cause a noise. Most studios will put a wind shield in front of mics to stop this. To a large extent these problems can be reduced by having the mic slightly to one side rather than straight in front, and this is called being off-axis. Sibilance is more difficult to control.

The mic will probably be on a stand with a gallows arm or boom suspending it over the table – assuming your speaker is sitting at a table. Some people will sound better, and project more, if they stand up. If the speaker is using a table then be careful about where he or she puts the script. It will probably be under the mic and so you could hear the paper rustling. Less obviously, the relatively hard surface of the paper will affect the acoustic around the voice. The movement of paper, and the movement of the speaker's head as he or she reads, can change the high-frequency component of the voice.

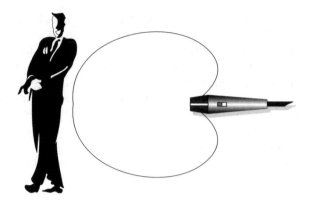

A cardioid microphone.

You can use most kinds of microphone for a voice recording, but the best kind is what is called a large-diaphragm condenser. Although these mics are very expensive they produce a smooth sound that is very easy on the ear.

There are basically three types of microphone, and their names come from the shape of their sensitivity, or polar response curves, as the following diagrams show. The further the curve is from the mic, the more sensitive the mic is in that direction. The reasons for the names will soon be apparent. In most cases you can assume that this curve is the same in three dimensions: a shape turned on the axis of the microphone. The exception is the bi-directional mic.

A cardioid mic will pick up more sound from in front than anywhere else. It is called cardioid because the polar response curve is shaped like a heart.

A bi-directional mic is sensitive on two sides, and this is also known as a figure of eight.

Finally there is the omnidirectional mic, which is equally sensitive all around. You should be able to speak closer to an omni mic than you would with a cardioid without bass tip-up and risk of popping. Some microphones can be switched between all these response types. To record a voice any of these microphone types can be used. A cardioid will have less pick-up from the room but may suffer from popping.

During the recording you, as producer, will be in the control room. The speaker may, or may not, be listening to the sound of his or her own voice in the headphones. Different people will want to hear themselves at different volumes (also called levels), and this can be critical to their ability to read well if they are inexperienced. Giving the speaker a volume control for their headphones is a good idea.

Most people's speaking voices will have quite a wide range between the quietest and loudest sounds. This is called the dynamic range. The engineer can control this dynamic range manually, by adjusting the volume control

A figure of eight microphone.

An omnidirectional microphone.

fader in the control room, or by using electronics to automatically compress or limit the signal.

Although the same word is used, audio compression is totally different from and unconnected with data compression. To avoid confusion, the term bit rate reduction is often used instead of data compression, especially in broadcasting. Compressors and limiters reduce the dynamic range of a sound. They are a sophisticated version of an automatic volume control in a tape recorder. A limiter is set to tightly control the volume of sounds that exceed a certain value, whereas a compressor operates over a wider range of levels but more gently. It is difficult to describe the effect of using these devices, but you will find some examples on the website.

You would choose to limit or compress a voice, and therefore reduce its dynamic range, for a number of reasons. You are most likely to choose to make the master recording with compression or limiting that is inaudible to the listener, and most often limiting is used to catch and reduce a few bursts of the loudest moments in the speech. In this way you can bring up the level of the whole speech (that is, make it all sound louder) without the few high points causing problems by overloading the electronics. With a digital signal, for which overloading causes more distortion than with analogue, limiting is useful as a back-stop to prevent accidental overload, especially if you can do only one take.

Both devices, but especially compression, can be used for effect. Because our ear's response to sound is not linear we tend to hear loud sounds with less dynamic range than quiet ones. You can fool the ear into thinking something is louder than it really is by compressing the sound. This is also useful if you want to put speech over some music and it is important that the speech is heard all the time without sounding shouted. However, remember to keep (and archive) a 'clean' copy of your master recording before you start to process it for delivery on your website or CD. This is an obvious thing to do if you are using tape, but if you are working entirely digitally in a computer it needs remembering.

If your sound is finally going to be played on a system with substantial bit rate reduction, as you might on a website, then processing it to reduce the dynamic range of the recording will make the playback sound better because there will be fewer quiet parts to disappear into the noise. For similar reasons, anything that will be played in a noisy environment, such as a point-of-information kiosk at a trade show, should be compressed to make it easier to hear.

If you are in doubt about using limiters or compressors, a basic recommendation is to use a little limiting to catch the loudest peaks. If the recording is quiet, with no background hiss or reverb, you can always compress it afterwards. However, you should remember that compression tends to exaggerate reverberation, and you have to be wary of this. If there is a high amount of background noise then compression and limiting will noticeably affect this by making it seem to get louder and softer depending on the foreground sound, leading to an effect called pumping. An example of this is also on the website. If the response time of the compressor/limiter is too slow, you will hear it pushing and pulling the sound as the amplification goes up and down. If it is too fast, it will distort the waveform of the sound.

Volume, otherwise known as level, has been mentioned already, but how do you measure it? There are two kinds of meters in use: VUs and PPMs. VU (pronounced vee-you) stands for volume unit, and PPM stands for peak programme meter. You will find them with a variety of displays such as dials, bars and sets of LED lights. Actually these kinds of meters are supposed to have a standardized response so you could say that there is third kind of meter which just gives you a 'general idea of levels' rather than truly following VU or PPM measuring.

VUs are the most common although they do not really tell you anything exact about the signal. However, an experienced engineer can judge the level of something very well with a VU, and it arguably gives a good representation of the loudness of the sound. A VU meter display will move around very quickly. A VU has a red band at the top (especially if it is a moving-pointer type of meter) and you will quite often see it running into the red. This is not necessarily an indication of overload, especially in an analogue system, even though it is supposed to be.

A PPM is a more exact kind of meter, and was developed by the BBC to control levels being fed into transmitters, although it is also used in recording. What a PPM does tell you is the actual peak signal going onto the tape or into the transmitter. PPMs are designed to have a fast rise time and a slower release. This helps you to read them. BBC PPMs also have an integration time (in other words they are not measuring the instantaneous level but an average over a small fraction of a second), which means that they will not detect very short peaks. This could be a problem for digital systems, but in practice, even though a short peak may be distorted if you look at the waveform, it will often sound fine because the ear may not hear a very short burst of distortion.

It is more usual now to find VU meters and PPMs that use lines of lights to show levels (sometimes called a bar-graph), but some would argue that a meter with a needle is easier to read. The meter may not be a real one, but could be an image of one on a computer or television screen. A particularly useful type of PPM is the dual stereo PPM, which has two meters side by side, each with two needles. One shows the left and right channels on two coincident needles while the other shows the sum and difference signals for stereo.

Measuring of levels for surround sound is more complex and while individual meters can be allocated to individual channels you can also produce a screen display that shows the levels around the sound stage with zero at the centre of a circle and full volume moving the display out to the circumference of a circle. This is called a 'Jelly Fish' display.

Besides level meters and a compressor/limiter, there will be equalization (usually just called EQ) in the channel of the desk through which the voice passes. This is a glorified bass and treble control, and will help the engineer

VU meter

PPM meter

Bar-graph

VU, PPM and bar-graph level meters.

to get a suitable sound out of the voice. Because of the ear's sensitivity you can often make a voice sound closer – have more 'presence' – by slightly boosting frequencies around 2 kHz.

■ Working with your voice-over artiste

Your recording might be used against a video, a sequence of still images, or in isolation. If you are recording a voice track that goes with a sequence of stills or even over a single image then there will be no problem in recording the voice without any reference to the sequence. This is sometimes called recording wild. In this case you can work your way through the script, one discrete section at a time, rehearsing and then recording. If the artiste makes a mistake (fluffs), all you need do is ask him or her to go back a sentence and read it again. This is best done as you go along rather than at the end. Anything that will be heard in a continuous sequence should be recorded as nearly as possible in that sequence so as to avoid subtle changes in tone or speed, which would be very apparent over an edit. You can mark up your copy of the script with timings for paragraphs, and you should also note where any fluffs occur and how many takes it took to get things right.

You can mark takes by using a diagonal line like this /, which you mark in at the point you will probably use for an edit, or the beginning of the sentence. If there are two takes you can put in two lines //, and you may also need to note timings by the lines. You can get timings from a stopwatch, or better still from the timer on the tape machine or digital recording system.

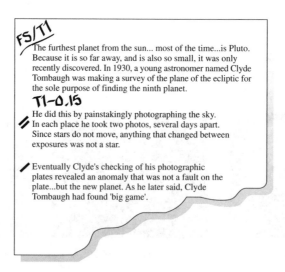

Marking a script.

Mini-disks, DAT machines and hard-disk recorders have a built-in time code that is recorded on the tape or disk (optionally with professional machines), and this is very useful for finding takes. A take that gets through only a few words and then falters is known as a false start (FS) and is not usually marked as a take. To assist editing, you should always record a few words in advance of where you know you will want to edit, to allow the speaker to get up to speed and give you a few choices of where to edit.

There is another way of dealing with takes, and that is to roll the tape back, play the preceding sentence and switch into record as the artiste speaks the lines again. This method avoids editing afterwards.

You might be recording a narration that has to be timed to a moving picture. In these cases you could bring in the computer and run the movie or animation or whatever, but an alternative is to record the movie onto a videocassette. In this way you can make use of a facility that has recording and mix-to-picture capability for TV or films so that the narrator can watch the movie as the recording is made.

Other things to remember about the session: check the spelling of the artiste's names for the credits and make sure that you have agreed the appropriate rights. If you have to go back to the artiste later to sort out rights you are at a disadvantage, and you cannot assume that because they came to the recording they have granted you the use of the material you require.

■ What can I ask the studio to do for me?

A recording studio will be able to do far more than just record your voice-over. If you want them to do so they can edit the takes together under your direction (and sometimes without) to produce a finished master. They can take your voice, script and music tracks and mix them together to produce a finished track for your application. Some facilities can even digitally compress the track into RealAudio or MPEG audio for you, but remember not to confuse audio dynamic range compression with data bit rate reduction. It is your choice as to how much you ask the facility to do, and how much you do yourself. This will depend on factors such as the tools you have available to you, your ability and your budget, because the facility will need to be paid, and this is an above-the-line cost.

■ Mono, stereo and surround sound

A lot of sound in new media is mono, which means single channel. This is because mono sound, by definition, takes up half the space of stereo sound. If you have the capability, stereo will be useful to you because, rather like moving images, it helps you build up the effect you want to convey in your application. If you decide to make your application with stereo sound you will need to know whether it might also be used in mono: if in doubt assume

A spaced pair.

A crossed pair.

it will. This is because a little care needs to be taken to make sure that stereo recordings are mono compatible and still sound correct when the left and right channels are added together to make mono. Similarly, if you want to avoid doing several mixes, you should ensure that surround sound recordings are stereo compatible (if not mono).

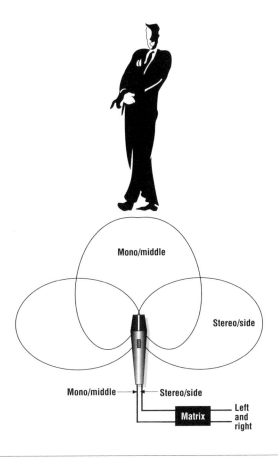

Mono/middle

Stereo/side

Mono/middle → | ← Stereo/side

Matrix

Left and right

The M and S method.

Stereophonic sound means two speakers. We allocate a position to a sound by a combination of time delay – the sound reaching one ear before the other – and level. Using level to give positioning is by far the most common way, and in mixing (which we will come on to later) the balance engineer will position sounds between the speakers by changing the amount of the sound fed to the left and right channels. This is known as panning, and the control on a mixing desk that does it is called a pan pot (for panning potentiometer). Most of the time this simple panning of sounds will work perfectly. Incidentally, we get our directional information at high frequencies rather than at low ones.

When recording a real sound in stereo things are a little different. There are three main ways of recording in stereo. They are called the spaced pair, the crossed pair and the M and S pair. The pair refers to a pair of microphones.

A spaced pair will be two omnidirectional microphones positioned several feet apart. For distant sounds, such as a crowd at a sports event, this will be fine, but the sound will tend to have a hole in the middle since, con-fusingly, a sound close to the microphones but between them is probably not close enough to either. (This kind of set-up sounds particularly good if you listen using headphones, but strictly speaking this then makes it a binaural sound system, not a stereo one.)

A crossed pair is also known as a Blumlein pair, after the English engineer who invented the technique. You take two cardioid directional microphones and place them as close together as you can but pointing 90° apart. This gives a good stereo image and no hole in the middle. For the best results the microphones need to have identical frequency responses.

You can do a simple calculation to show that M (which is mono, left + right) and S (stereo, left – right) can be combined, or matrixed, back to left and right. Left is M plus S and right is M minus S: you can ignore the factor of two here. This method combines a cardioid microphone pointing for-wards and a figure of eight microphone pointing sideways. This system has several advantages: mono compatibility is assured; good stereo can be obtained at a distance using a rifle mic (a very directional hyper-cardioid mic) for the M channel; and the stereo image is very good, especially at the centre. The microphones do not have to have an exactly matched response. You can in fact buy single microphones that use this technique and yet give left and right outputs as in the diagram.

One additional factor to consider is that, strictly speaking, a sound in the centre will sound twice as loud as one at the extreme left or right when the channels are combined into mono. This should be a factor in the mixing, and most panning controls compensate for this. If you want to position a voice off to one side for effect, or to have two voices discussing something, then the best position in the stereo sound field is half-way between the centre and a loudspeaker. This will also give you a good mono signal.

Although quadraphonic sound on record, with four channels, came and went in the mid-1970s, multichannel sound has made a comeback thanks to surround sound movies and DVDs. This is because surround sound sys-tems are being used on the soundtracks of movies to enhance the cinematic experience. More than four speakers are used. Originally, a speaker at the centre-front position was added to improve the stereo positioning for a cinema audience, since very few of them sit in the optimal place for good stereo sound when only two speakers are used, i.e. the middle. Basically a cinema audience is too big and spread out for conventional stereo. Having started with three speakers at the front and adding two at the back left and right to give a surround sound field, you can add what is called a sub-woofer, which gives out only very low-frequency sounds, and possibly two extra front speakers at the mid-left and right positions. This gives either a 5 + 1 or 7 + 1 surround sound field (usually referred to as 5.1 and 7.1) with the first number referring to the number of main speakers and the +1 referring to the sub-woofer, as used in the cinema and DVD. It is also possible to encode a version of surround sound into two channels, and this legacy of quadraphonic sound is still found in surround sound on TV and video and is used for the Dolby Surround format.

Although in theory mixing for one 5.1 sound field should be like mixing for another, it always makes sense if you can to at least check the mix using the delivery format. Since this could be Dolby Digital, Dolby Surround, TDS, MPEG multi-channel or plain old stereo or even mono, this is no trivial task. There is also a certification system for surround sound playback devised by Lucasfilm and called THX and since many movie theatres and home cinema systems are set up for this you might want to take it into account as well.

Recording surround sound is best done using a double-crossed pair with four cardioid mics facing in four directions 90° apart: double stereo. Otherwise a pan pot can be made that moves a sound source around a surround sound field, and some of the digital audio editing and mixing systems allow you to do this. It is possible to record two-channel sound for listening on headphones which gives a very realistic impression of a surround sound field. This is known as binaural recording and in principle, is recorded using a pair of omnidirectional microphones placed either side of a solid object like a cushion or even a plastic disk. This emulates your ears on either side of you head. In fact one famous binaural microphone set-up consisted of a realistic-sized dummy head with microphones in the ear channels. Audio recorded this way relies a lot on the minute phase relationships between the left and right channels and is not really mono compatible. It also sounds flat if you listen using loudspeakers instead of headphones but it is possible to process binaural sound using a complex arrangement of mixing, filtering and time delays to produce a very realistic sound field on speakers as well.

■ Tricks with sounds

There is a wide range of what are called psycho-acoustical effects which affect the way we hear sound, but it might be useful to describe a few potentially useful, or awkward, ones.

The ear's sensitivity to high and low frequencies diminishes at low volume levels. The 'loudness' button on your hi-fi amplifier takes account of this and lifts treble and bass to make it more pleasant to listen at low levels. Another effect of this phenomenon is that if you take a recording and then attenuate (drop the volume of) it, it will seem to lose top, or high, frequencies.

If you want to give a cheap imitation of a sound coming from behind the listener when you are working in stereo then it can be done by making the sound to the two loudspeakers out of phase. It might be that because we cannot detect a position for an out-of-phase sound, many people think it is coming from behind them. This is nothing like as good as real surround sound, of course. 'Out of phase' is the exact electrical opposite of mono, and is actually difficult to achieve except in a professional sound system. The website audio resources include an example of in- and out-of-phase sound so that you can compare them.

You may be tempted to work with headphones rather than speakers in order to cut down noise leakage and avoid irritating other people, especially if you are carrying out editing yourself in the office. Beware, however, that when it comes to judging sound quality and the balance of a mix, headphones are notoriously unreliable. They should be fine for editing.

One way in which we detect the loudness of a sound in the real world is by feeling the pressure of air on our bodies. For this reason it is dangerous to listen to sound loudly in headphones. The air pressure clue to loudness will not be there, and there is a tendency to turn up the volume to the ears to compensate.

A detailed knowledge of psycho-acoustics has led to high-quality and efficient ways of reducing the bit rate of digital audio files in systems such as MPEG audio. Sounds that we do not hear because they are, for example, masked by other sounds can be removed from a recording without noticeable effect.

The most-efficient layer of MPEG audio, layer 3, has become a popular standard for compressing audio and is known as MP3. This reduces the data and bit rate required for a sound recording by analysing the audio and doing its best to remove the parts of the sound that are not actually heard. How well it does this depends on the data rate and other factors in the compression. There is an example of an MP3 file on the website together with a recording of what the MP3 compression removed.

■ Digital basics

Digital technology has entered most aspects of sound recording and editing. The basics of digitization are that the continuously varying sound waveform (the electrical representation of the vibrating microphone diaphragm) is sampled. This means that many times a second the instantaneous voltage of the waveform is measured. Audio is usually sampled at 44.1 kHz, which is the sample rate for compact disk (and Minidisk), which means that 44,100 times per second the instantaneous value of the waveform is measured and stored as a 16-bit number. This is a technique known as pulse code modulation (PCM) and it has been a basis of digital audio since its inception. For reference, middle A on a piano is currently standardized at 440 Hz, and when you double the frequency of a sound its pitch goes up an octave. (This standard has changed gradually: in Mozart's time, middle A was 430 Hz.) So a single cycle of a 440 Hz sound will be sampled in about one hundred places. PCM isn't the only game in town as we'll see in a moment.

The highest frequency of sound that can be faithfully reproduced by a particular sample rate is just under half that sample rate (as discovered by a Swedish scientist named Nyquist and known as the Nyquist Theorem), so the range of frequencies, called the bandwidth, of a compact disk is 22 kHz.

The 22 kHz bandwidth of a compact disk should be enough to reproduce all the frequencies you could hear but there are higher quality audio formats now used professionally and even reaching the consumer market. Incidentally, the digital tape cassette format DAT uses 48 kHz as its standard sample rate, but most DAT machines can also record at 44.1 (after a while you stop saying kHz every time), and, if you have a choice, 44.1 is the better sample rate because any compact disks or digital transfers from MiniDisk that you include in your mixes will have to be at 44.1 and ought to stay that way to help keep the quality up.

This relatively simple sample rate picture has become more complex as more digital formats enter the professional market. Some professional audio is sampled at 88.2 and 96 (twice 44.1 and 48) and even higher to give a cleaner sound for reasons too esoteric to debate here and there are emerging super-CD formats using DVD disks that use these formats. Video formats with digital audio may use sample rates of 48 or even 32.

CDs and DAT share a bit depth of 16 bits. This means that the sound can, in theory, be digitized with a precision of 16 bits, or 65,536 levels.

So far we've been discussing PCM, whereby the actual value of the waveform is measured thousands of times a second and stored. One of the new DVD-based audio formats, SACD (Super Audio CD), takes a different approach and measures changes in the waveform's absolute value rather than the values themselves (sometimes called delta or difference coding or pulse density modulation) and in the case of SACD this is done over 2.8 million times a second. (The actual value was chosen so that it could easily be down-converted to PCM sample rates such as 32, 44.1, 48 and their multiples.) What is measured is a simple up or down value for the waveform. The system claims a frequency response from DC (a frequency of zero) to 100 KHz and unparalleled quality. By sampling at such a high frequency it is possible to move sampling artefacts and noise way out of the audible range without having to actually filter them out using imperfect real-world filters. They also use the DVD trick of dual layers to put both a CD audio and SACD layer on a disk, making them backwards compatible. SACD's rival in the Hi-Q audio stakes is DVD audio which in two-channel mode is 192 kHz sampling at 24-bits. Six-channel is 96 kHz/24-bit, which is still higher than a two-channel compact disc.

Until the advent of sophisticated audio compression for the Web, from the likes of MP3, Liquid Audio and RealAudio, one common way to get a smaller file size for audio on the desktop was to reduce to 8 bits and 22 kHz. These days, 8-bit has become less common although you may still find it used as a format for system alert sounds or WAV files on a PC.

You can work out the background (for which read 'error') noise of a PCM digital signal from the bit depth, since the maximum error between the 'real' sound and the digitized version of it is half the minimum step in the digitization. Since 16-bit has 65,536 steps and 8-bit has only 255 you can see that 8-bit will be 256 times as noisy as 16-bit. You can hear examples of the difference that is caused by some different sample rates and bit depth in a file on the website.

Fortunately our ears do not respond to sound levels in a linear fashion, which is why a logarithmic measurement, the decibel or dB, is used to measure it. This means that we do not actually hear 256 times more noise. In fact the signal-to-noise ratio of a 16-bit system is 98 dB (which basically means you will never usually hear it) whereas for an 8-bit system it is 50 dB. Since every 6 dB increment makes a sound twice as loud this means that 8-bit is eight times as noisy as 16-bit. Also, the noise only occurs in the sound, not in the silences (unlike analogue hiss which is usually relatively constant and caused mostly by random background electrical impulses in the amplifiers), but it will be very noticeable on slight noises like rustles, so these should be removed from any recording destined for 8-bit.

With digital audio recording a balance has to be struck between recording at so high a level that you risk overloading – which means clipping the waveform and producing distortion – and recording so quietly that noise becomes noticeable. As a result, the reference level at which audio is recorded on professional digital audio and video tape machines is set so as to give plenty of leeway for loud sounds. This is called 'headroom' and usually means that the peak audio levels may be as much as 10 dB below the maximum possible. Increasing the audio level in post-production to maximize the level, so that the loudest peak fills all the bits of the sample, is called normalizing. Professional systems usually record sound with 20 or even 24 bits (24 bits means that the noise is 150 dB down which is the difference between a jet engine close-up and a silent room), which gives the engineers the freedom to record at a safe level without noise. For distribution the sound will, in most instances, still be converted back to 16-bit.

To convert from, say, 16 to 8 bits the procedure is simply to divide each sample value by 256 and round the errors to the nearest whole number. To convert from 8 to 16 you multiply the sample value by 256. This will, unfortunately, also multiply the errors that cause noise, so your 16-bit version will not sound any better than the 8-bit original.

To get the best level out of a digital audio recording you should normalize it. This means finding the loudest part and adjusting the level of the whole file so that the loudest part fills all 16 bits of the sample (or something close to that). Most audio CDs have been normalized. However, professional audio source tapes may not have been. The standard peak level for professional videotape is about 12 dB below the normalized maximum. If your other audio has been normalized then this will result in a level difference between different files.

In principle, you should make sure that digital audio is normalized to full volume before encoding, although there are some exceptions. Some Web compression systems for audio will distort with a normalized file and so may some playback systems. To help avoid this you can normalize to less than 100%. RealNetworks, for example, suggest setting the maximum a little lower, say 95% of full level. This is equivalent to a level reduction of 0.5 dB. Also, files with the same levels can sound louder or softer since loudness does not completely depend on level. There is no hard-and-fast rule about this, especially when a user can choose the order in which things are heard. Perhaps the best approach is to normalize to 3 dB below peak, which will give a little leeway to boost quieter sounding files by normalizing them higher. DVD video disks usually have their average sound levels set lower so that the apparent loudness of dialogue is similar between movies and to allow for sound effects and music which will often be at a much higher level: explosions for example. The peak levels on a movie will be higher than the average level to a greater extent than would be the case on a rock album, so it will sound quieter most of the time.

The sample rate of a recording can be changed by recalculating the samples, and most audio editing and processing software will allow you to do this. When you take a sound file and process it with software such as Cleaner and RealProducer, any change in the sample rate will be recalculated. There are professional boxes that will do this as well and work from the standard digital audio interface connections. Reducing the sample rate of a file will reduce its frequency response and if the sound is not filtered first, following Nyquist's theorem, you will generate aliasing artefacts.

For reference, here are bit depths and sample rates that you might come across and where you might find them. This list is not exhaustive.

- 44.1 kHz 16-bit – CD, DAT and digital audio editing systems. As a rule of thumb this kind of digitized audio takes up 10 megabytes per minute. It is also known as Red Book after the name of the standard for compact disks and as PCM (Pulse Code Modulation).
- 48 kHz 16-bit – digital videotape formats, DAT, digital tracks on LaserDisks and some digital audio editing systems.
- 22 kHz 8-bit (or lower) – older personal computer sound and some streamed audio on the Internet.
- 44.1, 48, 88.2, 96, 176.4 or 192 kHz 20-bit (or more) – some professional audio systems and digital videotape recorders.
- 32 kHz 12-bit – long-play DAT and consumer DV.

There are what are termed DASH systems (digital audio stationary head), which you might come across in a recording studio, but these also use either 32, 44.1 or 48 for their sampling rate. Variants of DAT and hard-disk systems are now also using sample rates of 88.2 or 96. Sony used to sell a digital audio add-on for their Betamax video recorders called the F1. This was a 44.1 kHz 12-bit system. Other digital audio formats you may come across include:

- μ-law (used in telecommunications);
- NICAM (a 14-bit system used for stereo television sound);

- MPEG/ISO layers 1, 2 and 3 (layer 1 is very similar to PASC, which was used in Digital Compact Cassette; layer 2 is also called MUSICAM, and is used with MPEG-1 video and digital broadcasting and as an option for DVD; layer 3 – better known as MP3 – is used for telecommunications such as audio files on the Internet and broadcast radio contribution links down ISDN lines);
- ATRAC (used in MiniDisk);
- Dolby AC-3 (used on DVDs);
- MPEG-4 has an audio component and this includes more efficient compression but can also take an object-oriented approach to sound with separate parts of the 'mix' sent as separate objects and combined at the receiver. This way you could listen to an orchestra minus one instrument, for example, in case you want to play along.

Audio files can be downloaded (i.e. copied) across the Internet of course, but it is possible to stream audio on the Web using such formats as RealAudio and MP3. Streamed audio and streamed video are played in real time as the data arrives over the Internet. It is more like broadcasting than file transfer, and has the advantage (for rights owners) that a copy of the file is not usually left on the listener's computer.

The encoding for streamed audio over a modem is very efficient but results in an audio file with a very small audio bandwidth – as low as 4 kHz in the case of RealAudio for a 14.4 kBit modem – and high background noise levels. However, if you have two ISDN lines or a cable or DSL connection you can receive streamed audio of very high quality.

With the advent of DVD you will come across the two main standards for audio on the new digital video disks. Dolby AC-3 is the surround-sound format used for most DVDs, but a surround-sound version of MPEG audio (layer 2) is also possible as is a third format called DTS.

Finally, there are two common types of connection for digital audio: SPDIF and AES/EBU. SPDIF is the semi-professional system and is found on many consumer digital devices like CD players. It can use RCA/synch/ phono connectors or, occasionally, miniature jack plugs for the electrical version but there is also a popular optical fibre implementation. AES/EBU is the professional version and uses XLR connectors like those used on micro-phones.

■ Aliasing

The Nyquist theorem says that in order to accurately digitize a sound (or indeed any waveform) of frequency n you must sample at a frequency of at least $2n$. If this rule is not followed strange results can occur. The phenom-enon is called aliasing. (The effect on pictures will be discussed in Chapter 8 on graphics.) The result of aliasing is that the digital signal does not accurately represent the analogue original. If there are frequencies higher than n in the signal that you digitize with frequency $2n$ there will be spurious samples in the result, and in audio this will usually sound like squeaking, and the signal should be filtered to remove such high frequencies before digitizing. Aliasing is a common problem in digital systems but it can occur in analogue systems as well. A popular example of the effect is seen on film and video when the wheels of a wagon appear to move backwards, and this also underlies the principle of using a stroboscope (regular flashing light) to 'freeze' fast regular motion.

This aliasing is a particular problem if you down-sample, which is where you take a sound digitized at, say, 22 kHz and shift it down to 11 kHz. You will think you can hear sounds of higher frequency than 5.5 kHz in the result, but they are not genuine sounds from the input but aliasing artefacts. For this reason you need to filter before you down-sample. Not all software does this, and you will hear the distortion that results. Down-sampling and aliasing can also introduce other artefacts. One instance is if the original recording contains a small amount of television line whistle at around 15 kHz from an NTSC or PAL signal. This will be almost inaudible, but if it is shifted down by aliasing to around 7 kHz, which can happen in a 22 kHz down-sampled sound, it will suddenly become audible because although the actual volume of the sound is the same, the ear is more sensitive at 7 kHz than at 15 kHz.

■ MIDI

A slight diversion takes us into MIDI – Musical Instrument Digital Interface. MIDI is an alternative way of encoding music which works completely differently to digital recording. A MIDI file stores information about the music in much the same way as sheet music. It stores information like pitch, duration and the instrument that should be playing the note. The actual sound is not stored in a MIDI file, it is the responsibility of the playback system to provide the sounds.

MIDI is the core of modern music making and there are numerous packages which allow a composer to work on a computer to produce music. In many cases you can work with MIDI and real audio side by side in the same package and along the same time line. Arguably without MIDI there would be no Pet Shop Boys and no Moby, so central is it to contemporary music making.

Professional musicians using MIDI will have their own hardware to produce the sounds of the instruments. These could be 'real' instruments such as an electronic piano or they could be produced by a sampler (playing short recordings of the real thing) or even a synthesizer.

Desktop PCs, if they include a sound card, will also include some form of MIDI playback and in many cases the instruments provided are surprisingly natural. QuickTime now contains a set of instruments and, besides hardware solutions, you can also buy sets of instruments in software. There is a set called General MIDI which is defined as a minimum requirement of MIDI systems, so that a MIDI file using this set will play back sounding similar everywhere. The piano will be a piano even if you don't know if it will sound like a Steinway or a broken-down one from the corner of a bar on any particular system.

MIDI files do not take up much data since they are descriptive rather than literal and you can look on MIDI as the equivalent of text in its relationship with a sound recording. Web browsers will usually be able to play a MIDI file so one option for including music in a web page is to use MIDI. It won't take long to download and is an alternative to streamed audio.

■ Doing it on hard disk

Tapeless recording and editing systems are now commonplace in audio, and inexpensive (or even free) systems are available for desktop computers and lap tops. It is possible to record straight onto hard disk, and some audio facilities will do just that for you. These same facilities will edit your audio and prepare the tracks for use in a computer system by compressing them to RealAudio or MPEG audio (or whatever is appropriate).

Where the hard-disk systems come into their own is for editing because a digital hard disk audio package allows for more versatile editing than tape ever did.

■ Editing

Tape editing used to be done by physically cutting the tape with scissors or a razor blade. If you were editing yourself then you rocked and rolled the tape backwards and forwards across the playback head in order to locate exactly the point at which you wished to cut. This was sometimes called scrubbing. Then you marked the back of the tape with a soft chinagraph pencil and sliced the tape with a blade or scissors. You joined the bits you wanted together with adhesive tape. The adhesive tape was slightly narrower than the recording tape and had a non-leaking adhesive. A specially machined block was used to align the tape over the join. In many places you will still find analogue tape-based audio editing.

In a hard-disk-based digital system the sound is usually manipulated by working with a representation of the audio waveform on the computer screen. The sound is cut and pasted in much the same way as text in a word processor. You can still scrub to find the place to cut but now you are manipulating sound in a file rather than on a tape. One useful feature of professional digital systems is the ability to do a mix across the joins to 'soften' the cut, which can be used to make an otherwise impossible edit work.

Some places are easier to cut than others. You can fool the ear by cutting into a sharp sound, a transient such as a bang or a drum sound. By doing this you do not usually notice any cutting off of the preceding sound. In fact the incoming sound is more critical than the outgoing in most edits. For speech some sounds make for better cuts than others; 'p', 'k' and 't' work well, whereas vowels and the 's' sound are quite difficult. Vowels are especially difficult because they carry most of the intonation in the voice and so they can sound completely different each time they are said. Consonants are more consistent and often you can splice them around to help to clean up word endings.

You should listen to speech patterns to help with your editing. Many people miss out letters from their speech. If you were to say 'next time' you would probably not pronounce both 't' sounds, but would actually say 'nextime'. You can take advantage of these truncations to find places to join speech together. You will even find that just looking at the waveform will help you to find places because you can easily identify pauses and consonants by the shape of the waveform.

Rhythm is important in speech, and your edits should respect that rhythm and not cut across it. Although people do shift the rhythm of their speech, most of the time an edit will feel more natural if a speech rhythm is preserved. Rhythm obviously is very important in editing music, and some of the same rules apply to both music and speech. A few milliseconds can make all the difference to a music edit. You can hear an example of 'good' and 'bad' editing in the resources on the website.

It is not true to say that a good edit is a joy to hear – because you will not hear a good edit.

■ Judging quality

Sometimes you will be required to produce assets to a certain quality. This might be specifically mentioned in a contract. It is difficult to define the quality of audio in objective terms. You could say that the frequency response will be one thing and the signal-to-noise ratio another, but these facts will not cover how well a presenter reads a script or how well mixed is a piece of music. The best course, should this issue arise, is to say that you will apply 'appropriate' standards or even 'broadcast' standards. You, and your clients or customers, will be able to compare with what you hear on radio and on CDs. It is important for clients to realize, however, that sound heard on a computer and on the Internet will often be of poorer quality than broadcast simply because the computer or the method of distribution is not capable of that quality of reproduction, no matter how well the material is prepared. On the bright side, you will usually find that the quality issue can be handled by comparing your results with other similar applications.

■ Choosing a codec

In order to prepare a sound file for use on the Web or in a kiosk or CD-ROM, you need to decide what quality you will be able to use and then choose a format. The format will usually be determined by the codec (coder–decoder) that you choose. Quality is generally dependent on the amount of data you can use but also some codecs give better quality results than others. Apart from on the Web, sound can usually be left in an uncompressed format such as WAV or AIFF. For a small amount of compression there is a format called ADPCM (adaptive delta – or difference – pulse code modulation) which can compress a few-fold with very little effect on the sound. It is supported on PC and Macs under the name IMA 4:1. For the Internet, a fourfold reduction in data is usually not enough.

To compress audio for the Web, whether along with video or not, there is a bewildering range of choices. We have already discussed MP3 and RealAudio but there are other options. RealAudio, like some other codecs for web audio, has settings attuned to speech or to music. It helps to use different techniques if you want to get best results for speech on its own whereas a music codec basically does its best with the whole sound. The production guides for each codec will tell you how to judge the best settings depending on whether you want stereo or not, whether it's just speech, the frequency range of the result and the likely speed of the final connection. This last factor is especially important if the sound is going to be streamed although (with the notable exception of a streamed radio station) many audio files are small enough for users to download them. MP3 does not have such a wide range of options but you still need to choose sample rates and bit rates for the final file.

One practical advantage of MP3 is that it is treated as 'native' on PCs and Macs with the same raw MP3 file playing using both Windows Media and QuickTime.

Compared with the uncompressed bit rate of one megabit for stereo sound, codecs like MP3 and RealAudio will achieve more than 12 : 1 reduction in data.

A final reminder, as with all asset preparation: keep an archive copy of your audio at a high uncompressed quality such as the audio CD standard Red Book or better. You may need to recompress the audio again sometime using a different format.

THEORY INTO PRACTICE 6

Take the editing practice-recording on the website (download it in its MP3 format and use an audio utility to convert for editing) and, in whatever editing tool you have, try to make the speaker say the opposite of what he originally said. Listen to see how natural this sounds.

Listen to the examples of audio with different sample rates and bit depths and see if you can recognize any undesirable effects that result from them. This includes loss of high frequencies and addition of noise.

Search out some freely available encoders for MPEG audio and RealAudio and whatever you can find. Take a sound file and encode it with the different systems and compare the results.

■ Summary

- This chapter has looked at the background to sound recording, and has explained what you should expect when using a professional audio facility to record voices for your website or multimedia application. It has outlined the preparation you need to make to prepare for the session.

- The kind of microphone used, the way it is positioned and how the sound is treated will affect the way your recording sounds.

- Stereo and multichannel positioning is usually achieved by adjusting loudness between the channels.

- During recording, scripts should be marked up for later editing.

- Keep an archive master copy of any audio that you process for inclusion on a website or CD-ROM.

- In digitizing, the highest frequency that can be digitized with a sample rate of $2n$ is n, otherwise odd-sounding artefacts are likely to appear in the recording.

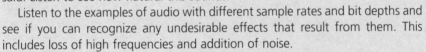

■ Recommended reading

Moore B.C.J. (1997). *Introduction to the Psychology of Hearing*. 4th edn London: Academic Press

Pohlmann K.C. (2000). *Principles of Digital Audio*. 4th edn, Maidenhead: McGraw-Hill

Watkinson J. (2001). *Art of Digital Audio*. 3rd edn, London: Focal Press

Information on RealAudio encoding is available at their website: www.real.com, the audio advice is at
http://service.real.com/help/library/guides/production8/htmfiles/audio.htm

The MIDI Manufacturers Association are at
http://www.midi.org/

MPEG Audio information (including FAQs), is available at
http://www.tnt.uni-hannover.de/js/project/mpeg/audio/

A document describing SADC can be found on Sony's website at
http://www.sel.sony.com/SEL/consumer/dsd/dsd.pdf

The DVD FAQ, including information on DVD audio, is at
http://dvddemystified.com/dvdfaq.html

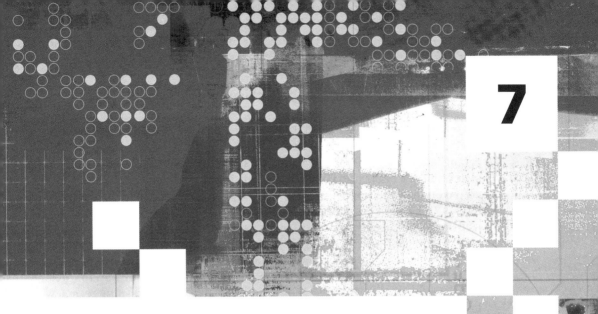

Video asset production

Project manager's responsibilities

- To book crews, help cast actors, presenters and subjects for recording interviews if necessary

- To explain to clients what quality of result to expect on the Web and desktop

- To make sure that the recording session is successful

- To make sure tapes are logged and prepared for editing

- To ensure that the material is prepared to the correct specification, recommending or selecting the appropriate formats

- To choose the most appropriate way of compressing video for the application and make sure it is done to an appropriate standard

- To understand the processes involved in producing this kind of asset

■ Managing asset production

The previous chapter has explored the production of sound in multimedia, paying special attention to the use of external facilities. For video, similar arrangements are likely to be made. It is possible that the video content of a multimedia application will be shot using a consumer camcorder and edited on the desktop, but in other cases the budget will allow a professional facility to be used and the production values will require it. As with audio, websites currently make less use of video than CD-ROMs did, but as bandwidth increases this will change.

One crucial aspect of video production is the amount of preparation required. For sound it is quite feasible for the producer to turn up to interview someone after having made the arrangements by telephone a few hours before. But for video there is much more that needs to be done and probably more people to involve. This chapter concentrates on the set-up for an interview because that is the most straightforward and arguably the most common use of video in multimedia. You might wish to shoot drama, or work on location, but unless you already have experience in these areas you are advised to hire specialized help to direct the shoot and therefore to manage it. Exterior location work is particularly difficult because of the range of permissions you need from people such as the police and local authority and because of the vagaries of the weather.

One managerial issue that rears its head in video more than in audio is the question of whether the client should attend the shoot or the edit. There is no simple answer to this but your relationship with the client should influence you. The main reason why the client should attend is to avoid arguments about changes later, since changes in a video edited at an outside facility are probably the most expensive to fix. This, of course, is a strong argument for making an offline edit to inexpensively preview the result and letting the client see it, or for editing on your desktop. If you are completely confident that the client respects your abilities then you might not need to involve them, but if you think that later changes are likely, and if you have agreed a fixed price for the project, then invite them. You should emphasize the costs associated with changing video after the edit. Of course, with a computer-based non-linear edit it is much easier to change things than it was in the old-fashioned assembly method of videotape editing, but it still takes time and costs money.

Moving pictures are a recent entrant into computing, although computers have long been a part of video, at least on the professional and broadcast television side. Engineers have for a long time been devising ways to manipulate and create images for broadcast television, starting with graphics and control of equipment. Today computers play a part in every aspect of broadcast television production.

Just as video is starting to take over as the dominant medium in the multimedia mix as inexpensive computers become more powerful, so multimedia is beginning tentatively to make its way into television. Video-on-demand is essentially a multimedia database system for the home; prime-time television programmes are using desktop computers to generate graphics and many television programmes are edited using desktop computers; and digital television is now being broadcast by cable, satellite and terrestrial transmitters to home consumers.

Television itself dates back to the 1920s, and moving film goes back into the nineteenth century. The Scottish television pioneer, John Logie Baird, devised a mechanical system of sending moving pictures down a wire and through the airwaves, at a time when radio broadcasting itself was in its infancy. Electronic scanning took over from his wheels and cogs, and the BBC launched the world's first regular scheduled television service in 1936 to a handful of very rich viewers in the southern part of England. A television set then cost more than a family car, and not many people had either.

This chapter deals with the way in which a television picture is made and how you might record and manipulate it. Some background on the way a video signal is built up, and the differences between the various formats and standards, will help you work with video. As with the last chapter on audio, it will concentrate on the kind of equipment and techniques that you, as a new media professional and practitioner, will come across when you make use of video.

◼ Basic principles of video

Because our brains are easily fooled, we see a rapid succession of still images as a continuous stream, and, with the right images, we see movement. The movies work like this, by showing us tiny slices of reality 24 times per second. The frames of a movie are those slices of reality. Television slices the reality a slightly different way because each of the frames in a TV signal is made up of hundreds of lines.

As a compromise between resolution (in pixels), the rate of change of the picture (in frames per second), and the amount of radio waves that a television signal would occupy (bandwidth), the engineers who designed electronic television made each frame out of two fields. The first field covers only half the picture by missing out alternate lines of the image as it scans down the screen. The second field fills in the gaps.

The beam that 'paints' the picture on the television screen starts at the top and scans from left to right at a very slight angle downwards. For the first line only, the beam starts in the middle rather than at the left. When it reaches the right it flies back to the left-hand side and starts again, a bit lower down. Eventually, after doing this a few hundred times, the beam reaches the bottom right of the screen and promptly flies back up to the top left and starts all over again. This time it will be scanning in between the lines it laid down last time; eventually it will reach the middle of the bottom line and fly back up to the middle of the top line, and the whole process starts again.

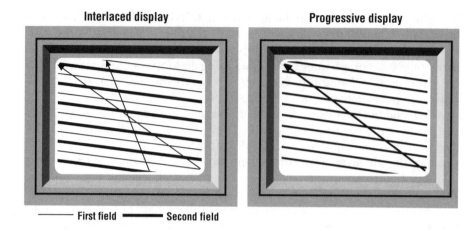

Interlaced display   Progressive display

——— First field ▬▬▬ Second field

So there are two comb-like scans, interleaved with each other, making up each frame, with each consisting of half the number of lines in the whole picture. Each of these scans is called a **field**. The complete picture will be refreshed only 30 or 25 times per second, which keeps the bandwidth down, while the apparent flicker of the picture is at the rate of the fields, which is twice as high and so is less noticeable. This is a neat trick; but, as will be shown later, this system of interlaced fields causes no end of problems when we get onto the computer because computers use a non-interlaced display, in which the lines are written in turn, left to right, from top to bottom of the screen. This is called progressive or sequential scan and one of the fiercest debates going on between broadcasters and the computing fraternity is about whether future television systems should have interlaced or progressive displays.

◼ Composite video television standards

These are the three main systems of analogue broadcast colour television. They are known as composite video (or just composite) because the brightness and colour information are mixed together into a single signal. The oldest colour system still in use is NTSC, which is used mostly in North America and Japan. The main European system is PAL, also used in places such as Australia and South Africa, and there is also SECAM, used in France (from whence it came), Eastern Europe and the Middle East.

For NTSC a constant-frequency signal at 3.58 MHz, called the colour subcarrier, is superimposed on the picture to carry the colour information. At the start of each line of the picture there is a short burst of the colour subcarrier. The colour at any point in the line (this is analogue so the concept of a pixel is not strictly valid) is determined by the phase relationship between the superimposed subcarrier at that point and the reference burst. The phase relationship is the difference between where one signal is in its positive/negative cycle and where the other one is.

There are 525 lines per frame in NTSC. Interlaced television pictures always have an odd number of lines so that one field can start in the middle of the screen (horizontally) and the other can start at the left-hand end so each field includes a half-line. In broadcast NTSC 487 lines have picture on them – half in each field – and these are called the active lines. You don't have to have an odd number of active lines and in multimedia practice, NTSC is considered to have 480 active lines rather than 487. In its earlier black-and-white incarnation, US television used 30 frames per second, but for colour this changed to 29.97. It was supposed to be 30, but obscure technical reasons to do with the subcarrier frequency changed all that.

PAL has a subtle, but significant, difference from NTSC in the way that the colour information in the subcarrier is encoded. NTSC suffers from colour shifts due to minute timing changes during a line which affect that phase relationship between the colour subcarrier in the picture and the reference burst: this causes changes in the colour. PAL compensates for this by reversing the phase of the colour encoding between alternate lines and so 'averaging' out the errors. PAL also has a higher-frequency subcarrier, at 4.43 MHz, and has 625 lines in a frame, of which 576 have picture on them: half in each field. PAL shows 25 frames per second exactly.

SECAM, the French-devised third system, uses a totally different method for transmitting the colour (it sends the two colour components alternately with each line) but is otherwise the same as PAL, so if you fed a SECAM signal into a PAL monitor you would see a black-and-white picture and vice versa. SECAM means 'Système en couleur avec mémoire' which literally means 'Colour System with Memory' although it is jokingly reputed to really mean 'System essentially contrary to the American method'. Although SECAM is still used as a transmission system, and gives very good results, it has problems for production, mainly because you cannot mix or fade a SECAM signal out because of the way the colour is encoded in the signal. Incidentally, NTSC is reputed to stand for 'Never twice the same colour', but actually it is National Television Standards Committee. (The digital equivalent in the USA is ATSC, Advanced Television Standards Committee but I have yet to hear the 'alternative' definition for this.)

There are some variations, particularly a South American variation of PAL called PAL-M, which is basically NTSC timing with PAL colour. You will sometimes see PAL-I and PAL-BG referred to, but these are different only in the way they are transmitted; the videotapes are compatible even though the televisions and VCRs are not, mainly because the sound is transmitted on a slightly different frequency, and that is why a European PAL television will not usually work in the UK and vice versa.

On European videocassette machines you may see a form of NTSC called NTSC 4.43 or Modified NTSC. This is a special version of NTSC, and it happens because the colour information on the videocassette is stored in a different way from the original composite signal: when it plays an NTSC tape the machine puts out what is basically a PAL signal but with NTSC timings. The subcarrier is at the PAL frequency. This saves having two sets of circuits for the colour in the VCR and the monitor. However, this modified NTSC will appear as black and white if you feed it into a real NTSC monitor, or a digitizer card that expects real NTSC. This can also happen with formats such as S-VHS and Hi8, which, although they separate the brightness and colour information, still use a subcarrier to encode the colour information. You will not come across this problem with broadcast videotape machines, and it is not applicable to the component systems we discuss in the next section, but it is the most likely cause of mystery colour disappearances when using NTSC videocassettes on multi-standard VCRs.

A single video cable can be used to carry a composite video signal since the colour information is encoded in with the luminance and the synchronization pulses are usually kept together with the picture information. Some equipment labels composite video, CVBS.

■ Component video

Professional colour videotape is now either digital or component, or both. Component video (often just called component) means that the colour (chrominance or chroma) and brightness (luminance) information are kept separate, having been mathematically derived from the red, green and blue (RGB) signals received from the camera imaging tube or chip.

The luminance part of a component signal is referred to as Y. The true colour components are red-Y and blue-Y. Red and blue signals are smaller in value than green so they make for larger (and therefore less noisy) components. Often the components are referred to as YIQ (in NTSC) and YUV (in PAL), but these are not strictly equivalent and the terms are often misused. Strictly speaking there is no such thing as NTSC or PAL component, but people do sometimes refer to component systems by their related composite system names in this way as they do with digital component systems. When it comes to components, PAL and SECAM tapes are the same.

Using colour components this way is useful for TV for two reasons. First, the luminance signal is exactly the same as the old black-and-white signal, and so the video is backwards compatible and easy to view on a monochrome monitor. Second, because we do not see as much detail in colour as we do in brightness, there is no need to have as high a definition for the chroma as for the luminance. This saves bandwidth, and is one of the two forms of information compression used in analogue TV: interlace is the other.

Component video offers better quality than composite because the colour information is kept separate from the luminance. It is possible for a colour television decoder to mistake some of the fine detail in the luminance information in a composite signal for colour, causing spurious coloured patterning. A presenter wearing a narrow-striped jacket would cause problems on a composite system. This also means that luminance information of similar frequency to the colour subcarrier will be missing from the composite picture as it will be filtered out.

Connectors for component analogue video are the same as for professional composite, only there are three of them: one for luminance (Y) and two for colour. The sync pulses are usually carried on the Y line.

Half-way between composite and component video is S-Video as used in Hi8 and SVHS. This has two signals, one being the Y and the other a combination of U and V usually referred to as C. So a connector for S-Video might have Y/C written on it. An S-Video connector is made either from two BNC or phono connectors or from a four-pin mini-D. Sync pulses are carried on the Y line. There are only two forms of S-Video since, once again, PAL and SECAM are the same at this level.

■ Blanking and time code

Besides the image information, making up the visible part of the lines, there are elements of the analogue television signal that tell a television monitor, and other equipment, where the lines, fields and frames begin and end, and provide reference information about the colour. The places in the television signal where the picture does not exist, but these signals do, are called horizontal (for lines) and vertical (for fields) blanking. This is because they are blank, although the vertical blanking interval (VBI) has become home to such things as Teletext, vertical interval time code (VITC, pronounced vit-see) and test signals.

Time code is very likely to be useful to you. When you look at a videotape to select extracts for digitizing, time code is the way to specify the sections you want. Every frame of a television signal can be allocated a unique number divided into hours, minutes, seconds and frames (of the form hh:mm:ss:ff, for example 05:46:35:19). This time code signal is recorded on the tape along with the video and audio.

Time code is sometimes referred to as SMPTE (Society of Motion Picture and Television Engineers, pronounced 'sempty') although, strictly speaking, SMPTE time code is for NTSC video only, and the PAL/SECAM version is EBU (European Broadcasting Union).

Burned in time code (BITC or bit-see) or time code in vision is a system whereby a character generator superimposes the numbers of the time code on the frames to which it refers. This is invaluable in choosing extracts and editing. Since a time code number can refer to either field in a frame, some readers will add a field indication, such as an asterisk, to the number you see. You can often look at the two fields of the picture separately because most videotape machines show you a field rather than the whole frame when the tape is in still 'frame'.

With NTSC time code you will see the term 'drop frame' used. Because NTSC does not have a whole number of frames every second the time code has to be adjusted every so often to keep it in step with real time. This is just like the extra day in February in leap years. In the case of NTSC a frame is dropped, hence the term. This is fine when it is important for the time code to show time-of-day, as it is called, or to know exactly how long a programme is, but you need to remember that some time code numbers will be skipped. For everyday video editing it is more straightforward to use non-drop-frame time code. You should know which type of time code your NTSC tapes have otherwise you will miscalculate the actual duration of your video. In PAL there is no need for drop-frame time code as PAL has exactly 25 frames per second.

■ In the studio and on location

You might use only a small amount of video in an interactive application but its use can be very powerful and effective. One common form is known as a talking head. This is where all you see on the screen is a single person talking. If you have a famous presenter for your application then you might see him or her a few times like this. Even if most of the time you only hear the voice, it is nice to show your viewers what the face behind the voice looks like.

The talking head might be recorded in a studio or on location (meaning not in a studio), and he or she might be positioned in front of a real scene (a bookshelf is a common one for a subject expert) or against a single colour. A single flat colour is useful because, in some circumstances, you can decide on the background later and add it in the edit suite or on your computer.

Since a human face does not contain any blue, blue is commonly used for this purpose. Television people call this chroma-key or colour separation overlay (CSO – hence CSO blue to denote the colour). Film people call it a matte (if it moves it is called a travelling matte – and yes, it was used for flying carpets in Arabian Nights films – and now you know the origin of the name of that character in *Fraggle Rock*). Another name for this technique is blue screen, although other colours can be used: broadcasters often use green, and the traditional colour for movies was the yellow light of a sodium discharge lamp.

One neat method of generating the flat colour is to put a reflective cloth behind the foreground object (such as a person being interviewed) – one of those cloths that reflects light straight back at the source – and illuminate this with a low powered ring of coloured lights fixed around the lens. This creates the coloured background easily but also makes it straightforward to light the foreground subject independently.

Although in film-making a travelling matte works using totally film-based methods and some clever work at the time of printing, in television an electronic circuit detects the blue and switches the signal to another source wherever there is blue. This substitutes the other image for the blue.

Colour separation overlay.

Common problems occur due to spillage of the blue light onto the person's face, shadows on the blue backcloth, and difficulties in coping with the fine detail in hair and with shadows. The most sophisticated colour separation systems, such as Ultimatte, can solve these difficulties but, in any case, good lighting helps to avoid them.

Sometimes it pays to shoot against black. This can be very effective to isolate the person speaking and emphasize their role as a specialist, and it can be less distracting than the ubiquitous rows of books. Black does not spill onto faces and, if you are careful, you can overlay onto black just like blue or green. In this case you need to watch out for shadows, especially under the eyebrows.

Although these are film and television techniques, the use of colour separation overlay extends easily onto the desktop, and video editing and manipulation programs usually allow you to clean up and replace coloured backgrounds in this way. When the video is digitized and compressed, a static background will compress very efficiently. This is especially true if it is free of noise, so it is common to shoot the interview against black and then replace the black with 'digital' or mixer black.

The simplest 'professional' way of lighting a single person uses three lights: one will be a spotlight on the face, one will flood the scene to lighten the shadows, and the third will be positioned behind to both light the blue screen (if you have one) and backlight the person to help lift them from the surroundings and give the scene a three-dimensional look. The spotlight in front needs to be high enough so as not to make your speaker want to shade his or her eyes but not so high as to cast shadows in the eye sockets. As usual, good lighting will look so natural on the screen that you will wonder just what you have paid for. The lights have names, and a redhead refers to a one-kilowatt lamp while a blonde is a two-kilowatt one. The lights will need to be set up, but it is bad manners to inflict this on the speaker, who will be under the lights for long enough later. One of the crew will stand (or sit) in for the speaker while the lights are moved and adjusted. Find someone the same height as the speaker. Also, you should make sure that the speaker does not wear clothing containing the colour of the background, if you are using overlay.

For a professional and hassle-free video shoot you should avail yourself of an experienced camera operator and crew. The smallest crew will be one that consists only of a cameraman and you, the director (so get yourself a chair and a megaphone). You should seriously consider having a sound recordist, who will also help the cameraman to set things up, and a PA (production assistant), who will take notes and carry out the little administrative chores and free the director to … direct. You can reasonably expect the crew to bring their own equipment and videotape (referred to as 'stock') but don't forget to check.

If your application needs more substantial shooting, such as some drama or location documentary filming, then you will probably need to bring in a specialist director. If you have the experience to direct this kind of material, you probably do not need to read this chapter anyway. Crews for drama shoots can be very large, and include workers with colourful names such as the gaffer, best boy and grips.

The kind of camera used for professional video is similar to a consumer video camcorder, but it is physically bigger with a better lens and will give a much better picture. The camera operator will probably connect up a monitor for you to see the picture. For an interview, don't put the monitor where the speaker can see the picture or they'll keep looking at it and not at the interviewer or camera or wherever you really want them to look.

Your speaker will need a microphone, and you will probably not want to see it. For this reason a common microphone used in filming is called a rifle mic, or hypercardioid. This is a long and thin microphone, although you will usually see it in a wind shield or wind sock. This makes it look like a big furry hotdog held on the end of a pole by the sound recordist. Alternatively a very small microphone can be clipped to the person's tie or jacket collar. These are usually omnidirectional, and it is not unusual to position them upside down to avoid blasts of breath.

■ Shooting an interview

Although an interview (and similarly a recording of a single speaker at, say, a conference) seems to be one of the simplest forms of television shooting it is still difficult to direct well. Part of the problem is that you will want to edit what you record for inclusion in the finished application. With a sound interview you can cut almost anywhere as long as it makes sense, but with video you have the added difficulty of having the picture to cut along with the sound. It is highly unlikely that two similar pictures will cut together. In the case of a person speaking you will see the join as a jump, which is quite disconcerting. One tactic is to make a feature out of this 'bug' and just show the jumps, or do a quick mix across them. You might do this if you want to clearly show that the interview has been edited. To hide the jumps you can do one of two things but you need to have recorded the material to do so. First, you can cut to a different view of the person who is speaking, known as changing the angle, or zoom or move closer (in) or further away (out). To disguise a cut, a zoom will work better than a simple change of angle, but ideally you should combine both. Sometimes two cameras can be used to shoot the interview, set up with different shots so you can cut between them. It's not unusual for a broadcast camera to be used for one and a consumer camcorder for the other; just for the quirky effect. It all depends on how obvious you think the cutting should be.

Changing the size of the shot has a curious side-effect. Zooming in on a person speaking, either as a real zoom or as a cut to a closer shot, makes what he or she says seem very dramatic, as if confiding in the viewer. Zooming out has the opposite effect.

The second method of covering an edit is known as the cutaway. You can cut away to anything relevant. This might be some footage of whatever the person is describing. Alternatively the cutaway can be to something as simple as a shot of the person's hands as they move to emphasize a point. Of course, while you are cutting away from the speaker's face you can edit the sound to your heart's content.

It is possible for the speaker to work from a script but not appear to be reading. This kind of technique with half-silvered mirrors has been of benefit to politicians everywhere since Ronald Reagan showed it to Margaret Thatcher, but in television it has been in use for decades. It is used extensively in news and current affairs programmes where the presenter has little opportunity to learn a script. Almost as useful is to photocopy the script, blow it up to a large size, and tape it just below the camera lens. This obviously works best with short scripts.

Prior to the interview you should run through the topics you want to cover, and you should have given the speaker time to research the answers, even if it is his or her specialist field. Rehearsing can reduce spontaneity, but retakes are always a possibility. You can change the shot for retakes to make editing between them possible.

The shorthand for describing the amount of the speaker you can see in a shot is roughly like this:

1. **Long shot** – you can see the whole person and maybe enough of the surroundings to see where you are.
2. **Mid-shot** – you can see most of the person speaking, including his or her hands.
3. **Medium close-up (MCU)** – you can see the top of the person, from the middle of the chest upwards. This is sometimes called a 'head and shoulders' shot, and is the basic shot for an interview or statement to camera.
4. **Close-up** – you can see little more than the head.
5. **Big close-up** – very close (tight) on the head, cutting off the forehead.

Incidentally, women who wear strapless dresses are difficult in interviews because the MCUs and close-ups make them look naked. This may not be the effect you want.

A very useful technique for interviews is to turn them into statements. This is used a lot in television documentaries, and basically means that the interviewer is neither seen nor heard in the edited result. This means, of course, that one place to which you cannot cut away is a picture of the interviewer nodding sagely (these shots are known as noddies). In this case it is important that the speaker never actually answers a question directly, and you should ask the interviewer to say things like 'Tell me about your adventures up the Limpopo river' rather than saying 'Was it fun up the

Limpopo?' A common tactic is to ask the interviewee to repeat the question as the first thing he or she says in reply.

It is possible that you might be conducting the interview yourself, especially if you are not including the interviewer in the final edited footage. Part of your role is therefore as much to put the speaker at his or her ease as it is to ask anything meaningful. You will nod encouragingly, but never say anything while the interviewee is speaking. Some subject experts are so used to appearing in front of a camera that they will respond accurately to a request like 'tell me about Jupiter's red spot in 30 seconds' with consummate ease. Subject experts like that can be worth their weight in gold.

If you have a PA with you, he or she can make notes of questions to set against the time code, which can usually be read on the side of the camcorder. You should resist the temptation to use time-of-day time code or drop-frame time code in NTSC, and you should start each new roll at a new hour on the time code. This way you can easily judge which roll is which (they are still called rolls even though they will be videocassettes) from the time code numbers. So the time code 04:23:01:10 is on roll 4 and 13:21:10:00 is on roll 13. It is vitally important that the time code always goes forwards as you work through a tape and that the code never passes through midnight. This is simply to make it possible for the editing system to know which way to spool a tape to find a number, and unfortunately 23:59:59:24 reads as being almost 24 hours after 00:00:00:00 instead of one second before it. When you digitize the footage for editing, the software might report a time code discontinuity as dropped or missing frames and may not tell you where the problem is. This means you will have to review the file to make sure it is OK. Better not to have any time-code discontinuities if at all possible.

■ Do it yourself

So far we've looked at video production as being something that you hire people to do, but you don't have to. DV camcorders can produce quality that is eminently suited to multimedia and this begs the question of how much can you just go out and shoot yourself?

The answer is, as much as you are able to do. The key to shooting good video lies as much in the camera operator as in the equipment – more so perhaps. Lighting is important as well, partly because normal room lighting will not necessarily work well with a camcorder but also because inexpensive cameras generally take better pictures if the scene is well lit.

Bright sunlight is good for general shots, but you might find it difficult to shoot a face, for example. If the sun is shining directly on the person then they will probably want to shade their eyes to compensate and frontal lighting does not usually look as nice as an offset lighting, which 'models' the shape a bit by producing shadows. If the light is behind the subject then the camera will probably show it as a silhouette. If the shadows are too dark then that will look wrong and you may have to use a white board to reflect some light into the shadows. Alternatively you can put a light on the camera but you need to be careful about the balance of the brightness and colour of the light so that the scene doesn't become unnatural.

Since many video compression techniques compare frames to help reduce data, it is a good idea to keep the camera steady and this is especially important with the high compression used for Internet video. In any case, a shaky camera is usually regarded as being a bit amateurish (or possibly the current fashion for access television). If you don't want to use a tripod and you can't afford a small Steadicam (and there are versions designed for camcorders) then you might get away with the shot steadying or shake compensation feature in the camera, especially if you shoot at the wide end of the zoom. Optical ones work best, but the electronic ones are surprisingly good as well, and only slightly reduce the quality. You should not use a shot steadier when on a tripod. This is because the smooth movements from the tripod will slightly confuse the system and it will counteract the start of, say, a pan and then have to quickly adjust. So, ironically, the steady shot can look jerky!

Beware of automatic focus, white balance and exposure on a camcorder. A camera's auto-focus might try to reset itself once in a while, so if you are shooting an interview and the person you are shooting is not moving, turn the auto-focus off. If you don't then there's a good chance that every so often the shot will go out of focus and then back into focus quickly, as the system resets. If you have your centre of interest at the edge of the frame the auto-focus may well try to focus on something else.

Auto white balance will be taking an average of the colours in the whole scene and adjusting the colour balance so that this average matches a pre-set average. If you take a shot of a face against a reddish wall then the colour will slowly drift away from red towards blue, to try to reach this preset goal, which will be something close to grey. Any strong background colour will affect the foreground. It is best either to use a colour balance fixed setting that is close enough – usually the choice is daylight or artificial light – and correct in the edit or to take a white card and set the colour balance on this, assuming the camcorder lets you. Fluorescent lights usually have a very strange colour spectrum and quite often faces will have a greenish tinge. Since these kinds of light do not produce a smooth continuous spectrum of colours to make up their 'white' light, unlike tungsten lamps or the sun, it may be impossible to completely correct the colour.

Auto-exposure will again be taking an average of the scene, or a weighted version of this, perhaps weighted to take more account of the centre of the picture (called centre-weighted). So if you have a brightly lit figure on a stage with the rest of the scene black then the camera will probably over-expose the figure. In these cases it is a good idea to zoom in so that the figure fills the frame, lock the exposure, and then zoom out again. That's a quick way of avoiding the problem if you don't actually have manual exposure.

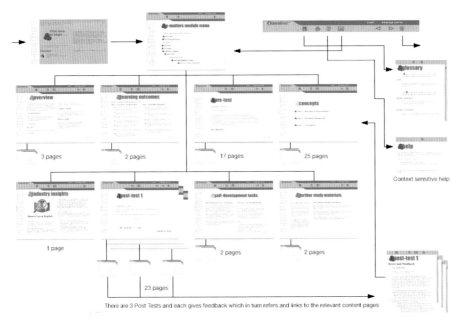

Colour versions of the site map and menu page for the **e-matters**
e-learning course described in Book 1 Chapter 6 – *Agreeing the Content*

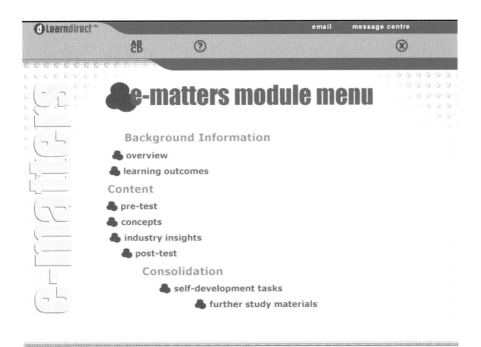

Courtesy of ATSF and Learn Direct

www.dtg.org.uk, the web site of the Digital Television Group is a compendium of news and other information about digital television. The front page (shown above) is built automatically from content elsewhere on the site and draws in relevant news headlines on the fly from www.moreover.com each time the page is displayed.

The award-winning site for Diesel clothes (www.diesel.com opposite) is a good example of a stylish site used to promote a product.

The online record store, Off the Record – www.otrvinyl.com – has a deceptively simple design but is very easy to use. If you know what you want and they have a copy, you can buy it there and then.

Courtesy of the Digital Television Group

STAY YOUNG / INHAIL OXYGEN

Discover how you too can stay looking young and beautiful forever
www.StayYoungForever.com

Eliza Higgins, born 1860
Reborn 1911, 1955, 1982

POCKO

The first 5 of a 98-book series from contributing artists now available in Diesel stores

Collect all and make all salute your superior artistic sensibility

STAY YOUNG
YOUTH PRESERVATION TECHNIQUES

FALL / WINTER
LATEST COLLECTION & DIGITAL EXPERIMENTS

STAY YOUNG /

INHALE OXYGEN

GUIDES
STOP AGING NOW
YOUR SECRET

"Breathing pure oxygen keeps us moist and clean. Who cares if the world is polluted? Thanks to our friend O2 we can ignore all the dirt and stay beautiful...forever."

Violet Goddard & James Kimble, born 1892

DIESEL.COM

Courtesy of ehsrealtime and DIESEL Spa

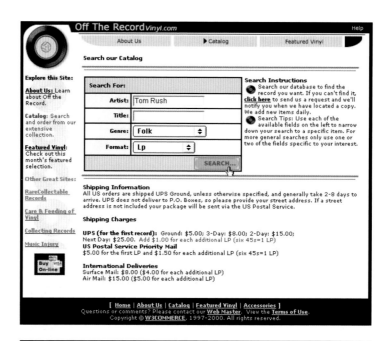

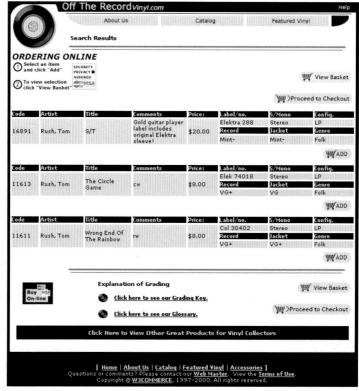

Courtesy of W3Commerce Inc and www.otrvinyl.com

These information kiosks installed a few years ago in the London Science Museum were designed to operate individually but could be centrally updated as the day progressed.

In many ways kiosks present the most difficult challenges because the users may only use a kiosk once and there is no opportunity to 'train' them.

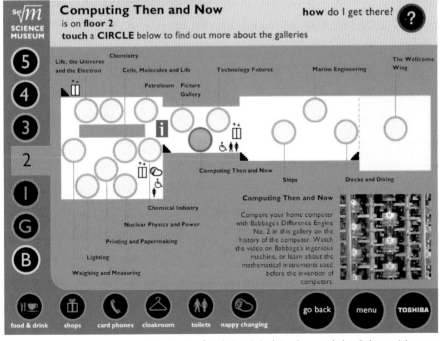

Courtesy of Nykris Digital Design and the Science Museum

Interactive soccer coverage from the UK satellite broadcaster, Sky.

Courtesy of BSkyB

A screen from the television version of ORB's Trimedia 'reality TV' programme *De Fritz Waldländer*.

Radio Fritz presenter Steffan Hallaschka and trimedia reporter André Noll during the *Waldländer* transmissions. André's reporter kit includes a broadband wireless LAN link, 'eye-phones' to monitor video and computer output and a DV camcorder for live feeds and recording.

Courtesy of Ostdeutscher Rundfunk Brandenburg and TRIMEDIA project

Conceptual 3rd Generation mobile devices from Nokia.

Images courtesy of Nokia

There is one thing that always caused headaches for video cameras, and that is computer monitors. In this business you are very likely to be taking shots which include a computer monitor. Here you may be out of luck. Some camcorders allow you to change the shutter speed which might help things, but with most of them the computer monitor will just flicker. Using electronic shot steadying will make this worse, so it helps to use a tripod and turn it off.

■ Preparing for editing

The tapes from your recording are known as rushes, from the time when they were shot on film and were rush-processed so that you could see the results the next morning. They will be dubbed onto videocassette, usually VHS, with burned-in time code (BITC) so that you can equate the time code to the parts of the material you are viewing. A time-coded transcript of the rushes is a useful first step in editing, and can help you to choose which parts of the interview you want to use.

There are usually three stages of videotape editing, although in the new media world you may not actually do any of them in a dedicated facility since more and more video processes can be carried out on the desktop. The first stage of the process is to prepare for the edit. This will involve looking through the recording in the cold light of day and choosing which parts of it to use. The odds are that you will have recorded much more than you need for the final application. The result of this stage is a list of extracts, probably marked on the transcript with their time code numbers.

☐ Offline

The second stage is the offline edit. Offline editing was originally introduced because of the high cost of editing equipment. Early offline systems used videocassettes, but offline editing was the first application of non-linear desktop video. The offline session is like a rehearsal for the online. Edits would be tried out, again and again, until the editor and the director settled on the ones that worked. The result of this stage was a list of the edit decisions.

The edit decision list can be taken into a 'real' edit suite and the edits carried out on the tapes. This is called conforming. If this process is done automatically it is called auto-conforming, and this technique came back into fashion in the early days of digital video tape machines because of their high cost.

Today an offline session is likely to take place on a computer, using a system like AVID or even Premiere, although the basic principle is the same. With a non-linear system the offline would be done using lower quality digitized video and for the auto-conform the full quality footage would be loaded up as needed. Although the same equipment is often used for offline and online editing, the amount (and cost) of hard-disk storage needed to hold everything at broadcast resolution usually means that high quality is reserved for the auto-conform.

Quite a substantial industry has grown up around these non-linear systems, as they are called. Non-linear is another way of describing what a computer person is more likely to call random access and the term is used to differentiate a hard-disk editing system from one using videotape. With tape your editing basically had to start at the beginning and work forwards, linearly, through the programme. Some non-linear editing systems are designed to seem familiar to video professionals, while other systems are more computer-like and so are not as popular with video editors but have their fans in the multimedia community because they feel familiar to them. Non-linear systems started as offline edit systems, although they have migrated upwards in quality, and have passed through news broadcasting to full acceptability as a high-quality editing medium.

☐ Online

With a non-linear system the only difference between offline and online is likely to be the sophistication of the editing software and whether it has features for compositing or video effects. Otherwise, as already outlined, at the end of the offline session you virtually just press a button to load up high-quality footage and auto-conform it and then, finally, copy it onto videotape or, possibly, produce a computer file you can take away and compress. Or the facility might compress it for you.

You might still find yourself using an edit suite with tape machines, or one configured to be like a tape suite rather than a computer. The videotape machines, with their whirring motors and fans, were kept in a separate room, called the machine room. This is sometimes still the case, but with the quieter videocassette-based systems the machines are now often kept in a rack next to the desk. In some facilities it is common practice to have a central pool of machines and allocate them to suites as required, rather than having machines dedicated to a particular suite. So you may not even see the machines being used for your session. You may not even know whether you are using tape or non-linear until the edit starts.

You, as the client, will be in the control room of the edit suite. There will be a bank of television monitors in front of you, with a control desk and a vision mixer. It is one of the standing jokes of the video industry that in *Star Wars*, when the denizens of the Death Star zapped a planet, they controlled the destructor beam with a Grass Valley vision mixer, common to many videotape editing suites around the world. (Computer people get their laughs from Scottie trying to use a Mac Plus in the *Star Trek* movie about saving the whale.) The staff of the suite will probably be two people: the editor and an assistant, also known as the tape-op if there are tapes. Almost without fail a character known as a runner will come in from time to time and offer you coffee or toast.

Computer-based non-linear edit suite.
(Photo courtesy of Sightline, Godalming)

The editor's skill is in working out how to cut your material, to your specification, so that it flows and so that the edits do not jar. There are little tricks, such as cutting just before a movement in the incoming picture, which distract the viewer's attention momentarily and can be used to disguise the cut. With an edit, the material you have before the edit is called the outgoing shot, and that after the edit is called the incoming shot. The edit is adjusted by tightening it (making it happen earlier) or loosening it (making it happen later).

The editor will be editing sound and video. Often the sound will be mixed across an edit even if the video is cut. This is done to soften the impact of the cut. If the sound is heard before the vision cut it is said to be leading it. An edit where sound and video are cut at different points is said to be split (a split A/V). Sometimes you will continue the sound and come back to drop a short cutaway shot to replace some of the video.

Online videotape editing is a linear process. You started at the beginning of the programme material, edit shot onto shot, and finally reach the end. This meant that you needed to be satisfied with each edit as you did it, since you do not have much option for changing it. Hard-disk systems allow you to edit in any order, and you can go back to an earlier edit to change it if you want to. Despite this versatility it is important that you are satisfied with the edited material when you leave the edit. The last thing you do should be to view the material all the way through to make sure it is cut to your satisfaction. You might do this while the videotape is produced, if you are confident that it is OK. To be honest you don't have anything to lose by doing this. You should always have two copies of the finished programme, one can then be a safety for the other in case of problems. You could also ask for a viewing cassette to show, perhaps, to your client. Do not transport the main and safety copies together.

Just as audio studios have signal processing equipment for echo and delay, so a videotape edit suite will have its equivalent either built-in to the editing software or as self-contained boxes of equipment. One very common piece of equipment is the digital video effects unit, or DVE. With a DVE attached to the vision mixer, the video can be processed to make it change size, appear to move with 3-D perspective, and even be wrapped around shapes in real time. Such devices have a variety of names and manufacturers, but one legendary name was for a piece of BBC hardware, never marketed, which was called TIPSE. This stood for Technical Investigations Picture Shuffling Engine.

One important thing to remember about digital processing of television pictures using external boxes is that, without exception, the picture will be delayed as it passes through the device. Usually it will be delayed by one frame, which in NTSC is just over 33 milliseconds and in PAL is exactly 40 milliseconds. This delaying of the picture will eventually make the sound lose its synchronism, so it is usual to delay the audio to match, and edit suites have audio delay lines for this purpose. There are many opportunities for sound and vision to lose synchronization so this is something you should watch for.

■ Analogue videotape machines

It is possible that you will come across a variety of videotape formats, depending on the kind of work you are doing. Some of them will only be used now for archive footage, but it may be useful to know what the terms mean. Unless otherwise stated these machines can be found in NTSC and PAL formats, although component formats should be referred to as 525/60 and 625/50 (for lines and fields) or simply 525 or 625. SECAM and PAL are the same at a component level so there is no difference between a Betacam-SP or Digi-Beta tape recorded in France and one recorded in Germany or the UK. Similarly SECAM SVHS is the same as PAL SVHS as far as the recording on the tape is concerned.

The oldest tape format still used, even if only for archive material, is 2-inch Quad. Originally the American company Ampex developed a system called Quadraplex, which used 2-inch tape, in 1956. Other companies also made 2-inch machines for this format. Long-established broadcasters such as the BBC have archive material on 2-inch, and it was in regular use until the 1970s, so it includes colour. Some stock deteriorated over time because of physical problems with the tape itself, and the Quadraplex system was relatively violent, spinning four heads rapidly across the width of the tape, so it is possible when playing a 2-inch tape to damage the tape, especially if the edge of the tape is already damaged a little. If the owners will still let you use this material, and they allow it to be played despite the risk, then it should be copied onto a more recent format as it is first played. Oxide from the tape can easily clog up the tape heads, and sometimes engineers will use a piece of card or even their thumbnail to remove oxide from the heads as the tape plays. The basic rule is to leave 2-inch to the specialists, and, in any case, very few facilities will handle it these days.

There was a 2-inch helical scan system that was used by a few broadcasters. This is incompatible with the 2-inch Quadraplex machines. A well-aligned 2-inch recording can be of extremely high quality with a sharper signal than later analogue formats.

After 2-inch came 1-inch. This was a helical scan format, which means that the tape heads are on a drum that moves in almost the same plane as the tape path. Videocassettes are helical scan as well. The main manufacturers of 1-inch machines were Ampex and Sony (who made C format machines) and Bosch (who made B format machines). Almost all 1-inch tapes in the UK and USA will be C format but some countries, such as Brazil, Germany and Austria, used B format. The essential thing to know is that the two are incompatible.

The 1-inch tape format was in use from the early 1980s until the early 1990s, by which time cassette-based formats like Betacam-SP had replaced it. Sony developed Betacam as a derivative of their ill-fated Betamax VCR system. There is a difference between Betacam and Betacam-SP, and although most engineers will use the words interchangeably (or just say 'Beta') you should always specify Betacam-SP if you mean Betacam-SP just in case the video library also handles the older Betacam format. This is mainly a problem in the USA rather than Europe, where PAL Betacam never really caught on.

Betacam-SP has been very successful. It is a very handy system to use, with small cassettes being used in camcorders (with 20 or 30 minutes of tape time) and larger tapes in console machines. Video quality is good, and since it is a component system unlike 1-inch or 2-inch, the pictures are better suited to digitization. There is another component cassette format that competed with Betacam-SP, and that is M-II (M-Two). Beta machines come from Sony, Ampex and Thomson and M-II from JVC and Panasonic.

As far as sound goes, 2-inch tape carried a single mono track with reasonable quality, although it suffered from a high-pitched whine caused by the video tracks, which lie at right angles to the sound track. The orientation of the tape oxide was optimized for video and lay across the tape rather than along it, and so was in the wrong direction for audio which affected audio quality. The 1-inch C format has either three or four tracks, depending on configuration. The performance is good, but Dolby noise reduction was often used to improve the signal-to-noise ratio.

Betacam-SP has four sound tracks. Two are very high quality but cannot be used during editing since they use the video track although they can be used for straight recording. So in practice the other two lower (but still good) quality tracks are used most.

■ Cassettes

Although virtually all professional videotape formats are now cassette-based rather than reel to reel (also known as open reel), there are videocassette formats that are regarded as consumer or industrial. There had been domestic and industrial open-reel videotape formats, notably from Philips and Ampex, which became available in the late 1960s, but the price was far too high for widespread use.

Videocassettes first came onto the market in the 1970s with the 1500 format from Philips and U-Matic from Sony. U-Matic has high-quality (Hi-Band and SP) versions. It is still also used for digital audio as the Sony 1630/1610 format. However, you are unlikely to find U-Matic tapes used in high-quality video today since variants of Betacam-SP, digital video cassette (DV) and S-VHS/Hi8 have taken that niche. U-Matic cassettes use $\frac{3}{4}$-inch tape, and are sometimes referred to as the $\frac{3}{4}$-inch format. One serious disadvantage of U-Matic is that the maximum tape length is 74 minutes. (Coincidentally this is the supposed maximum duration of a compact disk.)

The most common videocassette format for domestic and industrial use is the irrepressible VHS. The picture quality of VHS is relatively poor, with particularly fuzzy colour performance. Hi-fi sound tracks were retrofitted to VHS, and achieve very high quality even though they are analogue. S-VHS uses cassettes of the same size as VHS but with different tape. S-VHS gives much better results with higher bandwidth, resulting in sharper pictures and better colour. S-VHS machines can usually play and record VHS but not vice versa, and both systems use half-inch tape. JVC developed a higher-quality version called Professional-S.

Video-8 is Sony's successor to Betamax, and boasts the smallest analogue cassettes in video. There is a high-quality version, analogous to S-VHS, called Hi8. These formats sometimes have digital sound. The tape width is 8 mm – hence the 8 in the names. There is a digital version of Hi8 using DV encoding on Hi8 tapes.

There are industrial versions of Betacam-SP with a lower price and a lower, but still very good, quality. The gap between S-VHS and Betacam-SP is also narrowed by the high-quality version of S-VHS available from JVC. One advantage of the industrial Beta systems is that they are compatible with the full spec. version.

■ Videodisks

John Logie Baird actually sold 78 rpm videodisks in the 1920s, but it was not until the 1980s that commercially viable videodisk machines came onto the domestic market. In Europe the domestic market for videodisks never really caught on, although it was successful in a niche for film fans and classical music enthusiasts. This market virtually disappeared when high-quality digital video from a DVD became available. There is more on DVD video in Chapter 3 of this volume.

Interactive video, which uses videodisks with computer control, was the precursor of multimedia, and you are unlikely to be working with videodisks (in any case that is outside the scope of this book) any more. However, you might use videodisks as a source for video and audio for multimedia, and there are a few points to bear in mind.

PAL LaserDisks can, if they are older, have analogue soundtracks. In any case PAL disks can have only two tracks, analogue or digital but not both, whereas NTSC disks can have both and often do. If you are trying to digitize from an NTSC videodisk, check whether your player outputs real or modified NTSC. If your digitizer sees black and white then this might be the cause.

Sony produced a WORM (Write Once Read Many) videodisk that records component video and is considered to be of broadcast quality. This system has been used by some television stations to hold station identification sequences because of the random access and lack of deterioration (unlike tape) but has been superseded by digital storage.

Pioneer produced a magneto-optical recordable/erasable videodisk that also had two separate head assemblies, which can be used independently for playback. This is also a component system.

Both these machines exist in PAL and NTSC versions.

■ Digital formats

Video is digitized in much the same way as audio: the waveform is measured many times a second and the resulting value is stored as a digital number. It is possible to digitize composite video but the highest quality systems digitize the component signal. The standard for this has a sampling rate of 13.5 MHz (for both NTSC and PAL timings) for the luminance component. The two colour components are usually sampled at half of this rate. There are several ways of sampling the luminance and colour components which are all denoted as ratios with the number 4 representing the 13.5 MHz sample rate of the luminance. In the studio, where bandwidth is not such an issue, a configuration of $4:2:2$ is used meaning that the colour information is sampled at half the rate of the luminance. This is what happens along each line so the colour resolution is higher horizontally than vertically. On tape, and in MPEG-2, the colour is effectively sampled every other line, evening out the horizontal vertical resolutions and saving about 25% data. This is known as $4:2:0$.

For production it is important that the colour bandwidth is great enough for chroma-keying and $4:2:2$ sampling gives a chroma bandwidth of 3.37 MHz, which is high enough although there is a four channel system, $4:2:2:4$, with a separate key signal at high resolution added to the $4:2:2$ format.

Digital video is digitized with 8- (and occasionally 10-) bit resolution. To people coming from audio this seems crazy since eight bits gives a very noisy result with sound. But with a video image, noise is not perceived in the same way. The effect of noise is even reduced by the way the eye and brain are inherently turning the series of stills into a moving image so a movie will seem to have less noise (or grain in the case of film) than an individual frame will. So eight bits will suffice.

Digital video levels do not go between 0 and 255 in an 8-bit system as you might expect. Black is at 16 and white at 235. This is to minimize the effect of spikes and overshoots in the digitized waveform but it can lead to 'real' video seeming washed out when shown on a computer screen. Conversely computer-generated graphics can seem crushed at black and white levels unless the 16/235 limits are taken into account.

In the 1990s digital videotape formats began to replace analogue ones. First there were D1 and D2. D1 is a very high-quality component digital system developed by Sony, but unfortunately the cost of machinery and tape stock made it popular only with advertising agencies, film companies and video research. D2 was a derivative system, which recorded digitized composite signals (PAL or NTSC). As a result it could be easily integrated into existing systems, and was more popular. Neither D1 nor D2 compressed the data used to record the video or audio. However, it was the advent of half-inch digital systems that brought digital video within the cost range of the majority of broadcasters.

D3 is a composite digital system, D4 does not exist, and D5 is a component digital system without compression. There is a mode for D5 that supports high definition pictures with some compression. Digital Betacam is from Sony (of course) and uses a $2:1$ compression in the signal. Some Digi-Beta machines can play Betacam-SP tapes, which makes for versatility in editing. It is also possible to get Betacam-SP machines with digital inputs and outputs, but these are not Digital Betacam.

Even though there is a digital output from these tape formats, the usual way of copying the pictures into a multimedia system is by digitizing or grabbing the analogue output. This is partly because of the high data rate of professional digital video (270 megabits/second) and partly because of incompatibilities in the shape of the pixels between computers and the international standard for digital television.

A consumer digital videocassette format using 6 mm tapes, called DV, has become popular for high-end consumer, industrial and even some broadcasting applications, especially in news. The format is not fully component but uses the Y/C format which separates luminance and colour but only has a single colour channel. Two semi-compatible professional derivatives, DVCAM and DVCPRO (which also has a derivative high-quality version), together with a long-play derivative of basic DV, are also available. DV machines are now made by all the major camcorder manufacturers, and at its best with a three-chip camera and good lighting, DV produces results that are hard to distinguish from broadcast equipment. DV has a $5:1$ compression which does not compare succeeding frames. Sony has produced a digital version of its Hi8 system which uses DV encoding on Hi-8 tapes and gives owners a backwardly compatible path to their old recordings. As the tape is bigger than DV the Digital-8 camcorders cannot benefit from the same level of miniaturization. Most of the manufacturers provide a digital connection (using the new IEEE-1394 standard, better known as FireWire) with which video can be copied to and from a computer. This system provides a very cost-effective high-quality way of shooting and preparing video for multimedia on a website or CD-ROM. There is a limited interoperability between these formats, which mainly means that the professional formats can play back the domestic tapes. Some consumer DV machines can play back the professional tapes although the pro formats run the tape slightly faster – for example a 60-minute DV tape recorded in a DVCAM machine only lasts 40 minutes.

JVC has introduced a further broadcast digital cassette system called Digital-S, and has announced D-VHS as a time-shifting format for the home market. Sony has an industrial/news-gathering digital version of Betacam, Betacam-SX. An SX machine can play SP (i.e. analogue) tapes, and so an SX machine offers an upgrade option for anyone with a large archive of SP material. It is interesting to see how many competing digital videotape formats have been introduced in the past few years. The market is obviously now large enough for the manufacturers to try to shake out standards in a way that was not really possible 20 years ago. The most interesting aspect of these new formats for multimedia is that the inherent quality even of the consumer DV format is so high that the tape format is not really the limiting factor: the quality of the lens and camera chip (CCD) have the most effect.

■ Copying tapes for use in multimedia

Since it is extremely unlikely that you will be allowed direct access to a master videotape it will be useful to outline some suggestions for formats.

If the master is composite then your working copy can be either composite or component. Since, as we shall explain in a moment, it is better to digitize from a component source, in most cases you will want to ask for a component dub of the master. If you can work with a digital source then you should ask for a component digital copy. As discussed above, one very practical option for desktop video is to use a DV or DVCAM dub and work from this, especially if you can transfer the video to your computer using FireWire. The lack of tape noise on DV makes it especially attractive for compression, assuming the lighting was sufficient and did not lead to noise from the camera circuitry.

It is possible that you will be editing and possibly processing the video to make a new master tape. This might happen if you were to be encoding material for MPEG on DVD and wanted to prepare a master of your own first. This might include video noise reduction and re-editing. In this case a digital composite dub would be recommended (such as D3). In this way the decoding of the composite video to component can be done as part of your processing, and you will have more control over it.

Under no circumstances should you get a composite dub of a component tape; neither should you digitize from a dub on videocassette such as VHS, S-VHS or Hi8 unless you really have no alternative. Incidentally, you can save money by asking the facility house to dub a VHS with burned-in time code in vision, for your viewing, as they dub the master.

Finally you should not standards-convert a tape between PAL/SECAM and NTSC or vice versa. Your copy should be in the same standard as the original, assuming you can digitize from the format of course, so that you will not be encoding conversion artefacts.

A final note about DVD. DVD players have a system called Macrovision in them specifically to stop analogue copying and this is likely to interfere with any dubbing you try to do. The MPEG information on the DVD will also be encrypted so you can't just copy the file unless you legally have access to decryption. It may be that in future there will be legitimate reason to dub from a DVD because other versions no longer exist. But since you will be legally licensing the material (you will … won't you?) you have to ask for a copy in a format you can use, such as broadcast tape, or an unencrypted MPEG data file.

■ Digitizing video for multimedia

Digital video in multimedia can mean partial screen or full screen, full motion (that is, 25 or 30 frames per second) or partial motion (down to 10 or fewer frames per second). The details of digitizing from a video source are very much down to the particular equipment in use, but there are some general principles. Remember that here we're talking mostly about digitizing from a video source, not copying DV into the computer using FireWire.

'Recording' the video into the computer is called frame grabbing, and this grabbing should, if at all possible, be done at full frame and full frame rate. It is possible to frame grab uncompressed, but this requires very fast digitizing hardware and local storage. The kind of hard disk used in a desktop computer cannot work this fast unless several are joined together in an array. (When it comes to copying DV, the video is already compressed so most hard disks can cope with it but DV still takes up a lot of disk space: over 200 megabytes per minute for sound and vision.)

The pixels of a television picture and the pixels on a computer screen are not actually the same shape. This affects 525 and 625 line pictures differently, but essentially means that when copying a digital TV signal to the desktop, such as DV via FireWire, the aspect ratio of the image changes slightly. If you are editing on the computer and copying the finished video data back to the DV machine then this is not a big problem, but if you are going to distribute the video on a computer then you need to correct the aspect ratio change at some point. A frame grabber will sort out the pixel shape as it digitizes the video.

In order to play the video back on the computer it will have to be compressed and probably shrunk in size, but this is better done 'at leisure' rather than in real time. From a practical point of view high-quality JPEG can be used during the grabbing process, so that the movie becomes a series of JPEG stills, which will save disk space. The results from this will usually look very good.

One important point about frame grabbing is that the frames you store on your hard disk will be either component or RGB; they will not be composite. This means that if you are grabbing from a composite source the grabbing board will need to convert (decode) NTSC or PAL into component or RGB. This will involve filtering the incoming signal to separate out the colour from the luminance. Unfortunately, the cost of a good filter to do this would be much higher than the cost of the rest of the equipment put together, so the filtering in a commercially viable grabber board has to compromise on quality, and some artefacts may be noticeable.

First, the luminance bandwidth may be compromised by the filtering out of the colour subcarrier if the video input is a composite one. Many filters (including those in most television sets) remove the higher frequencies of the luminance signal, those above the subcarrier, as well as the subcarrier itself.

Second, filters 'ring' and this has an effect on vertical edges in the picture. A sharp vertical edge has high frequencies in it: the sharper the edge, the higher the frequencies involved. Passing such a signal through a filter can have a detrimental effect on the shape of the edge, and the signal can overshoot and ring (just like a bell). What you see is a dark band between a bright and a dark part of the picture, darker than the dark part. Now if the dark part is black this results in a small part of the picture that is blacker than black, which is possible in an analogue television signal as shown overleaf. For this reason, among others, black and white in a digital television signal are not set at 0 and 255.

A good filter can avoid these kinds of problems, but a better way is to avoid filtering altogether and always digitize from a component source, such as Betacam-SP or Digi-Beta. If the signal has to be converted from composite, because it was originally recorded that way, then a high-quality broadcast filter can be used during a dub from the original tape or a digital composite copy of the original tape to a component tape.

Taking a movie film and recording it onto videotape uses a machine called a telecine and the process of putting the film onto tape is called a transfer. For digital video in multimedia this telecine transfer should be done into a component videotape, and preferably a digital one. The film should be clean to avoid dust, and for top-quality transfer the imaging gate through which the film passes in the telecine machine can be submerged in a liquid with the same refractive index as the film base. This is called a wet gate, and produces excellent results. Many telecine facilities also have

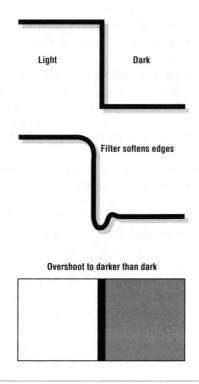

Light   Dark

Filter softens edges

Overshoot to darker than dark

Ringing.

digital noise reducer, which make use of the similarity between frames to 'remove' dust and scratches or have infrared sensors to detect dust and so help remove it.

Video digitization should be done from the original television standard- and not from a standards-converted videotape. This is because standards conversion changes the image, even if only slightly. In any case, for digital video, the computer controlling the playback is generating frames at its own rate, and the system will cope automatically with the input frame rate. Unfortunately it will do this by attempting to read out a frame when it needs one, even if there is not a new frame available. In this case it repeats the last frame. (The opposite may occur where frames are dropped.) There is nothing you can do about this, but you would make it worse by digitizing from a standards-converted source where this process, or a sophisticated version of it, has been carried out already.

A television standards converter will interpolate new frames, or combine old frames, in order to avoid the jerkiness that this basic 5–6 conversion has, but a computer display does not do this. This may suggest that, if you have the freedom of choice, you might actually use NTSC rather than PAL for your video in Europe, because the NTSC frame rate is more like that on the computer.

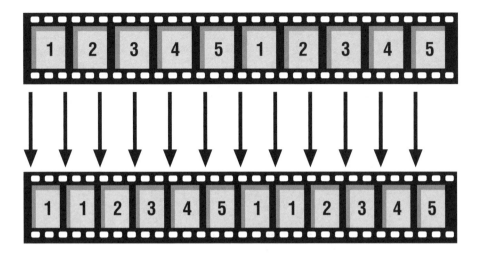

To read out six frames where five are available means that
one frame is repeated.

Another set of problems is caused by the television signal being interlaced. When a television camera captures motion during a frame it does so
in two separate slices of time, a 60th or 50th of a second apart. A moving
object will have changed position between those two slices, the fields. When
this is played back on an interlaced television screen there is no problem
because the output display is interlaced with two fields per frame in the
same way as the input camera. This does not happen when the full frame is
displayed on a computer screen because a computer screen is not interlaced, but writes the picture in one sweep from top to bottom, left to right.
The result is that horizontally moving objects can appear to break up like
a comb. Vertical filtering, also known as convolution, can be used to correct this fault but at the expense of resolution. It does not occur when the
camera was a film camera because a film camera exposes the whole frame
at once.

This situation will also only occur if the video on the computer screen is
the same size (has the same number of pixels) as the original video grabbed.
If it has been shrunk to half size, for example, to make a quarter-screen
image of 320 by 240 pixels, then the result will be a slight horizontal blurring
or a double image rather than a comb effect. Alternatively you could simply
drop one of the two fields, although this might produce artefacts.

When shrinking an image (it does not matter whether it is movie or still),
new pixels should be calculated from combinations of the old ones, rather
than by sub-sampling (that is, only selecting some of) the old pixels. If this
is not done then near-horizontal lines will 'staircase' and also appear and
disappear with movement of the picture, as they go from 'visible' pixels
to 'no longer visible' pixels and back again. This vertical filtering (to blend

Combing.

together information from the fields) is very important when dealing with television pictures in the digital domain.

Some computer systems will allow the computer display to be set up to be interlaced, but use of this is rare unless the application is going to be shown on a television monitor. Using an interlaced display with a computer causes flickering of fine detail in the picture (called twitter), and filtering this out reduces the effective resolution of the image.

■ Compression

Video in multimedia is, by definition, digital. For practical reasons it also has to be compressed, because it is impractical to handle the high data rate used by raw video. Broadcast technology is able to handle this, but at a price and even digital broadcast television is compressed. For multimedia we have a choice of various 'standard' methods of compression, and the choice available increases as time goes by. These standards use compression and decompression software or hardware called codecs.

Two of the international standards that are applied to video compression are JPEG and MPEG. JPEG, which is discussed in the chapter on graphics (Chapter 8), is a compression system used for still images. JPEG is attuned to work with photographic images, which have smooth gradations of tone rather than sharp lines. JPEG works in only two dimensions: the height and the width of a frame. MPEG adds further data reduction by comparing groups of successive frames. Since not all of an image changes – frame by frame – in a movie, this redundancy can be used in the compression.

With sufficient data bandwidth available, from a fast hard disk for example, JPEG images can be displayed fast enough to become a movie, and this is a pseudo-standard called M-JPEG and is often used for non-linear editing. MPEG uses less data but is more difficult to decompress (and compress). Both of these standards, when used for movies, require hardware or a fast processor. MPEG as used in video compression actually encompasses three variations, with MPEG-1 being the version designed for use on compact disc at 1.5 megabits per second. MPEG-2 is a higher-quality, higher-bandwidth version, which is used for digital television and DVD, and MPEG-4 is aimed at low-bandwidth applications and interactivity. Recently, codecs like DivX ;-) (which does include that smiley in its name), and 3ivx have appeared, based on MPEG-4, and are aimed at watching movies via broadband connections.

Several software video compression systems exist, making use of operating system architectures such as Windows Media and QuickTime. For use on the Internet the issue is how the systems will perform with a low bandwidth, and at the time of writing the most popular standard is RealVideo, which is designed to cope with modem or ISDN data rates. In this case the video is streamed across the Internet, rather like broadcasting, instead of being copied to the user's computer.

As a general rule, video codecs that give good results at one data rate will not perform as well at a very different one. This is called scalability (or lack of it), and means that increasing the data rate will not allow an increase in quality because the codec has a quality ceiling. Cinepak is a codec that behaves in this way and has been replaced by the Sorensen codec, which can also work at higher rates.

In fitting movies into an operating system environment, the manufacturers (such as Apple and Microsoft) define standard interfaces for control of the movie with VCR-like controls for play and fast forward and rewind. A progress bar, to show how far through a movie you are at any moment, is also a standard part of such an interface.

QuickTime and Windows Media both can work transparently with a range of video compression systems, since the operating systems present a consistent interface to your application. This means that you can switch from using, say, Indeo to using MPEG-1 without changing the application as long as the two videos have the same resolution and share the necessary control parameters. However, you have to be confident that your intended audience has the codec you use since few will be willing to download a new plug-in or codec especially for your video. On the Web this usually means RealVideo, although Sorensen (through QuickTime) or Windows Media's MPEG-4 codec are serious alternatives.

With the movie come sound and stills, since an audio file is basically a movie with no pictures and a still is a movie consisting of only one frame. It is MPEG that currently offers the best set of these features since MPEG audio and MPEG stills are of extremely high quality and are very efficiently compressed.

■ Judging quality

The points outlined in the previous chapter on quality as it applies to sound also apply to video. However, it is usually very difficult to achieve broadcast quality with video on a multimedia system (if not currently impossible on a website), and your client should be aware of this. Again, use of the term 'appropriate' to describe the quality may be the best option. Some of the quality issues are less tangible. The quality of editing and the camerawork are independent of the technical quality of the desktop video, and in these cases you should aim for a quality threshold similar to that of broadcast television. Explaining early on that the multimedia video will not look as good as TV, and showing the client some examples, will avoid this becoming an issue, but you should be prepared to explain why, especially to a client who has experience of corporate video or broadcasting.

THEORY INTO PRACTICE 7

One of the ways of building video skills is by watching. Look carefully at what you see on television. See how people are framed by the camera, and watch particularly how faces usually look into space within a frame. Look at how a movie is cut, and think about why a cut might occur in a particular place. Watch for the way the incoming shot often starts with an action that will distract your attention from the edit itself.

If you have a camcorder then you can try some of this out for yourself.

You should also look at good quality web video, such as that on the BBC site (www.bbc.co.uk) and compare how it looks with television.

■ Summary

- Moving pictures are a very effective way of conveying information in multimedia.
- You need to be aware of the different broadcast television standards that you might encounter and of the difference between composite and component video. NTSC and PAL are the main forms of composite video, and each has a component and digital equivalent.

- For a variety of reasons component video offers better quality than composite and is more suited to digitizing.
- Time code is a numbering system used in videotape recording that will also be useful to you. You can use it to show tape numbers as well as time.
- Shooting a video interview is one of the most likely kinds of video you will undertake. The subject can be separated from the background by shooting against blue or black.
- If you want to shoot video yourself using your camcorder then you need to take care over things like colour balance, focus and exposure.
- The stages of editing video are preparation, offline and online. New technology and non-linear editing systems using PCs have blurred the distinction between online and offline editing.
- Options for compressing video so that it can easily be handled on the desktop include moving JPEG, MPEG and software codecs. The most common equivalent for the Web is RealVideo with QuickTime and Windows Media as alternatives.
- Codecs will usually have a range of data rates and applications for which they are suited, so a web codec may not work well on CD-ROM and vice versa.

■ Recommended reading

Watkinson J. (2000). *Art of Digital Video*. 3rd edn, London: Focal Press

Watts H. (1998). *On Camera*. 2nd edn London: Focal Press

Quantel Ltd *The Digital Factbook*,
http://www.quantel.com/domisphere/infopool.nsf/DFB

Zoom Culture, a US Internet Video production company, have produced a quirky but excellent video (In Real format) showing the dos and don'ts of shooting video for the Internet. The URL is
http://www.zc.tv/clips/rams/046738.ram

8

Graphics asset production

Project manager's responsibilities

- To assemble the necessary graphics team
- To ensure that the project definition is in a form that adequately briefs the graphics team
- To monitor the development of the graphics, and liaise between the client and the team over changes and misunderstandings
- To make sure that 'proofreading', the checking of any written material in the graphics, is carried out
- To make sure that the source graphics are archived at the highest reasonable resolution, no matter how they are displayed in the application
- To understand the processes involved in producing this kind of asset

■ A picture is worth a thousand words

No matter how innovative your interface design, how sophisticated your programming or use of HTML, the public face of your web page, your inter-active television programme or multimedia application and the major make-or-break factor is going to be your graphics and design. (Possibly not a big issue for a WAP site at the moment however.) Your potential customer will feel able to make an instant judgement, for better or for worse, on the basis of that first impression on the screen.

Just as with software, the creation and manipulation of graphics is a com-plex business, and the purpose of this chapter is to provide some general background to the techniques and systems that you might wish to use, and to outline some of the problems that you might come across.

The two key parts of managing the production of graphics are the defini-tion of the task and the selection of the personnel. There should be some definition of the approach to graphics in the project plan. In some cases a graphics artist or art director will have taken part in the creative definition of the application. On the basis of the graphic requirements a team will be chosen. It may be that you are working in an organization that has graphics artists on the staff or a pool of freelancers. This situation is more common for graphics and programming than for sound or video. In this case you might find that the project plan evolved to fit in some way with the abilities of a particular graphics person.

There are many kinds of process that go to make up artwork, and after a brief explanation of terminology for colour, this chapter will look at the dif-ferences between them and how the way they are made may impact upon the management of a project. This will apply to two stages, because you should work with your images in the highest quality possible and then con-vert down if necessary to the standard required for delivery. Archiving should also be done so as to include the highest-quality versions.

■ Colour

A colour image on a computer or television screen – whether it is a cathode ray tube (CRT), liquid crystal (LCD) or gas plasma – is made up of red, green and blue dots or lines, which are close enough together to blend into each other when seen from a working distance. Red, green and blue (R, G and B) are what are called the primary colours for any colour displayed with light. You will find an example on the website of how a colour image is built in this way. (For pigments, such as paint and printing ink, the primaries are red, yellow and blue. For practical reasons printers work with secondary colours – cyan, magenta and yellow – to which black ink – called K – is usually added to avoid the muddy effects of trying to make black from the secondaries. This is known as CMYK.)

For this reason we refer to a colour image on the screen as an RGB image. (RGB is one of a number of ways of defining a colour, other so-called colour spaces include CMYK and hue-saturation-brightness which is known as HSB but in this discussion we will stick with RGB.) For most practical purposes, almost any colour can be produced by mixing the three primaries, and in a full-colour image on the screen each picture element or pixel is built up from varying amounts of red, green and blue light. Shades of grey are produced by making the amount of red, green and blue in the pixel equal. For black there is no light, and for white the light is 'full on'. In digital terms there are 256 shades to each of red, green and blue in a full-colour 24-bit image.

With fewer than 24 bits there will be fewer colours, but it is possible that each of the colours that can be shown can be predefined from the full range, or palette, of 24 bits.

■ Drawings

This word has a double meaning. To the person in the street, drawing is taking a pencil and creating a freehand work of art. Drawing, like painting, is the essence of fine art.

In computer terms a drawing is an image that consists of distinct segments or shapes, called draw objects. It is sometimes referred to as line art but this term could be ambiguous, sometimes also referring to an image on the screen that is made up of only black and white pixels.

The classic draw objects are lines, rectangles and arcs together with a range of wavy lines called curves, of which Bézier curves are perhaps the

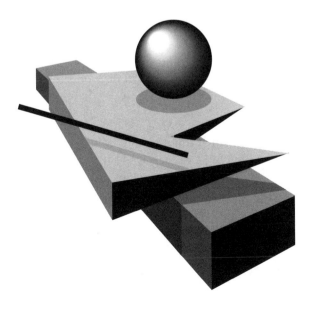

most familiar. Since the draw objects are based around lines they are sometimes called vector graphics. The important thing about a drawing is that the objects in it retain their separate identity, so that they can be manipulated independently of each other, even if, in the image as seen, the object is partially or completely hidden behind other objects.

Each object has characteristics, which can be changed. Drawing applications will allow you to rescale an object or a group of objects without a loss of quality. The width of a line, and the pattern with which it is drawn, called the pen, can be changed. If the object has an 'inside', it can be filled with a colour or a pattern. A polygonal shape or a curve can be altered by moving the corners or changing the controls on the curve.

Changing one object has no substantial repercussions on the other objects. If the circle in the diagram is moved it would reveal the polygon behind it. The image becomes a pattern of dots on the monitor only when it is displayed or when you choose to 'fix' it. By definition the drawing does not have a scale, and can be expanded or shrunk or distorted as required with no ill effects, as seen above. An exception to this scale independence is the thickness of lines, since that tends to be fixed. As a result you might wish to increase line thickness as the size of the final drawing increases, and conversely reduce line thickness for a small drawing.

If changes are required, drawings are relatively easy to modify. Because it is based around these distinct and almost unconnected objects a drawing package is said to be object-oriented.

In some computing systems, particularly the Apple Macintosh, these draw objects are supported by the operating system at a low level, which makes it easy for different programs to work with them and even exchange them.

Although most graphics on the Web are bitmapped, there is a small but important use of draw objects in making small animation files. Flash is a particularly popular example of this, and by describing the objects that go to make up an animation, and describing how they move and change, Flash is able to produce sophisticated animations from a very small amount of data.

■ Bitmap or painting

In contrast a bitmap, sometimes referred to in computing as a painting (hence paint packages as opposed to drawing packages) or rasterized graphics, exists only as the patterns of dots. To continue the example above, if the ellipse moves it leaves a hole. If the bitmap expands, the dots get bigger and the resolution of the image becomes cruder.

The bitmap may start out as a set of draw objects. It may be created in a drawing package and then turned into a bitmap, 'fixing' the pattern of lines and shapes. This process is also known as rasterizing. The bitmap could have been scanned in from a photograph. Scanners are devices that take a 'real' image such as a print, a slide, a transparency or even a photographic negative and scan across the image, from side to side and top to bottom, to produce a stream of dot information about the image, which can be stored in a computer file and so make its way onto the screen.

Making changes to a bitmap, such as changing text in the image, could have serious implications because of the holes left when parts of the image are removed. One way around this problem is to use a paint package which allows control of layers of an image and the way they are combined, or composited, together.

JPEG and GIF are the two most common bitmap formats for graphics, and both are used extensively on the Web. On CD-ROMs, JPEGs are also common, although GIFs are unusual. BMP (Windows) and PICT (Mac) are platform-specific bitmap formats used on CD-ROMs. The older TIFF format is often now found in digital still cameras as an uncompressed format. The new graphics format PNG supports up to 48 bits of colour (16 bits each for R, G and B), which allows the look of the graphic to be adjusted as it is displayed to compensate for differences between different computers' graphics displays.

■ Composites

The addition of alpha channels and layers into paintings has helped to bring some of the advantages of draw objects to the world of the bitmap. Separate bitmap objects can be combined into a composite image. Even though changing a bitmap object itself is still difficult, the relationship between objects can easily be changed. Text (one object) over a photographic background

(another object) can easily be changed. Each component of the final image is known as a layer, and the alpha channel determines how the layers blend with each other.

The simplest alpha channel is transparency or a simple mask, so-called because it masks or hides part of the image. The GIF format allows for a colour to be transparent, which allows the background to show through, and helps the image to blend into the background of the web page.

A true alpha channel is a graduated mask. It is essentially a fourth channel after red, green and blue, and it determines how much of the RGB image layer is shown at any point of the composite image and how much of whatever is underneath shows through. For most of the image the mask would be 'white', showing that all the RGB was visible and none of the underlying layers. Outside the image it would be 'black', showing that none of the RGB was visible there but the underlying layers were fully visible. At the edges of the image, where it would be designed to blend into its surroundings, the alpha channel would gradually change from white to black, and the depth of the 'grey' at any point would determine the visibility and mixing at that point. TIFF and PNG formats support an alpha channel, as does the Macintosh PICT format.

In a montage, where there might be several small images grouped together over a background, each of the small images would have its own alpha channel and would exist in a separate layer. In this way changes can be made to each of these elements independently of the whole composite image. A further refinement of this technique would allow layers to be completely transparent or translucent. A reflection in a window would be transparent, with the image behind the glass being opaque behind it.

As a result of using layers in this way an image becomes easier to change under some circumstances. Let's use the example where a final image consists of a photograph with some text superimposed on it. If there is no layering to the image in your archive then to change the text you will have to find the original image of the background and build the image again from scratch. With layers you can change the text, which will be in the foreground layer by itself, without having to touch the background. A recent innovation is to use a version of layers to hold changes to an image, so that the changes can be modified or even reversed.

Paint packages can be biased towards creation, retouching or both. For many graphic artists Adobe's PhotoShop defines the retouching package (although it is not alone), especially once it became available on the PC platform as well as on the Apple Macintosh. Recent versions of PhotoShop included Image Ready, which prepares graphics for the Web. An alternative web-oriented graphics package is Fireworks. In the Linux world there is an equivalent free package called the GIMP.

■ 3-D modelling and rendering

Quite often an application will have illustrations and montages that have a three-dimensional look. This may or may not include an animation such as a smooth movement of the viewpoint through a group of objects. 3-D packages are usually object-oriented like a drawing package. You can build a solid object using techniques analogous to building with bricks, to using a lathe to turn, or to extrude (like squeezing toothpaste). Just as two-dimensional draw objects once became part of low-level operating system tools (sometimes called primitives), in time three-dimensional objects are joining them. This makes the creation of 3-D objects easier and cheaper because, again, programs will be able to make use of the operating system's objects rather than having to define their own.

Often speed of display is more important than realism and it can be more convenient to work with a wireframe version of the three-dimensional shape. This can be very useful with a very complex picture but it takes some skill to visualize how the wireframe will look when it is fully rendered.

Once the scene is designed and the objects in it are built and positioned you can choose the surfaces for the objects. This can include texture mapping, where a bitmap is spread over the surface of an object, bump mapping, where the object is given a bumpy surface, and setting the reflectivity or opacity of the object.

Then the lighting conditions can be set up with a balance of ambient (general) lighting and spot and floodlights, and the viewpoint chosen. All these parts of the process are part of the modelling.

Finally the scene is rendered to produce the final image or images. Unlike other graphical processes, which work more or less in real time, rendering can be very slow. A single image can take minutes or even hours to be rendered as the computer works out the view (depending on the power of the computer being used of course) and if an animation is being produced this multiplies the time. To overcome this several computers are often used together to gain speed. The end result can be quite stunning, and can be genuinely referred to as photo-realistic. This is one reason why 3-D modelling is such a popular technique.

3-D images take a long time to render partly because of the time taken to work out the shadows and reflections in a scene. One very popular technique for determining reflections is ray tracing. In this case every ray of light in the view is traced as it 'bounces' from the light source, the objects in the scene and the viewer's eye. Ray tracing is very computationally intensive, and an alternative is environment mapping, where a view of 'the world as seen by the shiny object' is computed and wrapped around the object itself.

Three-dimensional modelling, like illustration and animation, is a special skill somewhat distinct from general graphics work, and you are likely to find artists who specialize in one or more of these areas.

A special case of 3-D modelling is VRML, Virtual Reality Modelling Language, which is available to be used on the Web to make virtual worlds that the viewer can navigate at will. The VRML data defines the environment, and this is modelled in real time by a plug-in to the viewer's browser. The process needs a lot of computing and so is usually somewhat clunky compared with a sophisticated 3-D rendered image, but the real-time response to movement is very engaging, and it is possible to provide simple shading to enhance the experience. VRML evolved to include animations and sound so that you can watch events unfold in front of you from whatever perspective you want but, as a web technology, it has had limited success.

A similar process to this kind of modelling is provided by QuickTime VR (QTVR), which is usually used to show the real world in a navigable way. The world is photographed as an interlinked series of 360° panoramas, allowing the user to look around and move from one panorama to another. QTVR can explore other worlds as well, since not only can the panoramas be computer-generated, but NASA published QTVR panoramas taken by a rover vehicle on Mars. QTVR is not the only such navigation software and with some it is possible to look around a whole spherical scene.

◼ DPI and bit depths

In computing terms you define an image in a number of ways. For a bitmap the most obvious defining parameter is size. In printing, graphics artists are used to defining an image by its size in inches or centimetres, and then saying what the resolution is. This means that if you have a scanned image that is 2 inches across, with a resolution of 300 lines (or dots) per inch, there are 600 dots across the image. Print is defined in this way because print has a fixed size: the size of the final image on the printed page. Computer displays are not necessarily like that, and television screens are definitely not like that. In these cases the size in inches is not important, but the size in pixels is. So the computer person will give the image size as 600 pixels across and not really be worried about its physical size in inches. Note that to a printer a screen is part of the process by which an image made of continuous gradations of colour, such as a photograph, is turned into something that an ink-based printing press can actually reproduce. This book uses the word 'screen' to mean the computer display.

Certainly a computer display has its equivalent of the printer's screen. Dots per inch are the usual way of defining a computer screen output as well. This is usually 72, 75, 80 or even as many as 120 dots per inch (dpi), and each dot is a pixel. For a computer display of 75 dpi, the 600-pixel image will be 8 inches across. You need to be clear in your mind about the relationship between the size of an image in pixels, in inches, and the connection between the two, which is its dpi. If the image on the screen is to be 2 inches across again, instead of 8, then it can be shrunk by half in a paint or photo-retouching package. (You can scale an image in a web browser when you display it of course, but that is inefficient and sometimes of poorer quality.)

There is a third dimension to computer screen images, which is the bit depth or colour depth. The number of bits in the screen display determines the number of colours or shades that can be shown. For a fixed size of image in pixels, the size of the file needed to store it doubles for most of the stages below.

- 1 bit gives you two colours (black and white).
- 2 bits give you four colours.
- 4 bits give you 16 colours.
- 8 bits give you 256 colours (GIFs are 8 bits or less).
- 16 bits give you 65,536 colours.
- 24 bits give you 16,777,216 colours (JPEGs are usually 24 bit but can be less).
- 48 bits give you 281,474,976,710,656 colours (PNG supports up to this depth).

Usually, when literature refers to 32-bit colour (as on the Apple Macintosh), this refers to 24 bits of colour information and 8 bits of alpha channel or mask, which is used for compositing. Also, a 16-bit system often gives five bits each to red, green and blue, and uses the sixteenth bit for a one-bit mask. Another technique is to give green more bits than red and blue because our eyes are more sensitive to green. The exact format of any particular graphics format will be found in its specification.

The book website includes examples of an image stored with different bit depths.

There are occasions when you will see a reference to colour of more than 24 bits, which is really just that. Colour scanners often scan at 10 or even 12 bits per colour, making 30 or 36 bits. This is because the colour rendition of the object being scanned will not usually match that of the computer, and it is handy to be able to adjust the scanning to compensate for this. The difference usually shows in the darker and lighter parts of the image. This becomes especially true when working with photographic negatives, which have a particularly wide latitude (the film equivalent of dynamic range). The relationship between the colours at the input of a device and its output – for example, as how a monitor displays shades of grey – is called the gamma of the device and is denoted as a number. Every display device has a gamma, and photographs, PCs, television sets and Macs all have different gammas. This means that a 'correct' image made on a Mac will not necessarily look good on a PC or a TV. You can adjust the gamma of an image, but doing this to a 24-bit image results in some colours disappearing – a phenomenon familiar to anyone who uses PhotoShop's 'Levels' facility. Since PNG has 48 bits it will allow changes of gamma as the browser displays an image without sacrificing visible quality. (A good explanation of the maths behind gamma can be found in the PNG specification in the references at the end of this chapter.)

Of course you can substitute 'shade of grey' for colour. It is generally assumed that the eye can distinguish fewer than 256 shades of grey, which would suggest that you could represent a smooth gradation from black to white with 256 shades. Unfortunately this does not always work, because our vision is extremely sensitive to the transition between very similar shades. However, 256 grey levels are reckoned to be far and away good enough, and it certainly works for everyday images. For colour images the boundary lies between 16-bit and 24-bit.

Although 24 bits are best for a colour display, you can make do with fewer bits if the individual colours are chosen carefully from a 24-bit palette of colours, to match the colours in the image. Very few images run across the whole 16 million colours, and so using a custom (or adaptive) palette, as this is called, is a useful way of getting the bit depth, and also the size of the file, down. Often you can go down to 256 colours with a custom palette and the results will be virtually indistinguishable from a full 24-bit image. Unfortunately a custom palette is not always a practical idea, especially if several images with different custom palettes, and even the windows on the screen, are expected to share the same screen display and the screen is not a 24-bit one. The result will, at best, be an attempt by the operating system to reconcile the different palettes but, at worst, some of the images will turn psychedelic. There is a well-known palette for web design that contains the 216 colours 'native' to Netscape Navigator under Windows as a kind of 'lowest common denominator'.

Dithering.

The basic rule of reproduction, and this applies to print as well as to computer displays, is that you can trade spatial information for bit-depth information, which you could call colour resolution. This means that you can group pixels together and use the group, averaged between the individual pixels in the group, to show more colours than an individual pixel can. The group of pixels acts like a larger pixel that is capable of showing more colours. This technique has versions such as half-toning and dithering, which you can use as well as or instead of a custom palette. It is even possible to dither a one-bit image to make it look almost photographic, if the screen resolution is high enough and you do not look too closely.

As an extreme example, the illustration shows a grey-scale image of the Matterhorn that has been dithered from eight bits (256 shades of grey) to one bit (black and white). This is called a diffusion dither. You really have to squint and imagine really hard to see this as a grey-scale image, but the basic principle of dithering is there: groups of dots simulating greys. If you are trying to use a photographic image on the display of a mobile phone then this kind of dither is what you will probably need to do.

■ Using what, when and why

For the designer of a computer-based application there are times when you will need to think very carefully about how your images are stored and reproduced.

In an ideal world, apart from special effects, you would always be able to use 24-bit (or better) images in your web pages and multimedia applications. However, you could run into problems in doing this, for reasons of display incompatibility and file size and/or download times. If the display of your target delivery system is not 24-bit then you need to know how it will react when fed a 24-bit image. If the display does not gracefully degrade it by, for example, dithering it, you might be better off dithering the images yourself. If there are palette problems, which are common in applications using windowing interfaces because of differing requirements of the windows on the screen, this can make your images look poor to the point of being psychedelic when their window is not active.

Custom palettes, especially when viewed on a display with less than 16-bit colour, present a potential difficulty in that, when switching from one picture to another in a sequence, the palette may not switch at the same time as the picture. This can lead to a brief flash of weird colours on the screen as the palette settles down. There is a brief moment while the beam scanning the image onto the monitor switches off as the display scan moves from the bottom of the screen back to the top, called the vertical blanking interval or VBI and this happens with all monitor displays including televisions. The VBI allows a short period during which both screen image and palette can be changed so that the palette flash is not seen – as long as the necessary changes can be made quickly enough.

File size is important for reasons of capacity and loading time. As well as taking up three times the space of an 8-bit image on your website or CD-ROM, a 24-bit image takes three times as long to load. This could be crucial if you are expecting very fast response times and, of course, this is especially important on a website. As we have already discussed, you can reduce the size of an image by reducing the number of colours, and we discuss data reduction or compression of still images below.

You should also think carefully about whether you want to use 24-bit if it is available. It may be that some of your images will work very well in 8-bit, and so you should consider using them this way. This is particularly true of animations, where you might need to reap the benefit of smaller file sizes, or even use simple but fast compression methods (run-length encoding, for example) to avoid having to move too much data too quickly.

Even though your final delivery may not be a full 24-bit colour image, you should carry out all the retouching and compositing operations in 24-bit. Working on an 8-bit or a 16-bit version of an image will never give as good a result as working on the 24-bit original. This argument also extends to the archiving of graphics, and they should be kept at the highest reasonable quality as well as in their final form.

■ Anti-aliasing

Although text is essentially a one-bit image, there are circumstances when you would want to display text with more bits. It is all part of that trade-off between spatial and colour resolution. When converting from an object (such as text or a drawing) to a bitmap you have to fit the edges of the object to the pixels on the screen. If you do this and set the pixels black or white depending on whether the majority of the pixel is covered by the line or not, you get jagged lines on the screen, known as jaggies or staircasing.

The alternative is to colour the pixels along the edge in different shades according to how much of each one is covered. This will disguise the jaggies, and usually renders them inconspicuous at the risk of the edges seeming a bit soft. The shades are blends of the foreground and background colours.

Because the effect of the mismatch between the real line and the 'quantizing' caused by trying to fit it onto the pixels in the image is known as aliasing, the kind of rendering that puts the grey pixels around the edge to smooth it out is known as anti-aliasing. Anti-aliased text, particularly, has become very popular with computer typographers and designers because it looks more like words on paper and less like a screen bitmap.

Some computer operating systems can render text to the screen in an anti-aliased fashion in real time, but in other cases the text needs to be built into the image as a graphic.

There are some occasions when you should think carefully about using anti-aliased text. This is especially the case when the text is small, because the grey wedges around the edge tend to make small text look fuzzy. This problem increases with the reducing of text size because the 'grey' pixels around the edge have a fixed size and so become a bigger proportion of the

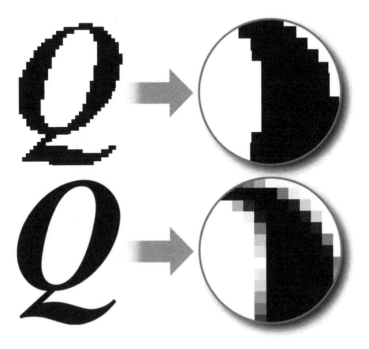

Anti-aliasing.

text size as the text shrinks. In some cases, more careful alignment of the text on the screen will optimize the appearance. The worst-case scenario is where the text is small enough, and misaligned enough, for some of the strokes of the characters to be almost completely grey. In this case they just look out of focus. Making the size of the characters such that their top and bottom edges lie exactly at pixel boundaries reduces this effect, but few characters have straight lines at their edges. Basically you have to check the images carefully.

■ Look before you leap

Any graphic should be checked on the delivery system. Reducing the bit depth of an image can have all sorts of undesirable side-effects, particularly quantization. This is sometimes also called posterization or contouring. It is the result of taking a smooth transition from one colour to another and replacing that with a series of discrete steps.

In this image, as an example, you see an extreme case of posterization. There is a risk that the image on the left (subject to the vagaries of repro-

Posterization.

duction in print), which has 256 shades of grey in it, would come out looking like the one on the right if that computer screen could display only four levels of grey.

Unfortunately you can only be sure of this kind of compatibility if you have checked your image on every screen format, which is a bit problematic for a website because there are so many computers with so many browsers and even Web on TV to consider. As I've already mentioned, there is a well-known group of colours, known as the web safe palette, which can be used for 8-bit images to minimize the risk of unforeseen changes. This palette also eases cross-platform compatibility between the PC and Mac. However, there is a final Mac/PC issue that often catches people out, and that is the difference in the display gamma between the two platforms. As has been discussed earlier in this chapter, gamma is the way in which brightness levels are shown on the display, and the result of Macs and PCs having different gamma curves is that images look darker on a PC than they do on a Mac. To overcome this you must either tailor the image to the platform – a CGI program or JavaScript can find out what platform a viewer's web browser is using and call up appropriate image files – or accept dark or light images or attempt to compromise. In the future it will be possible to detect the characteristics of the computer display and adjust the gamma of a PNG image accordingly.

☐ Taking less space

You will usually need to reduce the size of graphics files. This can be for reasons of space, for example on a compact disk. It can also affect the time it takes to access the files, whether from the Web or from a CD.

One way of reducing the size of a graphic is by degrading it. The size of the file, in pixels, can be reduced. A 640 by 480 file could be shrunk to 320 by 240 and blown back up on display. This will lead to a dramatic reduction in quality. The colour depth of the picture can be reduced. One quite effective way is to change from a 24-bit image to an 8-bit one with only 256 colours. If the palette for the picture is carefully chosen a 256-colour version of a 24-bit picture can be a very effective substitute. This is known as an adaptive palette.

JPEG compresses photographic images substantially by losing the less visible elements of the picture using a process called a discrete cosine transform (DCT) to identify fine detail and remove it. JPEG at relatively low compression rates, such as 5 to 1, will usually be indistinguishable from the original. This means that JPEG is even more efficient than 8-bit with an adaptive palette.

Compare the two images on the next page.

The first image was compressed using a high-quality JPEG compressor, but if we subtract this image from the original, and the range of brightness in the result is expanded so that the changes are easier to see, a mosaic pattern becomes visible.

JPEG Matterhorn.

JPEG artefacts.

In the second image, the finer the dots are, the more detail has been removed by the JPEG DCT algorithm. The reduction achieved by JPEG here is a factor of 3. If the image was colour the difference would be greater. You can find these images on the website.

Reducing the size of a file reduces the time it takes to load that file. If the image needs to be decoded, as a JPEG image would, then you have to take account of the decoding time. Despite this, on a website you will find that the time taken to download and decode a JPEG image is still less than the time taken to download an uncompressed version – if your browser could display the uncompressed file type.

◼ Animated graphics on the Web

Animated graphics are somewhat different from movies, although an animation can be a movie. By animation what we mean is an animated line drawing, like a cartoon, rather than something that is, or looks, photographic. Some forms of animation can be efficiently compressed for use on the Web. We have already mentioned Flash, which takes draw object shapes and text and allows sophisticated animations to be made using them that require very little data. Animated titles or bullet point slides can be made this way with little data overhead over and above the web page itself. The only disadvantage is that the viewer needs to have downloaded the relevant plug-in for the browser and to have installed it correctly otherwise an error results. All browsers can display animated GIF files, so this is an option although, as usual, you need to be careful about download times.

Another form of animation that is web-friendly is sprite animation. A small animated object, called a sprite, can be moved around a larger stage. This sprite could be an animation of a walking figure, and the stage could be a line representing a road. Shockwave, which is based on Macromedia Director, allows animations of this kind to be made and distributed on a web page. Director itself animates by using a sprite-based system, which translates well to the Web. Again, the plug-in is required.

Of course you could devise an animation that runs as a Java applet, and in this case it could be as sophisticated as your programming skill allowed. No plug-in is needed because many browsers support Java, but quite a few users disable it and some companies restrict or ban its use for security reasons.

◼ Which graphics format should I use?

To cut to the chase, you have two reasons why one format might be better-suited than another. First, the end-user's browsers may or may not support it. At the time of writing PNG is supported in newer browsers but you can't assume people out there are using them in sufficient numbers. That will change quickly.

Second, the way the image is compressed lends itself to a particular kind of image. GIF is a format that can only handle 256 colours and uses run-length encoding (RLE) compression. This is most efficient when dealing with repeating patterns or large areas of flat colour (because RLE works best with repeating sequences of identical pixels). So things like company logos and cartoons are usually suitable for GIF.

JPEG is designed for photographs but as these have textures, smooth soft edges and a somewhat arbitrary notion of which parts of the image are sharp and which are soft, you can also use JPEG for any image which does not have hard sharp lines in it, such as a watercolour (or an imitation watercolour) or an air-brush painting.

PNG is still something of a dark horse (at least for most of us). Since it has no lossy compression it will not compress as much as JPEG so it will probably be used as a direct higher quality and more versatile alternative to GIF.

Because GIF and PNG compress an their images with no loss (so you can exactly recreate the original on decompression) you don't really have any trade-off between compression and quality whereas this is a basic choice with JPEG which is a lossy compression standard. However, you can reduce the range of colours in a GIF or PNG and if you can produce a result which looks good then you have successfully reduced the size of the file. Graphics tools for preparing web graphics will usually let you compare versions of the image with different levels of compression. There is also a useful JPEG and GIF fine-tuning tool available on the Net Mechanic website, called GIFBot.

■ Asset management

It is possible that the number of graphics files you might have in your application is large. It could be the largest number of files, and if you take into account versions, sections of composite images, and animations then the number can easily run into thousands.

For this reason it is vital that from the beginning you adopt a known system of naming files. This was especially difficult with filing systems that did not allow long names, such as DOS, but is less of a problem now (although don't be tempted to use very long names since you are likely to run up against a limit of 31 characters on Windows CDs and Macs). It is tempting to use paths in your directory structure to identify files, but this has risks since files can become separated from their directories. Some kind of coding is probably going to be the only safe solution to this problem, with a short code identifying the image and its status. A suffix or extension should be reserved for the file type since some filing systems recognize files only by this extension. The resources in Apple files are potentially very useful, and very detailed information about a file can be put there as a special resource, but this does not help you if you are working on a PC. Also you will have to consider the problems of recognizing files from lists, including lists in archives.

In particularly complex cases a database may be required to handle the assets in an application, and several software companies have been addressing the problems of handling an image database of this kind. You may wish to write a system of your own, which can be used for different applications.

Image compatibility and quality

Since it is possible to display a photographic-quality image on a 24-bit display, you will need to take care that any compression does not noticeably degrade the image. In agreeing quality standards with a client you will need, as with audio and video, to align your quality with what the delivery system can display. However, there may be times, such as with a website, when the delivery system will encompass a range of displays, and under these circumstances you will need to check how the images look on all the platforms and try to make sure that they degrade gracefully as the display capabilities decline.

From a practical point of view the days of image standards for still pictures being incompatible are almost over, since there are a number of good conversion packages that can take an image in one format and convert it to another with no loss. You should be aware, however, of differences between uncompressed, compressed but lossless, and compressed with loss (or lossy).

An image that is compressed without loss, such as one compressed with run-length encoding, will be the same as an uncompressed one when the latter is expanded. Such a system can be used for archiving and a key example is PNG. Lossy systems are more unpredictable but the good ones, such as Photo-CD and JPEG, can be used as if they were uncompressed as far as delivery of the image is concerned. (There is a lossless JPEG standard but it is rarely used.)

There is a caveat. If you are going to manipulate an image you should start from an uncompressed or lossless-compressed image. Exceptionally, Photo-CD can be used for origination, as the compression system used for it is visually lossless, even though it does lose some information. This loss amounts only to information that we do not see since our eyes do not resolve colour as well as the brightness information.

Proofreeding!

In software they say that 'there is always one more bug', and the typo is the graphical equivalent. It will be important to check for any errors in the graphics, just as you will do with any voice-over script. Any text on screen should be checked for spelling and consistency of presentation before it is passed on to the graphics team for display on the screen. However, even the most experienced typographer can make a mistake, and if proper names or foreign languages are involved, extra care is needed.

Proofreading is a skill and, in any event, should not be carried out by the person who wrote the text because they will sometimes see what they expect to see rather than what is really there. You cannot rely on spell-checkers because spell checking does not usually pick up misused words or typos that are valid words, such as 'if' for 'of' or 'reed' for 'read' and in any case a spell checker can't check text in a graphic. But it is still worth running a spell-checker to catch obvious mistakes, missed spaces and such like. You do remember that there was a printing of the Bible which contained the commandment 'Thou shall commit adultery' don't you?

THEORY INTO PRACTICE 8

The website contains examples of images with different resolutions and bit depths. You should familiarize yourself with the effects on different kinds of material and, using whatever image manipulation software you have, experiment with changes in the number of colours.

If you have access to a range of machines with different graphics capabilities, or if you can easily change the display on your computer, you can take a couple of graphic-oriented websites and see how they look under differing conditions.

The GIFBot feature on Net Mechanic (see below) can also be used to directly compare compression options for JPEGs and GIFs.

 ## ■ Summary

- There are two basic types of image, one that is object-oriented and known as a drawing or vector graphics, and can be changed relatively easily, and one that consists only of the exact dots displayed on the screen. This is a bitmap or painting, and is less easily manipulated.

- Working with a composite image in a package that uses layers and alpha channels can give you the best of both worlds because you can separate the sections of the image and work on them independently.

- Unless you are working with photographic images (usually 24-bit colour), you will have to select a range of colours carefully for representation of the image. This is known as the palette.

- In transferring a 24-bit image to a smaller palette, say 8-bit, there are compromises that have to be made. However, the resulting file will also be smaller.

- Reducing the number of colours in an image is not the only way of shrinking the file, since JPEG compression, which is an international standard, can achieve a shrinkage with less visible artefacts.

■ Whatever you do with images, it is vital always to check how the image will look when it reaches your end-user. And don't forget to proofread any text.

■ Recommended reading

Foley J.D., van Dam A., Feiner S.K. and Hughes J.F. (1996). *Computer Graphics, Principles and Practice*, 2nd edn. Reading, MA: Addison-Wesley

Siegel D. (1997). *Creating Killer Web Sites*, 2nd edn. Indianapolis, IN: Hayden Books

The PNG specification, which has detailed explanations about gamma and other issues, is at
http://www.w3.org/TR/REC-png.html

Net Mechanic's GIFBot is at
http://www.netmechanic.com/accelerate.htm

Integration

9

Project manager's responsibilities

- To assemble the necessary software engineering team to implement the application
- To ensure that the project definition is in a form that can be implemented in software
- To monitor the development of the programming, and liaise between the client and programming team over changes and misunderstandings
- To define the testing to be carried out, and oversee that process
- To understand the basics of programming logic so as to better understand the problems facing the programmers

■ New media fusion or confusion?

Interactive media can be said to gather the best, and the worst, aspects of both computing and the audiovisual industry, and they have to be fused together in the core stage of multimedia development. This is the integration of the application, whether it is getting the parts of a website to work together or producing an iTV programme, a kiosk or CD-ROM. Here the underlying computer software is applied to the assets and/or the data, and this is often the first time that anyone, including the designer, sees the jigsaw puzzle fitting together. This chapter explores this integration and looks at programming as it applies to websites and offline projects: for simplicity I'll just call them all 'applications'.

The writing of HTML for a website is not often regarded as programming, especially because it is often carried out by another specialist, such as a graphics artist. However, JavaScript or CGI applications on the Web server certainly constitute programming, and can be just about as arcane as multimedia gets. So once you get beyond HTML you soon run into programming.

Managing a team in software development has much in common with the general principles covered in Chapter 14 of Book 1, *Team management principles*. The software team involved in an application can range from a single person upwards, although in multimedia software teams are often no larger than four or five. If you have a single person working on your project it will be beneficial for that person to have contact with other programmers so that any sticky problems can be sorted out. Within a team you may wish to have one person who manages the team's work. Software is often written on a modular basis, with separate but self-contained parts of the application being written by different people. It is often necessary for someone with software knowledge to distribute the work and make sure the modules fit together.

The choice of people to program your project will depend on how it will be carried out. Different software engineers will have experience of using different languages and tools and working in different environments. For example, dynamic websites need software engineers experienced in server-side or back-end programming while a kiosk is likely to need someone with experience of a package like Director. Interactive television might need C++ skills, or HTML/XML depending on the particular platform. WAP uses a markup language similar to HTML and written in XML. So people with HTML, XML, Java or C++ experience can fit into teams in many areas. Ideally you will have enough experience, or be able to get suitably impartial advice, to choose the environment and therefore know what kind of programmer to recruit.

A second part of managing software involves the specifying of what needs to be done and ensuring that it is carried out. Taking advice from a programmer during the early stages of the design can avoid problems later and can help you to describe the application in ways that a programmer can clearly understand. When specifying an application there will be input from every part of your team and from your client. For a consumer product your client's input could be augmented by information on what customers want, but the basic management principle remains the same.

The purpose of this chapter is to give an overview of the software aspects of websites and multimedia, but it does not set out to show how to actually carry out the programming. Just as in the audio and video chapters, this chapter aims to help non-programming specialists to understand the processes and problems that arise in multimedia software development.

A computer program is a series of operations and decisions. Something happens as a result of the user carrying out an action, and the software will respond. It is the task of the designer to decide what that response will be, and of the software engineer, or programmer, to implement this as code. The software engineer will write the software that carries out this integration by using either an authoring tool or a programming language.

■ Authoring versus programming

There is no hard-and-fast rule about what constitutes authoring as distinct from programming. Packages with which you can write multimedia applications range from graphical packages such as Director and ToolBook to Java and C++. With the first you can build basic interactive structures with a few clicks of the mouse button and a few pulled-down menus, through scripting and mark-up languages such as HTML, which is not unlike English, to the hard stuff, such as Java and C++. In general the versatility and performance of your application will increase as you move towards a full-blown programming language such as C++, but it will be more difficult to implement.

Offline applications have traditionally been a homogenous environment for programming in that many of them were written using a package like

Director and it was rare to need to go outside this particular environment. A website is now a heterogeneous environment, needing a working knowledge of more than just HTML. Dynamic HTML (DHTML) goes further by allowing sections of a web page to be defined and labelled so that they can be dynamically changed or moved around under JavaScript control. Cascading Style Sheets (CSS) provide a site-wide mechanism for controlling the look of a site. JavaScript is a programming language with great power and can work with DHTML and CSS to manipulate web pages. Currently, an increasing number of websites are moving away from HTML towards XML and the combination of XML to describe the page content with CSS to define how it should be displayed. Unfortunately the implementations of these technologies by the makers of web browsers are different. In one key area Netscape and Internet Explorer have used a different version of what is called the Document Object Model to describe the elements of a web page which makes it difficult to write JavaScript that will work successfully across all browsers.

Even if you program in a sophisticated language like C++ or Java, it doesn't mean that you have to write everything from scratch. You will have access to libraries of self-contained code routines or objects. You might write these and reuse them from project to project, they might be a constant part of the operating system you are writing for or they might be libraries of code you buy to enable to program a particular system. (See a discussion on copyright in computer code in Book 1 Chapter 15.)

The objects in the libraries will have a known and probably simple function and will come with instructions telling you how to call the routine and pass parameters to it and what it will do and/or return to you after it has run. These objects are often like 'black boxes' in that you don't need to know how they do their job, you just need to know exactly what they do and how to instruct (program) them.

An authoring package often lends its own look and feel to the application, and experienced authors can sometimes look at a program and say 'Oh, that was developed using Macromedia Director' or 'That's a typical ToolBook application'. This is partly the result of early users of such tools making good use of the facilities the tools provide – a package-led approach. Using authoring packages for web pages has an extra aspect, in that often the HTML they produce is quirky in some way, even though it usually still does the job. (Also some packages leave their footprints in the HTML, either in the creator meta tag at the top of the web page source or because they name JavaScript functions in a certain way.)

As time has gone by, the desired functionality has become more of a driving force than the obvious abilities of the tools. It must be said, however, that authoring tools do have their limits, especially when it comes to performance of offline applications.

So, how do you choose between the different options? In the end some kind of risk–benefit analysis needs to be done to compare your options, but there are a couple of underlying factors that you need to take into account.

As a general rule, the lower the level of coding you undertake, the longer it will take. This is partly because the code will take longer to write, but it will also be more prone to bugs that are difficult to track down. To counter this, if you have software engineers working in your team who have experience of lower-level coding then they may program very quickly. You, or your software team, should be building up a library of objects, or routines for your programming. This is particularly true if you are working in Java or C++. As we've mentioned earlier, you can incorporate these libraries in future projects as well. This is the main reason why it is a good idea for you to only license your code to your clients rather than grant them all rights; otherwise you will find it difficult to make use of your basic routines from earlier projects.

Besides the inherent abilities of the team at your disposal, you will also be judging the requirements of the particular application. In some cases it may demand low-level coding, for instance if there are any gaming elements, but for less responsive and more asset-led applications an authoring tool may be very appropriate.

■ The authoring tree

A good graphical authoring package or structure editor will have an underlying scripting language, and a good scripting language will allow you to build new commands with a lower-level language such as C. (The web-authoring package Dreamweaver allows you to write extensions to itself in JavaScript for example.) At the bottom of this pile, rather like the court of ultimate appeal, the low-level language could call routines in machine code for speed. Machine code written as part of an application is common in games but much less so in multimedia.

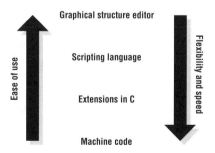

A graphical structure editor, or similar, lets you define the flow of an application's logic by drawing it on the screen in some way, often just like a flow chart in traditional logic. Examples of this kind of authoring package include Icon Author and Authorware.

Alternatively the flow could be predetermined, as in a card-based hyper-linked system, where you define hot-spots or buttons and then have a new card that is displayed as a result of activating the button. The buttons can also trigger other things besides jumps to other cards, and you can trigger events on opening or closing cards as well. Examples of this kind of system include ToolBook and HyperCard.

A third kind of authoring system uses a time line onto which you put events. The hyperlinks in this kind of system jump around on the time line. Macromedia Director is an authoring system of this kind.

Although these are in fact three different kinds of authoring system, what they have in common is that you can build a simple application or define the outline of a more complex one without typing in any programming commands. In almost every case, these authoring tools have scripting languages underneath, such as Lingo with Director and Hypertalk with HyperCard.

There is no hard-and-fast definition of an authoring or scripting language as opposed to a programming language. One possible definition is that a scripting language is a special type of computer language in that it usually appears to be in English. HTML is sometimes considered to be a scripting language, although it actually sets out to mark up text to say how it should be displayed. As HTML has evolved to allow designers to control more of the look of a page it has become more of a program and less of a mark-up. (However, since HTML has no true variables or structures to allow conditional looping and testing it falls outside any real definition of a computer programming language.) Scripting languages can also offer intuitive variables like 'it' so that when you 'get the time' the value of 'the time' is held in a variable automatically called 'it'. Then when the next command is 'show it' the value of the time will be displayed. Since the script says 'get the time, show it', it reads like English.

The definition falls down partly because well-written code in computer languages can sometimes be as relatively easy to read as English. There are even poems written in Perl which constitute 'legal' programs. Also C++, which is a very powerful programming language, has a variable 'this', which always refers to the current object. JavaScript and Perl are two languages used on the Web. JavaScript usually runs in the browser and is often embedded in the HTML, whereas Perl always runs on the server. Both these languages are often referred to as producing scripts rather than code, but this just serves to illustrate how blurred the boundaries are since their syntax can be decidedly cryptic at times.

Another definition is that a scripting language will only be able to carry out a defined range of tasks, whereas a programming language is versatile. This one is closer to the truth but still not accurate. As long as a language can carry out basic arithmetic and logic it can, in theory, be applied to any task – even being used to write itself, just as C can be used to write a C compiler. But that may be the key. In practice, most scripting languages are good at some tasks but very inefficient in others.

To help with their core task, scripting languages for multimedia will have built-in support for sound and video, which would have to be specially programmed in a more general-purpose programming language.

Because of the hyperlinked nature of the HTML documents used on the World Wide Web, you could argue that HTML is a scripting language, and the kind of programs that read HTML (Web browsers) can handle pictures, sound and movies. It is possible to use HTML as a simple form of multimedia authoring on CD-ROM (as we did on the CD in earlier editions of this book and has become increasingly popular over the last few years). HTML is designed to work in a distributed system – the Internet – and distributed multimedia is becoming increasingly important.

In an authoring environment you, as author, do not really have any control over the way your program interacts with the computer's memory, filing system and so on. This can result in problems if the authoring package you are using has any faults in the way it interacts with the computer. One example is where the program takes some memory to carry out a task but does not correctly free that memory after use. In this way it is possible for a program to very slowly eat into free memory until the computer runs out of usable memory and crashes. This kind of error, known as a memory leak, is extremely difficult to track down, and can be the cause of inexplicable crashes that also seem to be unrepeatable. In this case, using a utility program to monitor the computer can help. If you are working in a computer language that allows direct control of such things, such as C, then you have to take care of memory usage yourself.

JavaScript has its own issues with memory. The JavaScript in a web page has to run in the available browser memory and it is entirely possible for several JavaScript routines to be active simultaneously depending on how the website is designed. Browsers behave unpredictably under such duress.

A final analogy for programming versus authoring: you might be able to use a screwdriver (a low-level and versatile tool) to dig a hole in the street, but would you want to do so? The jackhammer or pneumatic drill (a rather blunt analogue of the authoring tool) is better suited to the job, but less versatile than the screwdriver. Conversely, think about trying to turn a screw with a jackhammer.

■ Stages

There is some confusion as to the stages of software development, since some of the terms mean different things to different people. In practice, because of the diverse backgrounds of people working in multimedia, a strict software-oriented development cycle might not be followed, or indeed be appropriate, as has been discussed earlier in Table 2.1 (Book 1 Chapter 2, *Multimedia and project management*). It is up to the development team as to how they manage their programming, but some clients will expect some of the more formal elements of software design. To help understand this, what follows is a brief outline of a more software-oriented procedure. Although this is primarily appropriate for an offline application don't forget that a dynamic website also behaves as a single application when the client (browser) and server-side functions are taken together.

In addition, the quality standards (such as ISO 9000) that can be applied to any process lay down definite meanings. One common software approach is to write a user requirements document and a functional specification. The proposal to the client may well have covered some aspects of this, since the application structure might have been outlined. Ideally someone from the software team would have been involved in this process, or else the structure would have been based on previous work and therefore would be, to a large extent, tried and tested.

☐ User requirements

'User requirements' is an ambiguous expression, and if it is mentioned, you will need to be sure of what is actually meant. There are two meanings, both of which are useful, and you might consider including both in the software process.

The first meaning is 'What are the needs of the user that the application can satisfy?' In this way the user requirement of a word processor is basically the ability to write and manipulate text, and this kind of information follows from the scoping of the project when the needs and objectives of the user are determined.

This is a very general interpretation, which allows the design team to lay down the functionality of the software in a general way. Sometimes this

stage is called a user specification, and in order to help a potential client or sponsor understand what the application will do, it could include short scenarios that describe (hypothetically) what it would be like to use the application.

The second meaning is 'What does the user require of the application?', which is a much more specific question. Here the answers are things such as 'a user-friendly interface', 'spell checking', and 'automatic saving of work on a regular basis'. It may be that your client will have very specific requirements that the complete application must fulfil, and a strict user requirements list like this is a good way of expressing those. The software team uses the list as input saying what needs to be done. It is their task to work out how to do it, which leads to the functional specification.

☐ Functional specification

Whereas the user requirements outline what needs to be done, the functional specification gives much more detail about how a task will be carried out. At its fullest a functional specification will list the outcome of every action carried out by the user, and will say how that is to be achieved.

With a website some things are taken for granted: the way the links operate and the graphics are displayed are outside your control since the browser does that. However, the client and the developer need to agree on the structure of the site and the way it looks. So a specification for a simple static website might concentrate on the look of the graphics – perhaps with template designs for page layouts – and the hierarchical structure of the site. Once a website moves beyond HTML then a more formal functional specification becomes a possibility. This can happen because the user interface is going to make use of JavaScript to improve the user experience. Or the site might be very large and dynamic with online shopping, perhaps something like a catalogue, with many pages that have a standardized layout. In such cases the website might be built dynamically by a database. The database will organize the site content, and the responses to queries will be output as HTML or HTML and JavaScript so that the browser receives what seem to be ordinary web pages.

For a major software project (and this would include a big e-commerce website, for example), the functional specification will be a very large document, and will be carefully researched and written. It can take many months to write the specification, and it is the document that defines the application. If clients have a software background, they may ask for such a document and often the developer will insist on one in any case. Otherwise, the programmers will perform the same sort of task if not necessarily on the same scale. In this case the clients may not be given the programming specification as part of the documentation because its use to them without a programming background would be minimal. If clients have requested a functional specification, then once this document is agreed and signed off, any changes have to be similarly discussed, agreed and signed off as change requests. A change request can then be evaluated in terms of its impact on time, quality and budget as discussed in Book 1 Chapter 5, *Contract issues 1*.

There is a basic difficulty in applying a strict functional specification of this type to multimedia, which is why its use is intermittent in the industry. This results partly from the audiovisual nature of multimedia. A lot of the content of the application lies in the assets, and they can be very difficult to specify since, at the start, they will not have been researched. Also, time-based media such as movies are notoriously difficult to specify since the performance of the integrated application depends on so many factors, including the exact nature of the time-based asset itself. We are not yet at the stage in multimedia where our clients and viewers can take as read the quality thresholds that apply to assets in the way they can for radio or television. The vague but widely understood concept of broadcast quality cannot yet automatically apply to multimedia simply because of the variety of display systems on people's desks and restrictions of delivery. Instead, custom and practice and easily available examples of quality in other applications and websites help to demonstrate that the best quality possible in the circumstances is being achieved.

A second problem with the functional specification lies in the difficulty of writing down what is a very dynamic process. For this reason many developers use prototypes, or demonstrator applications sometimes also called animatics, to define the task to be carried out. Even then there is an acceptance that not everything intended can be achieved. Sometimes for multimedia the only accurate definition of an application will be the application itself.

Finally, a recent trend in software design has been to forgo a functional specification altogether. With object-oriented programming, where distinct modules of the program are defined carefully so that they operate as independent objects and just communicate with each other, the important thing to define is the way the program will work. The exact detail of how the objects are coded is left to the software engineers.

For these reasons any kind of functional specification, and also the user requirements, are likely to be internal rather than external documents in a multimedia development. Their primary purpose is to help the software team to build the application rather than to define the application for the client. As a result the documents may even be called something completely different but would fulfil broadly the same purpose.

Alpha and omega

The actual development, as distinct from the talking about the development, also has names. Again, there is some variance as to what the terms really mean, but this is one set of meanings which is possibly more common with offline projects than with online. Software people will sometimes refer to stages of a project in terms such as pre-alpha, alpha, beta, and golden master. A wider approach to testing than a pure software approach is discussed in Book 1 Chapter 11, *Testing*. Using this as a reference, the point at which you would put your project out for external testing is what would be referred to as a beta version by software-oriented developers and can happen with a website just as with any offline application.

An alpha is more for testing internally in the team, and you might not even show it to the client. To extend the meaning of alpha into multimedia you might say that an alpha is structurally complete but does not have all its content in place, only enough to test functionality while you are waiting for the complete content. With a website this stage might be a graphical mockup or static prototype, done in something like PhotoShop, to show the design, after which and on approval, the HTML is done to build the page. This is part of the type of testing referred to as developmental testing in Book 1 Chapter 11.

In offline projects, the golden master is the one that is actually going to be sent for replication and distribution. The equivalent stage for a website is the point at which the complete site is ready to go online. It is fully tested and has survived all the testing you, and possibly your client, has thrown at it. The project is signed off or gets final acceptance and might even be packaged and sent off to the client's IT people to go onto their web server.

As the software team gets bigger, the difficulties of keeping track of the development increase. In new media this problem of version control or version tracking, as this is called, increases as well because most of your assets will be going through changes too. As part of your version control you will need to devise a numbering scheme for everything you do, including the documentation. Here are some suggestions:

- Anything that is unfinished has a version number smaller than one, for example 0.3 or 0.99 (for 'almost there'). You can have more numbers after the decimal point to show very small changes but this is a rather subjective concept.

- A more complex numbering system, such as 1.2 B 24 would denote that this is the beta version of version 1.2 of the specification, and this is the 24th build of the application. The term 'build' implies a compiling process or some process that takes the software in one form and turns it into another.

- An odd or an even number beyond the decimal point could indicate whether the change from the last number was due to new functionality or a bug fix.

In a modular piece of software a version number should be given to every module, especially if different people are writing different modules. Use comments in code freely to explain what is going on, including the basics of what the module does. Images built as montages of other images will also require version numbers.

▓ Bugs

Computers are, at best, very stupid but very logical. They never know what you mean, they only know what you say in your programs, and this can be extremely frustrating when something goes wrong with a program and it has to be investigated.

Legend has it that the use of the word 'bug', meaning a problem in a computer program, dates from Admiral Grace Hopper, who was one of the very early computer pioneers (and sometimes credited with inventing the software computer program back in the days when computers were programmed by changing the wiring). A big computer failed at 1545 on 9 September 1947, and the cause was an insect (bug) which had crawled onto a logic module and died as a result of the heat, voltage or just being trapped by a relay. The legend is only partly true, since engineers have been finding technical 'bugs' in things since the nineteenth century (the modern use of the term is reputed to have originated in telegraphy) and the log entry only says that this was the 'first actual case of a bug being found'. Hopper's insect bug (a moth) did, however, die its legendary death and now lies taped to her log book in the Smithsonian. You can see the log page, complete with moth attached, at http://www.waterholes.com/~dennette/1996/hopper/bug.htm.

There is a saying in programming, 'There is always one more bug', and unfortunately the reliability of complex systems decreases geometrically with the number of component parts. Since a computer program does not wear out like a car engine, its reliability is better defined as correct operation under all conditions. Things the user is not supposed to do – such as illegal keystrokes – should be catered for during software development; but reliability tends to decrease with the increasing complexity of

the program. Even changing the delivery medium can show up a bug. As an example consider an application developed under Windows that is to be delivered on CD-ROM. Windows now allows very long file names, and it is a temptation to use them, but a Windows CD-ROM that uses what are called the Joliet extensions to allow long file names still allows only up to 31 characters in the name, so the program that worked on a hard disk may not work on the CD-ROM. It now seems to be accepted that a complex computer program can never be tested for absolutely every eventuality.

This can be difficult for clients to understand. If they come from an area where it seems that absolute quality is achievable they might overreact to a bug. The onus is on the software team and the project manager to test as thoroughly as possible, bearing in mind cost and time constraints.

One option is to allow the client to use the software 'in anger' for some time and delay final acceptance until that period is finished. If you are going to do this then it is vital that the schedule and cost allow for it and that this has been agreed up front, not as an afterthought. See Book 1 Chapter 11, *Testing*, for how to specify a full testing strategy.

If it is any consolation, even long-established software can have bugs, some known and some unknown. One very common microprocessor, which was for a long time a mainstay of 8-bit computing, had a low-level addressing bug that was never fixed. If a bug is known about, and software works around the bug, it is possible that the bug will never be fixed because this would affect the existing programs that are working around the bug.

With a web page, the difficulty in testing lies in the many different browsers and machine combinations that people will use. A regular survey of visitors to the Browser Watch website turns up so many differently identified browsers visiting the site (this information is sent to the server with the page request) that four different web pages are needed to list them. This survey shows that there are still people out there using version 2 browsers or earlier – but not many of them fortunately.

Of course you can test and validate the syntax of your web page. Programs such as WebLint (which runs under Perl) will do this for you, and track down unbalanced tags (opened but not closed and vice versa) and the like: there are others, and equivalent validators for JavaScript. If you are using a web authoring tool like Dreamweaver then this should prevent you generating bad code and to a great extent will validate your existing code but, because Dreamweaver doesn't mess with your existing code unless it is incorrect, you can sometimes find problems which are more of an idiosyncrasy than a bug.

Sometimes a bug can appear out of a clear blue sky. The author suffered from crashes of a website that suddenly started for no apparent reason, only when using Netscape, and could not be replicated on the local machine, only over the network. This was eventually traced to a background graphic that had somehow become corrupted and was only affecting Netscape under certain circumstances. The graphic was replaced and the bug went away. Bugs like that are hard to find and, as usual, require a complex process of trial and error testing using a staged process of elimination. This process isn't helped with websites by the various caches in the system that can lead to you seeing a different version of a page to the one you think. Putting a version number in a comment at the top of a page can help.

It can be difficult to test CGI programs because they need to run on the server and get data such as environment variables over the network. Environment variables can be passed to a CGI program so that the program can act on them. This makes it difficult to test them offline prior to installation. Often when a CGI has a bug and does not return the correct result you will not see anything on the browser because the server does not allow the CGI to return anything at all. For this reason some servers allow you to run your CGIs in a debugging mode, which allows you to see remote results clearly. This might be done by prefixing the program name with something that identifies it as a debugging run.

A further consideration is that the Web itself suffers from the equivalent of bugs. Some days it slows down and very occasionally it suffers from a major problem. The server could malfunction: it could have crashed because of some external event you could not control, or your CGI program may have seized up, perhaps waiting for a key-press acknowledgement that will never come. If you have an ongoing responsibility for a site it is a good idea to have someone check it every morning or set up an automatic monitoring system. That way, if the client telephones you can already be on the case.

For more on Testing you should refer to Book 1 Chapter 11, *Testing*.

▧ The demo factor

In many organizations and projects there will be pressures to demonstrate websites or offline applications. This could be for the client, or other clients, or the board, or at a trade show. The demo factor brings two major implications to the development of the application.

First, and this is a negative factor, the timing is likely to be such that you will have to assemble a special version for demonstration. This is very likely to be the case if the demo is taking place early in the development cycle. If it is a networked application you may have to produce a stand-alone version, or you may have to put it on the Internet with password protection.

Second, and this is a positive factor, a demo can be a very good bug finder. There is something about letting a member of the company management demonstrate the software that brings the bugs out from the woodwork. Of course this means that the demo should be 'scripted' so that nothing untoward happens. Unfortunately people doing demonstrations do not always follow instructions. The author was involved in a project where the demonstrator was warned that under no circumstances should he do a certain thing because it was known to crash the program. He, of course, did just that – at the beginning of his demonstration to the chairman of the multinational company for which he worked.

However, this is a lesson that you learn very quickly the hard way, and it is a lot easier to lose a client than to gain one. The best approach is not to be press-ganged into giving demos too early.

The only other solution is to make sure that even a demo is solid enough to continue working and not crash completely. Do not have buttons that call a routine that crashes; rather, make them 'blind' and not do anything. It takes minutes to restart most multimedia systems.

▧ The jigsaw

Software engineering is becoming more and more like a mix-and-match jigsaw puzzle. Programs are made up of objects that interact with each other and can be reused in other applications. Multimedia applications will have three main sections that need to be fitted together:

- The **user interface** is the means by which the user controls the program. It may or may not include assets of its own.

- The **program logic** runs behind the user interface and carries out the tasks the user interface requests, and will possibly have an agenda of its own if, for example, the application includes any simulations.

■ The **assets** are the textual, graphical and audiovisual components of the program that the program logic will choose and activate, usually on the instructions of the user interface. In a database-driven application there could easily be tens of thousands of these.

Even if the application does not easily break down into these three sections, there are reasons why you might wish to separate them from a logical point of view. The user interface may run remotely from the core program logic in a networked application. A web page is essentially a user interface that runs on a web browser. Assets will need to be proofread or otherwise checked, which is their equivalent of debugging. Replacing assets on a CD-ROM is easy if they are not inexorably entwined in the software, unless of course you have a CD-ROM that has just been shipped out to a thousand customers. Replacing assets on a web page is fairly trivial at any time. Program logic is less platform dependent than the user interface and so is easier to port from one platform to another.

■ Risky business

There is a wish in most software teams for them to be exploring new territory and not continuously reworking the same old routines time and time again. It is considered a matter of pride to be asked to beta-test some new software tool or operating system extension. When surfing the Web you will often come across websites that require either a just-released browser or some plug-in or other. In many cases Web browser plug-ins – and this is also true of Java – provide tiny run-time environments in which the small programs can run, sometimes called virtual machines if they are particularly versatile. In fact these small programs have even been given a name: applets. Ironically, as you move further and further away from HTML, your online programming becomes more and more like programming for offline multimedia.

'Pushing the envelope' can be a dangerous business. The envelope is your current level of expertise, and when you push the envelope you try something newer and more challenging. To build an application you need to be able to plan and move forward through the development cycle, and if the sands shift beneath you because of bugs in the tools or changes in their functionality then you are in trouble. There are few things worse in computing than chasing a program bug for months only to find eventually that the problem lies in the operating system, or the language, or some other third-party software such as a low-level driver. Code that links (or glues together) two different pieces of software can be especially awkward to debug. It is not unusual for two companies whose software will not work together to blame each other for the problem.

Of course there always has to be a first time to use a new tool, so you can never be completely sure. The message is to think very carefully of the implications of using something new, and to allow for extra time for the learning curve in your planning. The time when you use a new version of a tried and trusted tool or of the operating system can also be problematic, and as a general rule upgrading should not be carried out in mid-project unless there is no alternative.

It is also possible that using a previously untried feature of familiar software can cause difficulties. Unfortunately it is not always possible to rely on documentation since a complex program, by definition, is very difficult to document fully. And as already mentioned, there can also be bugs in long-established software and even the operating system or processor.

■ The link between software and the client

The project manager's dilemma.

More than in any other area of new development, the project manager or producer has to be able to act both as a buffer and as a translator between the client and the software team. As project manager you have to trust your team to truly represent the status of the software. Sometimes they will give you what seems completely counter-intuitive advice as a result of some esoteric way the browser, compiler or authoring tool works or because of a known problem with the delivery system. The risk is that the client, if not familiar with software engineering and programming, will sometimes think that there is no substance to the real problems you will face. You are the liaison between the team and the client, and you need to be able to understand the problems the software hits in order to explain such things. There is a fine line between explaining a complicated problem to clients and blinding them with science, and the position of that line depends a great deal on your relationship with the client.

THEORY INTO PRACTICE 9

Talk to people you know who have programmed multimedia applications and ask them what they liked and disliked about the process and about the tools and languages they used. You should take any opportunity you have to try new tools, and you will find demonstration examples of some on the Internet.

■ Summary

- Integration is the core stage of multimedia development, where assets and software are fused together to make the application.
- Choosing the software package, programming language or authoring system is key to this stage. Multimedia authoring systems will have built-in support for different kinds of asset.
- You will need to define names and numbering conventions for the different stages of your development and testing.
- Testing and fixing bugs in complex code will be time-consuming and it is essential to avoid the possibility of bugs in tools and operating system routines as they will confuse the testing.
- Making use of browser plug-ins and Java results in a programming process more like offline multimedia than online web page design.
- 'Pushing the envelope' is risky.
- The software development in multimedia is likely to be the least understood part of the process for a client.

Recommended reading

Apple Computer Inc. (1987). *The Apple Macintosh Human Interface Guidelines*. Reading, MA: Addison-Wesley or see http://developer.apple.com/techpubs/mac/HIGuidelines/HIGuidelines-2.html for a downloadable version.

Niedernst J (1999). *Web Design in a Nutshell*. Sebastopol, CA: O'Reilly & Associates

Sebesta R.W. (2001). *Programming the World Wide Web*. Reading, MA: Addison-Wesley

Spainhour S. and Eckstein R. (1999). *Webmaster in a Nutshell*, 2nd edn. Sebastopol, CA: O'Reilly & Associates

Vaughan T. (2001). *Multimedia: Making it Work*, 5th edn. Berkeley, CA: Osborne McGraw-Hill

The BrowserWatch website is at http://browserwatch.internet.com/ (Note: there is no www in the URL)

2.5G Intermediate stage between current mobile telephones and **3G**. See **HSCSD, GPRS, EDGE**

3-D Three-dimensional, appearing to have depth.

3-DO Obsolete consumer multimedia player.

3G Third generation mobile telephone systems, another name for **UMTS – Universal Mobile Telecommunications Services**.

8-, 16-, 24- or 48-bit image The more bits a colour image has, the more colours can be shown in it. An 8-bit image can have 256 colours because 8 bits can be used for numbers from zero (00000000 in binary arithmetic) to 255 (11111111 in binary arithmetic). However, these colours can usually be chosen from a larger palette of perhaps millions of colours. If the 256 colours are all shades of grey then a photographic-quality monochrome image can be reproduced. A 16-bit image will have thousands of colours, and can look photographic in many circumstances. For a truly photographic colour image the millions of colours available in 24 bits is necessary (or even more). Note that on the Apple Macintosh an 8-bit matte or alpha channel can be added to the 24 bits, and the image can be referred to as being 32-bit. Also the PNG graphics format can handle 48-bit colour images with an alpha channel.

- 1 bit gives you two colours (usually black and white).
- 2 bits give you 4 colours.
- 4 bits give you 16 colours.
- 8 bits give you 256 colours
- 16 bits give you 65,536 colours.
- 24 bits give you 16,777,216 colours.
- 48 bits give you 281,474,976,710,656 colours.

16 by 9 Aspect ratio (width to height) of widescreen television (conventional TV has an aspect ratio of 4 by 3).

above-the-line cost A cost that you would not be paying as part of the overhead of running the company. Your in-house resources and/or staff are a below-the-line cost whereas a freelancer hired for a particular job is an above-the-line cost. These two kinds of cost are both real, since somebody has to pay them, but your attitude to them is likely to be different.

acceptance testing This is testing that is applied according to pre-determined parameters agreed with the client at the end of the project to show the project conforms to the standard expected and warrants payment.

accessibility Designing websites and other programs to give equal access to them by people with disabilities. In the case of web design it includes designing the page or a version of the page that makes sense when read by a speaking web browser (screen reader).

adaptive palette A relatively limited palette of colours that is calculated so as to best reproduce a full colour image. Often 256 colours but sometimes less.

ADPCM Adaptive delta (or difference) pulse code modulation. Delta PCM is a sound-encoding method that reduces the data rate by storing only changes in the size of samples rather than the absolute value of the sample. The adaptive part is where the encoding of the difference values adapts so as to more accurately follow large changes between samples.

ADSL Asymmetric subscriber line (or loop) which is a means of carrying very high speed data down a conventional copper telephone cable over distances of a few kilometres.

agent A piece of software that is empowered to act on the user's behalf, to carry out tasks like network maintenance or to book a holiday. A mobile agent is an agent which is able to move around a network from computer to computer in order to do its job.

aliasing Occurs when the way something is recorded produces errors that look or sound as if they should be parts of the real thing. The wheels of racing covered wagons in a Western movie, which often seem to be going backwards, do so because of aliasing. In this case the 24 frames per second of the film is not fast enough to accurately record the motion of the wheel. In digital audio it is possible to produce false sounds if the rate at which the sound is sampled is not fast enough to accurately represent the waveform. See **anti-aliasing**.

alpha channel Besides the red, green and blue channels of an image that determine the colour of each pixel, there can be another channel that sets how transparent the pixel is. This is known as the alpha channel. The effect is similar to a matte except that a matte is usually only 1 bit deep so that the transparency is either full (so the background shows through) or opaque. In television this is known as *keying*.

alpha disk The disk on which an alpha version of an offline application is distributed.

alpha test The first test of a complete or near-complete application, usually by internal users. The term originates from computing, and is not always used by web agencies and multimedia companies originating from other disciplines.

always-on A mobile phone system where data connections are charged by data transferred rather than by duration of connection. Also used to describe an Internet connection using, for example, ADSL where users do not have to dial in to connect.

ambient noise or **ambience** Extraneous sounds intruding on a sound recording due to such things as traffic, distant voices, bird song and the like, possibly including the **echo** and/or **reverberation** of the room.

analogue Strictly speaking an analogue is any kind of representation or similarity. However, analogue is used in multimedia (and in audio and video and electronics in general) to differentiate from digital. In digital, a signal is turned into a series of numbers, and the numbers are stored or transmitted. In analogue the signal itself is either stored or transmitted directly as a waveform, or is converted into another medium that can follow its variations and itself be stored or transmitted. Whereas analogue systems are prone to distortion and noise, digital systems are much less susceptible.

animatic An application that demonstrates and prototypes the final application.

animation Simulated movement of objects using computer or video effects. A simulation of a building rising from its outline foundations to completion is an example of an animation.

anti-aliasing In graphics it is possible for edges of objects to look jagged because the resolution screen display is unable to accurately represent the object itself. To alleviate this problem the colours of the pixels around the edge of the object are mixed gradually between the object and its background. In this way the colour resolution compensates for the lack of spatial resolution that causes the jagged edges. By definition, this technique cannot be used where only pure black-and-white pixels are available. Some computer displays will now automatically anti-alias text to make it look cleaner on the screen.

applet A very small computer application (usually in the Java language) downloaded from a website to run on the user's computer as part of a web page.

application A general term for a multimedia (or any kind of software) title or project.

application-based program A program that is either self-contained or which runs entirely within one environment, such as an authoring package.

artefacts Disturbances and defects to an image or sound that are not supposed to be there, but which are the results of errors in digitization or display.

ASCII American Standard Code for Information Interchange – the main standard for representing letters and numbers in computing.

assets The media components of an application or web page – audio, video, graphics, animations, text – that combine to form the content.

authoring tool A computer program designed to be simple to use when building an application. Supposedly no programming knowledge is needed, but usually common sense and an understanding of basic logic are necessary.

B2B Business to business: trading between two businesses carried out electronically. See **B2C** and **C2C**.

B2C Business to consumer: trading between a business and consumers carried out electronically. See **B2B** and **C2C**.

back-end A computer program whose operation is not apparent to the user, such as a supporting program on the server which provides information that the web server can send to the user over the Internet.

bandwidth The amount of data passed along a cable or communications channel of any kind. Sometimes the data channel, or pipe, is described as *fat* if it has a high bandwidth and can carry a lot of data quickly, or *thin* if it cannot. Bandwidth is usually expressed in bits per second or bytes per second. Because of this confusion you should be clear whether bandwidth is being expressed in bits or bytes to understand how fast the data can be transmitted.

banner advertisment An elongated narrow advertisement placed on a web page. There is a 'standard' size for banners of 468 by 60 pixels. Usually, clicking on a banner takes the user to the advertiser's website.

BCPL A computer language, one of the ancestors of C and C++.

bearer A protocol that transparently carries another protocol.

beta If your application or website has 'gone beta' then it should be finished but needs testing. This testing may be carried out by people outside the production team and even outside the production company.

bi-directional language Enabling a computer to cope with a language that reads and writes from right to left – like Arabic or Hebrew – as well as left to right as in English. The individual languages would of course be uni-directional. This goes hand-in-hand with being able to handle many more characters than the standard European-centred ASCII text. See also **double byte.**

bit The smallest unit in binary numbers. A bit can have a value of either 0 or 1. The number of bits used to represent a binary number limit the maximum value it can have. For example a 4-bit number can have values from 0000 to 1111 (0 to 15 in decimal).

bit depth In graphics, the more bits a colour image has, the more colours can be used in it. An 8-bit image can have 256 colours, but you can usually choose those colours from a larger palette of perhaps millions of colours. If your 256 colours are all shades of grey then a photographic-quality monochrome image can be reproduced. A 16-bit image will have thousands of colours, and can look photographic in many circumstances. However, for a truly photographic colour image, the millions of colours available in 24 bits is necessary (or even more). Note that on the Apple Macintosh an 8-bit matte or alpha channel can be associated with the 24 bits, making 32 bits. See also **8-, 16-, 24- or 48-bit image**.

bit rate reduction Audio and video engineers often use this term to mean compression of data, as the term 'compression' has another meaning, especially in audio. See **compression**.

bitmap A graphic image that represents the image by a matrix of pixels, usually going from top to bottom, left to right. Bitmap images usually have a resolution in pixels per inch and a size in pixels.

blanking In analogue television, the time between the end of one TV line and the start of the next (horizontal blanking) or the end of one field and the start of the next (vertical blanking or vertical interval).

Bluetooth A short-range high-speed wireless data standard especially promoted for consumer and mobile telephony use. Named after a Scandinavian king. See also **Wi-Fi.**

boiler plate A standard form of contract that is then modified or qualified to make up the contract for a particular agreement.

Bookmark A function of an application whereby users can store their place so that they can quickly go back there later, even saving the Bookmark for retrieval many days later. The electronic equivalent of a piece of paper between pages of a book.

browser A piece of software that allows the user to look through a number of resources, usually held in a variety of formats. A web browser is designed for viewing World Wide Web pages on the Internet. Netscape Navigator, Internet Explorer and Opera are examples of web browsers.

buffer A place for temporary storage of data, often to smooth out differences in speed between a data input and output.

build The process of taking all the component parts of a multimedia application (or indeed any piece of software) and making the finished version.

bump mapping In computer graphics, a technique for giving a surface texture to objects by slightly distorting the shape.

buy-out Paying for all the necessary rights in one go rather than paying royalties.

byte In binary arithmetic, and hence in computing, a byte is an 8-bit number and can have a value between 0 and 255.

C, C++ Powerful computer languages, often used to write sophisticated code to carry out specialized or difficult tasks in multimedia applications. C++ is more recent and is designed for object-oriented programming. Java is based on C.

C2C Consumer to consumer: trading carried out between consumers, like auctions or jumble/yard sales, carried out electronically. Also see **B2B** and **B2C**.

cache Computer memory or disk space used for temporary storage of data in order to speed up a task. A web browser has a cache on disk to hold recently downloaded pages and graphics so that if a page is revisited and has not changed the information can be quickly loaded from the local disk rather than downloaded again over the network.

call centre A centralized enquiry centre that people phone for information relating to a business, its services and/or products.

carousel A model for interactive television where a sequence of information is transmitted repeatedly.

cartogram A style of illustration in which a map shows statistical information in a diagrammatic way.

CD burner A machine that can write compact disks, including CD-ROMs. The disks were originally called WORMs (write once read many) and so sometimes the machines are called WORM burners. The term CD-R is more common now, and there is a re-recordable version called CD-RW, which has limited compatibility with standard CD-ROM drives.

CD-i Compact Disk-Interactive is an obsolete interactive multimedia platform that uses a television monitor with a CD-i player as the delivery system. Primarily developed by Philips for the consumer market, it allows use of all media on the system. It has its own set of authoring tools, and conforms to the Green Book technical specification standards. With the decline of consumer CD-

ROM, CD-i remained in a niche market for training and other professional applications primarily because of its inexpensive player cost and use of a television set rather than a computer monitor.

CD-ROM Compact disk read-only memory has progressed from allowing only text and data onto the disk to now include audio, graphics, animations and video. It conforms to the Yellow Book and ISO 9660 technical specifications. CD-ROM drives vary in the speed for transferring data but for multimedia delivery you need to allow for potential users having drives that are not the fastest available.

CD-TV A short-lived obsolete consumer multimedia system based on the Commodore Amiga.

cellular radio A system for radio communication that uses a large number of low-powered transmitters, each operating in a small area called a cell. Mobile telephones use this system and as the telephones move their connections move from one cell to another.

certificate An electronic document that authoritatively identifies a web server so that secure (HTTPS) transactions can take place. Without a valid certificate a web browser will not set up a secure link.

CGI Common gateway interface: Internet standards for the passing of information between applications such as web browsers and pages and the server. Programs that make use of this, called CGI programs, allow sophisticated generation of web pages based on dynamic data, and mean that such things as forms and databases can be used on the Web.

change management A system set up by developers to monitor and control the number and type of changes made during development, whether the changes originate in-house or from the client. Also known as *change control*.

change request form The document used to request a modification to an already agreed specification. Used in **change management**.

channel See **distribution channel**.

character generator A piece of software or hardware designed to make captions for video and superimpose them on the picture.

chat and chuck Name given to very cheap and disposable mobile telephones.

chrominance The colour part of a colour television signal, as distinct from the brightness part, which is luminance. Often abbreviated to chroma.

circuit switched data In mobile telephony, a dial-up call where users have continuous use of the circuit and pay by duration of call. See also **always-on**.

clearances The overall term for copyright and similar permissions.

client side A process, such as display of a web page, which happens on the user's local computer rather than on the server.

clip art/media Illustrations, photographs or any other media items available, usually inexpensively or even free, for use in productions with no further payment. See **royalty-free.**

codec A piece of software that compresses and/or decompresses audio or video. Stands for coder-decoder.

coincident needles A stereo meter for showing volume of sound where the two needles of the meter, representing left and right signals, revolve around the same point.

coloured In audio, the detrimental change in a sound due to the influence of the physical environment (such as the room) or distortions in the recording system.

competences The definition of skills evident from practices carried out in the workplace. This term has become prominent in training circles through the link to NVQs (National Vocational Qualifications). These are new-style qualifications that are concerned with accrediting people for the skills they employ naturally as they carry out their work.

compile To take the source code of a computer program and turn it into machine code using a compiler. The source code is written by the programmer. Extra code from programming libraries is incorporated at this time. The opposite is **interpreted**.

component A video image in which the colour information is kept separate from the luminance or brightness information. Usually two signals are used to represent the colour information. This is similar to RGB, and the RGB signals can be extracted from the three components. The components are also specified to take into account the eye's response to different colours.

composite A video signal in which colour and brightness are encoded together in the same signal. PAL and NTSC are composite television systems.

composite image In video, an image in which colour and brightness are encoded together in the same signal; in graphics, an image made up of several other images, blended together.

compressed but lossless A compressed signal from which the original signal can be retrieved without any changes or errors.

compressed with loss A compressed signal from which it is impossible to retrieve the original signal, in which a version of the original is retrieved that is satisfactory for its intended purpose. Also known as **lossy**.

compression In computing, reducing the amount of data needed to carry something; also known as **bit rate reduction**. When the term 'video compression' is used it will almost certainly have this meaning, and will refer to such systems as MPEG and Sorensen. In audio, reducing the dynamic range (range of loudness) of a sound recording.

computer-based training Often referred to as CBT, computer-based training is a method in which some or all of the training content of a course is turned into an interactive computer program.

concept map A visual representation to help show relationships between different items.

concept testing Testing of ideas on an audience chosen from a sample market. The aim is to check the feasibility of the ideas for the market before incurring expense implementing them. The method for implementation can but may not involve interactive methods. Concept testing originated with marketing, and may be called *focus groups*.

conforming In video editing, taking the edits noted from an offline edit session and using them to edit the real high quality recording for final distribution. If done automatically based on the list of edits it is known as auto-conforming.

contention ratio In an ADSL connection, a measure of the number of other users sharing your connection to the Internet. This will be a small number, typically less than 100, and it assumes that few users will be demanding bandwidth at any moment. Not all ADSL systems make the users share the connection.

contingency In project management, predicting the need and reserving funds, time and/or resources to cope with unforeseen circumstances that affect the project schedule. Multimedia project management needs more contingency than many other forms of project because it is a volatile environment.

contouring An artefact in graphics reproduction whereby smooth changes of brightness or colour become changed so that discrete steps are seen. Sometimes also called **posterization** (especially when used for artistic effect) or **quantization**.

convergence The gradual merging of computing, broadcast media and telecommunications technologies.

cookie A small amount of data stored by a browser on behalf of a web server to help track a visit to a website.

copyright The right of a creator of a work of art, literature, music, and so on to have control over the reproduction and exploitation of the work.

credit The linking of people to the tasks they performed. This is normally done by listing the name and function performed, as in credits at the end of a television programme. The crediting of personnel in media is very important and is often governed by agreements between production companies and unions.

critical path The identification of the optimum sequence to carry out tasks to achieve a project on time and within budget. See also **task analysis** and **network analysis**.

CRM Customer Relationship Management. A system based on collecting information on each customer from many sources within an organization into a central electronic file and using this to tailor information on goods and services to their needs.

cross-platform Describes the development of applications that will run on more than one delivery platform.

CUI Concept User Interface. These are tools that help a group of people debate, define and rank their most common important concepts. These tools can be helpful in the analysis of requirements for a project.

custom palette A palette of colours chosen specifically to represent an image.

DAT Digital audio tape, a format using 4 mm tape in cassettes originally designed for digital audio (48 kHz sampling 16-bit) but also used to store data when it operates as a streamer tape format.

data protection The concept in European law whereby personal information is protected and the organizations who use this data and the use they can make of the data are registered and regulated. See **safe harbour.**

debug To study an application with the intention of removing any errors found.

deck The equivalent of a website in **WAP**. The analogy is a deck of cards.

decompile To take the machine code version of a program and change it back into something a human can understand.

decryption To remove the encryption from something so that the original is produced.

delivery medium The system used to distribute an application. The World Wide Web can be considered to be a delivery medium.

delivery platform The multimedia system or systems that people will use to interact with the application. The total specification of the platform is important so that the application is developed within the capabilities. A web browser can be considered to be a delivery platform.

development platform The multimedia system that is used to develop the application. This may not be the same as the delivery platform. It is important that the final application is tested on the delivery system to check that it will perform on the specified platform.

development testing This is iterative testing applied naturally during the development of a project to ensure that all the pieces work.

diaphragm In a microphone, the membrane that is vibrated by sound and so causes the production of an electrical signal that represents the sound.

digital In a digital system, the signal (including such things as sounds and pictures) is turned into a series of numbers, and it is these numbers that are stored or transmitted. In an **analogue** system the signal itself is either stored or transmitted directly, or is converted into another medium that can follow its variations and itself be stored or transmitted. Whereas analogue systems are prone to distortion and noise, digital systems are much less susceptible.

direct competitors Companies that are in the same line of business, competing for sales from the same people.

discovery learning A learning situation that is structured to allow the learner to explore and find answers rather than be told the information.

discrete cosine transform or **DCT** A mathematical technique for transforming a bitmap of an image, which contains individual dots of the image from left-to-right and top-to-bottom. The DCT analyses the image block by block to find the large areas of colour and the fine detail in them. The resulting file can then be analysed to determine what can be removed without seriously affecting the look of the image. This is the basis of **JPEG** and the first stage of **MPEG** compression.

distance learning A learning situation in which the student studies a course away from the institution using any medium that is provided. This may include interactive programs. See also **open learning centres**.

distribution channel A well-defined and sustained system for moving goods from production out to the people who will buy the products.

dither Small, seemingly random perturbations to a signal or image designed to fool the eye or ear into thinking that it has greater quality than it really does. In graphics a dither is a seemingly random pattern of dots of a limited range of colours that, when viewed from a distance, appear to have a greater range of colours. When digitizing a signal, a dither is used to reduce the effect of digitizing errors because our eyes and ears are less distressed by noise (which dither looks like) than by the sharp changes in a signal that the dither disguises.

DLT A streaming tape format used for data backup and also used to send DVD masters to replication facilities. Has replaced **Exabyte** for these purposes where large quantities of data are involved.

document-based programming Programming in which the format of the document is standardized and one or more applications can be used in concert to read or display it. The World Wide Web is an example of this.

Dolby The company (and inventor) famous for a system for reducing noise in an audio recording and for systems providing multichannel (surround) sound in cinemas and the home. The name is often used ambiguously for either. Dolby is a trade mark.

domain name The Internet equivalent of a street address, showing the route to a particular computer. The name will end with the top level domain name (**TLD**), which designates a user sector, primarily in the USA, such as .com for commercial, .gov for government or .edu for education. There are also internationally agreed country names used as TLDs such as .us, .uk, .fr and .dk, and a machine will usually be situated in that country. New TLDs are occasionally added. The US sector top level domains are often used by organizations wishing to show an international presence even if they are based outside the USA. In an e-mail address the domain name appears after the @ symbol. An individual computer can have a fully qualified domain name (FQDN), which uniquely identifies it. Every FQDN must have a corresponding **IP address** but the reverse is not true.

Domain Name Registrar A company authorized to sell domain names and arrange for them to be made available on the Internet.

Domain name system Usually just called DNS, this is a distributed database on the Internet that maps domain names to IP addresses and vice versa.

dot com company Usually used to refer to a company that exists and trades solely in cyberspace. The name comes from the top level domain where many businesses have their domain names.

dot pitch The distance between dots of phosphor on a colour television or monitor tube. Figures of 0.23 to 0.28 millimetres are common and a smaller dot pitch means a higher resolution is possible.

double byte The use of 16 bits (two bytes) that allows all the characters needed for all world languages to be represented in software. This includes Hindi, Thai, Chinese and Japanese, for example and the standard for this is called Unicode. Most Western European languages can be represented in 8 bits using the **ASCII** standard. Also see **bi-directional**.

dpi The density of dots in an image or on a computer screen. Most computer screen displays are 72 or 96 dpi (dots per inch).

draw object In graphics, an image that is defined in terms of simple graphics 'primitives' such as lines, arcs and fills.

drop frame In NTSC television time code. A time code format which adjusts to compensate for NTSC not having a whole number of frames per second by dropping some time code numbers to keep in step.

dub To copy something, usually an audio or videotape recording. A dub is the copy itself. In digital terminology a direct digital copy is often called a *clone* since it will be indistinguishable from the original.

dumb terminal A computer terminal with a keyboard and screen that does nothing other than show a display generated at a distant computer and send back your typed input.

DVB Digital video broadcasting system used in most of the world apart from the USA. Also a mark used on European digital televisions to show that they will receive digital TV programmes.

DVD Digital versatile disk. Originally called digital video disk, this is the successor to CD-ROM and has many incarnations. The capacity of a DVD disk is much greater than that of a CD-ROM because the system packs the information more tightly on the disk, has the possibility of two information layers per side, and can have information on both sides of the disk. As with CD, recordable, re-writeable, audio and ROM versions are possible. DVD Audio is one of two new formats designed to supersede compact disc audio, the other is **SACD**.

DVD-ROM Use of DVD to hold a large amount of data (up to almost 18 gigabytes), which can then be accessed by a computer. Basically the equivalent of a big CD-ROM.

dynamic range In audio, the range of loudness or volume of a sound.

dynamic web page A web page that is composed by a program running on the web

server computer based on factors such as the kind of request from the browser and what information is currently available. To the browser it looks exactly like a static page.

e-business or e-commerce Business involving goods and services carried out electronically, usually via the World Wide Web.

echo In audio, delayed and distinct individual repeats of the original sound, either due to sound bouncing off the walls of the room or deliberately added electronically. Famously used on the vocal of Elvis Presley's 'Heartbreak Hotel'. See also **reverberation**.

EDGE Enhanced Data Rate for GSM Evolution, a 2.5G mobile technology.

educational technology The study of the ways in which the use of media and structured approaches to organizing material can aid teaching and learning.

edutainment A term derived from the words *education* and *entertainment* coined to describe a category of interactive titles. These are designed to be used in the home to inform and motivate through the use of media.

electronic programme guide A guide to what is available on the channels of a digital television system, shown on the system itself and enabling viewers to actually call up programmes. More usually called EPG. In a multi-channel world, if a channel is not listed in the EPG it is virtually invisible to viewers.

electrostatic Describes a system for microphones, and less commonly, loudspeakers and headphones, whereby electrostatic charge is used to detect or cause the movement of the diaphragm.

emulator A system that pretends to be something it is not, such as a software system that pretends to be a piece of hardware or a software system that pretends to be another software system.

encryption Changing a data file so that it is unrecognizable but can be turned back into its original form on receipt, if the receiver has the key to decode it.

environment map In computer graphics, a method of reproducing reflections on the surface of an object by determining an image of what the object 'sees' from its position and wrapping the object in this image.

environment variable Information passed to a web server when a distant browser requests a 'page'. It includes information on the computer making the request and what web page included the link being followed (if any).

EPG See **electronic programme guide**.

evaluation Often confused with the term 'testing' and used interchangeably, but when used in a strict technical sense, there are differences. Evaluation of an application is the broad appraisal of any factors that influence the development, delivery and reaction to it. See also **testing**.

Exabyte A type of computer streamer tape using 8 mm cassette tape in the same format as Video-8 but now largely replaced for professional applications by a format called **DLT**.

exclusively assigned rights Copyright passed on to someone else so that the original copyright owner no longer has rights in the material.

external clients People who are not part of your organization who commission you to do a piece of work. They define the brief and specifications. Budgets are agreed and negotiated between you.

Extranet A private network whereby the main company allows some other companies to share some or all data on their **intranet** with strict controls on access.

e-zine An electronic equivalent of a magazine.

fair dealing or **fair use** In copyright law, an exception to infringement under certain limited circumstances because your usage of the material is very slight and/or under circumstances where free usage is seen as reasonable. Examples of this include use of

extracts from books in a review and limited use in education. What constitutes fair use differs from country to country and is often misunderstood.

feature creep A gradual and insidious increase in the capability of a piece of software as it is developed, usually without any overall plan of implementation.

field trials The use of the product *in situ* with the intended users prior to release to identify problems for correction.

file path The combination of disk or volume name, directory names and filename that uniquely identifies a file on a computer.

firewall In networks, a computer which monitors traffic flowing between the Internet and an internal network so as to prevent unwanted connections such as hacking.

fixed-term contract A contract that cannot be extended beyond its original duration without positive action being taken by both parties. To extend the term either a new contract would be written or a new clause added to the original contract.

flowchart A diagram that shows step-by-step progression through the content blocks of the proposed website or program.

focus groups See **concept testing**.

force majeure A condition in a contract where neither party has control over the circumstances. This might include war, loss of electrical power and acts of God.

formative A term used to describe evaluation processes carried out during the development cycle. These are contrasted with summative evaluation processes, which occur at the end of development. In this context, team review meetings that occur during the project could be called a formative evaluation process. See **summative**.

frame-grabbing Synonymous with digitization of video but dating back to the days when computers had to digitize frames individually.

frames In video a complete single image, which forms part of a moving sequence of images. On the Web, a technique that allows several distinct parts of a web page to be defined, and which can be defined separately by the author. Often used to allow an index to be shown alongside the different things referred to in the index.

front-end A computer program that provides interface and setup procedures for a less user-friendly but probably more powerful back-end program. On a web server this might be the programme that formats web pages having drawn information from a back-end database.

FTP File Transfer Protocol. Protocol for transferring files between computers over the Internet.

fully qualified domain name (FQDN) see **domain name**.

functional specification A document that says how an application works. The application will be written by referring to this if part of company policy.

gallows arm A kind of microphone stand with a vertical part to which is connected a horizontal extension. This is like the arm of a gallows, and it is used to extend across a table (for example). The mic is fixed to the end of the arm.

gamma The relationship between the brightness of an original (such as a digital image) and the way that signal is displayed by a monitor or on a printed page.

Gantt chart This is a chart that shows progress in relation to a timescale, often used in planning and tracking a project. It was named after Henry Lawrence Gantt, an American engineer.

gateway A computer which connects one system to another, for example a local network to the Internet. In **WAP** a gateway translates and mediates between web pages using **HTML** and WAP phones which use **WML**.

GIF Graphics Interchange Format: a standard for 8-bit graphics, widely used on the Web.

One version of the standard allows part of the image to be defined as transparent.

gigabyte 1024 megabytes.

global culture An international group of people who share similar needs for communication based on profession, business sector, hobby, interests, or whatever.

golden master The final version of an application; the one that will be distributed.

GPRS General Packet Radio Service, a 2.5G mobile technology.

GPS Global Positioning System, a satellite-based system provided by the US Government (mainly military) which allows a GPS receiver to pinpoint its location and altitude on Earth. Precision of the system was initially limited to protect military interests but this has been improved. It is also possible to use a local fixed beacon to augment the satellites and give very high accuracy. May eventually be incorporated into mobile telephones and motor vehicles.

grabber board A piece of hardware that takes in an analogue signal, usually audio or video (where it is a frame grabber), and digitizes it for storage in the computer. Incorporation of audio-visual ports in computers and the advent of DV (digital video camcorder format) make this kind of card obsolescent.

graduated mask In graphics, a mask that determines how much of a second image shows through the first. It is graduated because it has values such that a mix of the two images is seen.

graphical structure editor In programming, a programming environment whereby the author can lay out the relationship between sections of the application in a graphical way, like a flowchart.

GUI Graphical User Interface.

hacker A person who uses considerable computing skill in deviant ways, including introducing computer viruses into a computing community. The term is also used less often, and informally, to denote a skilled computer programmer with no malicious intent. Similarly *hacking*.

half-toning In graphics, a method for reproducing shades of grey by using black dots of varying sizes. See **dither.**

hardware A piece of equipment; as distinct from software.

HCI Human Computer Interaction.

header The invisible part of a web page in which formatting information for the page and meta tags are placed. See also **meta tag**.

high-level design A first attempt to define the interactive structure and content of a program. The term comes from software engineering. See also **outline design**.

hits, hit rate Either the number of individual requests for data that a web page receives or the number of different visitors who have called that page up. This latter is now more usually called **page impressions**.

host machine The computer on which a program runs.

hot-spot A section of an image on the screen that instigates an action when the pointer enters or clicks in it.

HSCSD High Speed Circuit Switched Data, a higher speed version of GSM and a **2.5G** mobile technology.

HTML Hypertext mark-up language: the system used in web pages to describe a web page and its contents. Eventually a combination of XML and Cascading Style Sheets (CSS) will together describe the contents and define how they should be displayed.

HTTP Hypertext transfer protocol: the Internet communications protocol used in the World Wide Web. Basically, a browser calls up a web page by sending an HTTP request to the server. HTTPS is the encrypted and secure version of HTTP.

hybrid Web/CD A multimedia application that needs both a web connection and a CD to function fully. This could be a CD-ROM that updates itself from a website or a website that uses a CD-ROM to hold large multimedia assets such as movies.

hypertext Non-linear text that is read by following jumps and links in the text itself.

icon A pictorial symbol or representation used on the screen to denote an active area. It will allow access to further data or trigger an interactive reaction of some type. It has become common for a text explanation to appear when the user positions the cursor over the icon to help the user understand its significance. See also **picon** and **micon**.

ICT Information and Communication Technologies. Term used as shorthand in describing aspects of convergent technologies.

image map A graphical menu of a website usually put on the front page. This has fallen out of favour as it often took so long to download.

IMAP Internet Message Access Protocol. A recent alternative to **POP** for e-mail.

i-mode Web service provided by NTT DoCoMo in Japan for mobile telephones.

implied licence In the context of a website it is usually assumed that the web pages are published so that they can be viewed across the Internet. Any other use of the pages, such as extracting images from them or displaying them out of context, would breach this implied licence to view. Many websites now have an explicit set of terms and conditions under which the site is viewed.

in-bound communication Communication that only needs to be understood enough by the person receiving it to fulfil a specific need. The need can be linked to various levels of understanding – gist, relevance, decision, action, etc. Here the context is understanding a level of another language enough to understand the message without actually seeing a correct translation.

indemnity A guarantee that if any cost is incurred as a result of your action, you will cover it.

indirect competitors Companies that are in related lines of business to you who may win sales from your potential customers with their products.

information architect Helps users find and manage information successfully by designing organizational and navigational systems (also called *information analyst* or *information strategist*).

inlining Linking to someone else's image so that it appears to be part of your web page even though it does not reside on your server. Potentially a breach of copyright because of a breach of the **implied licence** under which web pages are published on the Internet.

instructional design The study of methods of teaching and learning with particular reference to the selection and use of media to aid instruction. The term is widely used in the USA. Europe tends to use the term **educational technology**.

instructional designer A person who applies the principles of instructional design to convey information using a variety of media and methods.

insubstantial portion In copyright, a small proportion of a literary work that can be reproduced without infringing copyright.

integrity (of moral rights) The author's right for the work not to be changed.

intellectual property A general term for rights such as those protected by copyright and patents.

interactive design The definition of how to structure the content and interactive paths through the material for an interactive application.

interactive television Interactivity applied to broadcast television. As yet this is ill defined, but certainly includes multimedia electronic programme guides, information systems, and adjuncts to the transmitted programmes allowing viewers more involvement.

interactive video An interactive system that uses an interactive videodisk to deliver sound and pictures and combines them with text, sound and graphics from a computer source. More a system of the 1980s, used by large corporations for training, its use has declined. Also denoted by IV.

interface The way an application is designed for people to use. This includes the screen designs, the use of icons or menus, the way interactivity is set up, and the overall structure of the application.

interlaced Describes a television picture that is made of two halves, which interlace with each other like the teeth of a comb and the spaces between.

internal clients People – part of your own organization – who define a piece of work for you to do. Budgeting for the work might be affected by company practices.

Internationalization producing software in a way that facilitates adaptation to suit other languages and cultures without the need for re-programming.

Internet A worldwide interconnection of computer networks, originally set up between the American military, its suppliers and research base to make a network that, by virtue of its multiple interconnections, would be safe from destruction. Up to the 1990s the Internet was largely the preserve of the academic and research communities, but the invention of HTTP, HTML and the World Wide Web has made the Internet the latest mass communications medium.

interpreted In computing, a computer program where each individual command is translated into machine code instructions for the computer before moving on to the next one. The opposite is **compiled**.

intranet A local area network, such as in a company, which operates using Internet protocols and systems. This will now usually include a local implementation of the World Wide Web with web pages read by browsers. Intranets have changed the way most large companies communicate with their staff.

ionizing The process of electrically charging something by removing or adding electrons.

IP address A number, in the form 123.123.123.123, which uniquely identifies a computer on the Internet. See **domain name**.

IRC Internet Relay Chat, a protocol for typing messages between computers in real time.

IrDA Infrared communications standard used in mobile telephones, **PDAs** and lap-top computers for interconnections and connection to fixed devices such as printers.

ISDN A digital phone line which provides a link of either 64 kilobits per second (European standard) or 56 (US standard) per channel with a minimum of two channels. ISDN stands for Integrated Services Digital Network.

ISP Internet service provider: the organization that connects you to the Internet, usually by means of a dial-up telephone connection with a modem. Some ISPs operate nationally and internationally (such as AOL, MSN and Demon), while others operate locally.

iTV See **interactive television**.

jaggies See **staircasing**.

Java A computer language based on C and devised by engineers at Sun originally for use in cable television set-top boxes. It allows efficient sending of small applications (applets) across the Internet, which are then executed on the user's computer.

JavaScript A scripting language that runs in recent browsers and allows more sophisticated control of pages and interaction than HTML. No relation to Java.

JPEG A standardized method for compressing still photographic images with high rates of compression. Almost always **lossy**. The acronym JPEG stands for Joint Photographic Experts Group.

kilobyte 1024 bytes of data (not 1000).

layer (of graphics) Several layers of images can be combined together in graphics to make a new single image. The relationship between the layers is controlled by their alpha channels.

leadership The employment of appropriate management styles to ensure and maintain progress of a team towards common goals.

lean back Like watching television, at a distance, as distinct from **lean forward** and sometimes known as couch potato.

lean forward Like using a computer, close to the screen, as distinct from **lean back**.

learning styles Part of the theory of learning, which indicates that people develop preferred ways of learning. This has implications for designing learning materials so that people can process the information in ways appropriate for their preferred style.

letters patent Formal term for the document that defines a patent.

library music Recorded music produced especially for use in film television and other audiovisual productions. Usually available for licence based on a standard rate card. Also known as **production music**.

limiter In audio, an electronic circuit that automatically controls volume to stop short peaks of volume exceeding a certain amount.

link On the Web a word, phrase or graphic on a web page that, when clicked by the user, sends an HTTP request to the server, usually calling up another web page. Sometimes referred to as a *hot link*.

load balancing Sharing the traffic on a website between a number of server computers in order to handle very high numbers of hits. See **scalability**.

localization Using translation and cultural adaptation to produce software and support materials ready for use in particular languages and cultures.

location-aware or **location-based services** Services provided to a mobile telephone which take account of where the phone is located, to offer lists of nearby restaurants for example.

log Record kept by a web server of every HTTP request it receives, with details including the time and date, who asked for the page, and how much data was transferred.

look and feel Common name for the interface of an application. See **interface**.

lossy In compression this means that the original data cannot exactly be retrieved from the compressed version. This does not necessarily mean that the effects of the compression are visible or audible.

luminance The black-and-white or monochrome part of a colour television signal or picture.

machine code Zeros and ones in a program that a computer can execute directly.

magneto-optical disk A type of disk used for data storage for which both a laser and a magnetic field are required to write data.

mainframe A very large computer – in capability if not in size. Probably run by a dedicated team of people and able to handle many tasks simultaneously.

market research Information about the changing behaviour of people and their habits, gathered by a variety of methods and organized into statistical or analytical representations.

mark-up language A system of marking text so that it can be understood or displayed correctly using a computer. **HTML** is hypertext mark-up language.

master tape The definitive and original recording of something.

mechanical right The right to record a piece of music.

megabyte 1,048,576 bytes of data – 1024 kilobytes.

memory leak A bug in a computer program which causes it to gradually fill up its available memory and finally crash.

menu A set of options listed or otherwise available on screen for the user to select. A main decision point in an application might be called a *menu screen* even if it does not contain a conventional menu list.

merchant services Service to facilitate trading, primarily used to mean accepting payment using credit cards. The merchant service is usually provided by a bank and ultimately has to link to a bank. May include online validation of the credit card transaction so that the merchant (i.e the online shop) can safely dispatch the goods.

meta tag A tag which is placed in the header of a web page to pass control or similar information to the web browser or indexing program that reads the page.

MHEG ISO standard for the definition of multimedia and hypermedia objects.

micon An icon that has moving images. Few make the distinction between icon and micon and generally icon is used to cover all selection images. See also **icon** and **picon**.

middleware Software that manages interaction between different programs, especially in a network. It might link a web server and a database.

MIDI Musical Instrument Digital Interface. A standardized way of describing music and how it is played so that a MIDI-compatible instrument can then provide the sound.

milestone Defined key points of the project's development. Milestones are often linked to the end of a phase of development, and can be linked to phased payment stages of the project as well.

MIME Multipurpose Internet Mail Extension. A standard way of identifying what a file is so that it is handled correctly by web servers and other computers.

mirror site A website that contains the same content as another website. This is usually done so that access speeds can be optimized depending on where in the world the user is. Mirroring a website requires permission, otherwise it is infringement of copyright.

mobile agent See **agent**.

modelling In 3-D graphics, building a scene by defining objects in the scene and arranging them and their environment.

modem Stands for modulate-demodulate and usually refers to a device that takes digital data and converts it into an analogue audio signal so it can pass through the telephone system. The signal is converted back using another modem at the other end. The term is also used for any similar translation and so an ADSL system would include ADSL modems (see **ADSL**).

montage A single graphic made from several sources.

moral rights Rights, related to copyright, which protect a work from unauthorized changes or misattribution without the author's permission. This is currently mainly a European concept but is applied to works of art in US law.

morph To change one shape into another in a smooth transitional movement.

MoSCoW This is an example of one approach to eliciting client needs in a project where you define the items the client *Must have*, *Should have*, *Could have* and *Would like to have*. This approach derives from Rapid Application Development programming techniques.

MP3 MPEG Audio Layer 3. One of the ways of compressing audio in the MPEG family of standards, widely used on the Internet.

MPEG Motion Picture Experts Group; a group of ISO standards for compression of video and definitions of multimedia objects.

MPEG audio The MPEG standard includes three levels of audio. Level 1 is used for DCC (digital compact cassette), Level 2 is usd in DVD and digital broadcasting and level 3 (better known as **MP3**) gives the best compression and is widely used to compress audio on the Internet.

MPEG-1 The version of MPEG that compresses video to a data rate of around one megabit per second. The quality is similar to that of S-VHS.

MPEG-2 The version of MPEG for broadcast quality video at bit rates of the order of 5 megabits per second. Digital television, digital versatile disks (DVD) and Sony's Betacam-SX use MPEG-2. (MPEG-3 was to have dealt with high definition but it was eventually included in MPEG-2.)

MPEG-4 An extension to MPEG introducing object-oriented structures to audio and video and compression for low bit rates.

MPEG-7 An extension to MPEG to provide a standard framework for indexing audio-visual material. (There is no MPEG-5 or 6 and the number 7 is the sum of 1, 2 and 4. The next MPEG is MPEG-21 which is a multimedia framework allowing an overview of all aspects of content delivery covered by the other MPEGs.)

multicultural Communication that needs to be produced specifically for different languages and cultures.

multimedia narrative The structure underpinning forms of interactive communication. Interactive narrative allows the user to take control of the sequencing of information and this is what differentiates multimedia narrative from more traditional forms of narrative.

multiscan Referring to a computer monitor that can work with a range of displays.

multi-session disk A CD-ROM that can be/is written to more than once with each new set of data being added onto the end of the rest until the disk is full.

multitasking Able to do more than one task at once.

needs analysis The primary stage of a training project where the definition of the criteria for success takes place. The competence level of the target audience and the gap between this and the proficiency needed is analysed.

Network Address Translation (NAT) A way of 'hiding' the IP addresses of the computers on a network from the Internet at large. This might be done for security or to avoid unnecessarily using up Internet IP addresses.

network analysis Also referred to as *critical path analysis*; this is the definition of the core tasks and the dependent tasks needed to complete the project. These are mapped out in a network diagram to show their relationship to each other. See **critical path**.

newsgroups See **UseNet groups**.

non-disclosure agreement A contract, usually brief, whereby one party agrees not to disclose information given to it by the other party. Usually known as an NDA.

non-exclusive rights A licensing of rights that still allows licensing to other people.

non-linear In audio-visual production, the use of a computer to edit digitized sound and/or vision. Synonymous with *random-access*.

normalizing In audio, adjusting the volume of a digital audio file so that the loudest parts have a predetermined value, often 100%.

NTSC The analogue colour television system used in North America and Japan, with 525 lines in a frame and approximately 30 frames per second. See also **PAL/SECAM**.

objective A precise definition of a result that is wanted, in terms that will allow the result to be measured. Objectives are used particularly in education and training applications where the results of learning need to be stated, and ultimately measured, to demonstrate the effectiveness of the materials. Objectives are often confused with aims. Aims are more general statements of direction rather than measurable statements.

objective evaluation Evaluation carried out with preset criteria that give a measurable indication of the results. See **subjective evaluation**, **qualitative evaluation** and **quantitative evaluation**.

object-oriented programming Programming as interaction between self-contained mini-programs or objects.

offline A multimedia application that works in isolation on a computer and does not need a network connection. A CD-ROM application is an example of offline.

offline editing Video editing with working copies of the 'real' videotapes and low-quality equipment in order to prepare for **online editing**.

on-demand services A method of providing entertainment and other audiovisual material to consumers (and others) whereby they can demand a particular item, such as a film, and it will be sent to them immediately down a communications link. Some early video-on-demand systems even sent MPEG-1 video to consumers down their telephone lines.

online Applications that operate over a network, particularly the World Wide Web.

online editing Video editing with the 'real' videotapes on high-quality equipment or using a computerized system but with high quality digitized audio and video.

open learning centres Centres usually set up in the workplace where a variety of learning and training materials are gathered for people to use. They can have access to the materials as and when they want. Many use interactive materials as well as videos and books. This approach to learning reflects the need for quick access to training in organizations that are changing faster than ever before.

open plan An office arrangement that assigns space according to changing need. There are no or few permanent partitions between desks, so that the space can be reorganized efficiently when needed. An extension of this principle allocates desks and even computers to workers as they are needed, and is known as *hot desking*.

operating system The lowest level of computer software in a computer. It manages the operation of the hardware and provides the programmer with ways of controlling the machine. Often the term *operating system* is taken to include the graphical user interface as well.

option bars Part of a graphic on the screen that provides hot-spots, buttons or icons grouped together for the user to make a choice.

OS Operating system.

out-bound communication Information that is distributed to numerous people who are likely to have specific uses for the communication. Therefore the accuracy of the information is important and in this context the accuracy of any translation from another language to retain its integrity becomes important.

outline design The first attempt to define the interactive structure and content of a program. The term comes from interactive training design. The later stage from this discipline is called the *detailed design*. See also **high-level design**.

palette The colours available for use in a graphic.

PAL/SECAM The analogue colour television systems used in Europe and most of the world outside North America and Japan, with 625 lines in a frame and 25 frames per second. See also **NTSC**. SECAM encodes the colour information differently to PAL and is used mostly in France, the Middle East and Eastern Europe.

pan Moving the viewpoint of a camera from side to side by swivelling it and not actually changing the location of the camera.

Pareto method An analytical representation of data in graphical form; used to help identify the products that can make the best contribution to the company.

patent The right to exclusive implementation of a process as defined in the patent document.

patent agent A lawyer who drafts letters patent.

paternity The moral right whereby you have a right to be identified as author: also known as *attribution*.

PDA Personal Digital Assistant. Very small hand-held computer also known as a palm top.

peer review Appraisal by colleagues or people performing similar jobs, where the sharing of experience and insights is used to adjust, in this case, the design and functionality of the application.

perceptual map Analytical representation of the results of a survey; used to understand the relative positions of two variables plotted in a matrix.

perceptual matrix See **perceptual map**.

performance monitoring A management process in which people agree criteria of acceptable achievements for a period and review performance according to the criteria at the end of the time. The performance agreement might be linked to bonus payments. Any shortfall of performance accredited to lack of skill might prompt training initiatives.

performing right The right to perform a piece of music to an audience.

Perl A computer language widely used on web servers to produce dynamic web pages based on data received from users. It has powerful string manipulation capabilities, which make it well suited to generating HTML on the fly.

personal construct Term originating with George Kelly, a psychologist from the 1950s who devised techniques for people to define and prioritize concepts that were important to them. A personal construct is the construction and interpretation of meaning by an individual.

personal video recorder (PVR) A set-top box television receiver which also contains hard disk storage and can record programmes for time shifting just as a VCR does. But a PVR can do more than this; the two main features being the ability to pause live programming and for the box to learn your viewing habits and record programmes speculatively to offer you later.

picon An icon that shows a realistic image or picture rather than a representation or symbolic image. Few make the distinction between picon and icon, and generally icon is used to denote all selection images. See also **icon** and **micon**.

pilot projects Experimental projects designed as a run-up to a full-blown development.

pixels Picture elements, the basic building blocks of a picture: sometimes used to be called *pels*.

placeholders A temporary use of images, audio and/or text that are representational of the navigational feel of the final version but not part of the real content.

plug-ins Small extensions to the functionality of a piece of software such as a web browser. The use of the term *plug-in* refers to the ease with which they can be added, usually involving simply copying the plug-in into a particular computer directory.

PNG Portable Network Graphics. A graphics standard devised to replace GIF but giving much higher quality and more versatility. PNG can be used as an archive format.

POP Post Office Protocol, one system used to handle mail boxes for e-mail users. An alternative is **IMAP**.

port (number) A software identifier saying how a computer should treat an Internet request. Web pages are usually requested from port 80.

port (to and **a)** Move a computer program from one machine/platform to another.

portable document format A standard for encoding documents in a file so that the look of the document, including its fonts and graphics, is retained no matter which computer it is shown on. Devised by Adobe.

posterization Reduction of the smooth variation in colours in an image to a series of discrete steps. Also known as **quantization** and **contouring**. Although this effect is usually seen as an error, posterization is sometimes used for artistic effect.

POTS and PANS Light-hearted terms used to describe changes in telecommunications. POTS are Plain Old Telephone System and PANS are Positively Amazing New Stuff (or similar).

pre-alpha A very incomplete version of an offline program.

pricing policy The decisions made on the price of goods based on the understanding of the market, competitors' prices and what people are prepared to pay.

primary colours The smallest set of colours which can be combined to produce virtually all other colours. For light these are red, green and blue and when combined produce white. For pigments they are red, yellow and blue and when combined these colours produce black.

primitives Basic building blocks of a computer system.

prior art In patents, a patent can be invalidated or refused if the idea has been publicized before or already existed (uses 'art' in the same way as the term state-of-the-art).

production music Recorded music produced especially for use in film television and other audio-visual productions. Usually available for licence, based on a standard rate card. Also known as **library music**.

programming language Since computers can work only with zeros and ones it is rather difficult for mere mortals to program them. To alleviate this problem, programming languages have been developed that understand almost real English.

progressive scan A television picture that scans each line in order as distinct from **interlaced**.

project management The specification, planning and control of time, cost, quality and resource issues to complete a project on time and within budget.

project manager A person who carries out project management. Used here to describe the leader of a multimedia team.

proposal The document in which the developers outline the application content, development schedule and cost for the commissioners of a project.

prototype A limited working version of the application; used early in the project to get reaction to the general design and interface so that adjustments can be made.

proxy server A computer that sits between a computer and the Internet and helping to handle transactions such as web page accesses. A proxy is commonly used to locally store distant web pages that are frequently called up so as to speed up the apparent web access and reduce network traffic.

psycho-acoustics The science of hearing, taking into account the psychological aspects of the way the brain interprets sounds as well as the pure acoustics and physics.

psychometric tests Psychological tests that use measurable factors to attribute a score for the person being tested. The tests are used in recruitment and career management decisions, particularly in large organizations.

public domain Used to mean out of copyright and so freely available for use. This is not strictly true since copyright material can be placed in the public domain by the owner with the intention of it being freely available but while still retaining the copyright.

pushing the envelope Trying something new, usually without sufficient experience and with an element of risk.

qualitative data Information collected by less structured means than quantitative data, e.g. free response questions, and relating more to impressions and feelings.

qualitative evaluation Evaluation that takes into account a wide variety of factors that might influence the results being analysed. The attitudes of the users, the culture of the institution or country and the general environment would be examples of qualitative factors. See also **quantitative evaluation**.

quantitative data Information collected by methods that can then be processed and represented numerically or statistically.

quantitative evaluation Evaluation that is concerned with measuring the results against predetermined criteria to assess whether they have been achieved. The number of times that Help is used might be used as an indicator of how effective the interface of an application is, and the percentage of correct responses after obtaining Help might be used to indicate the effectiveness of the Help messages. These would be examples of quantitative measures of evaluation for multimedia packages. See also **qualitative evaluation**.

quantization An artefact in graphics reproduction whereby smooth changes of brightness or colour become changed so that discrete steps are seen. Sometimes also called **posterization** (especially when used for artistic effect) or **contouring.**

quantizing Inaccuracies in the digitizing of a signal caused by the integer distance between levels of sampling.

RAM Random Access Memory; basically the memory in a computer.

ray tracing A technique used in computer graphics to produce realistic images by following the path of light as it travels from the light source, via the objects in the scene, to the observer.

refractive index The amount by which light changes velocity when it passes between media, usually between air and glass or water. The refractive index is different at different frequencies and therefore colours; hence a prism is able to break white light into its constituent colours.

relational database A database with a complex structure allowing the data items to relate to each other in many ways. If the relationship is simple the database is often called a *flat-file* since its structure resembles that of a card index.

render In computer graphics, to build an image.

requirements agreement A document explaining what the client wants from the program that indicates the range and scope of the work you will produce according to the time and cost you define.

residuals Extra rights in a licence that are not involved in the primary use but which may be applied later. Also called *secondary rights*.

return on investment (ROI) A measure of the effectiveness of capital invested in a project, calculated by expressing average profits from the project as a percentage of average capital invested in it.

return path In an interactive system, the way a user can send data back to the interactive system in order to control it.

reverberation In audio, delayed repeats of the original sound, either due to sound bouncing off the walls of the room or deliberately added electronically, which are so close together as to be indistinguishable. See also **echo**.

RGB Red, green, blue: the three primary colours of light from which virtually all colours can be built. Also refers to an image that stores the three primary colour components separately.

rights Permission to reproduce and/or sell something.

RISC Reduced instruction set computer: a microprocessor with relatively few built-in operations but which can execute what it has extremely quickly.

ROI See **return on investment**.

role-play A technique used in teaching and psychology, in which a person acts out a situation, perhaps from different perspectives, to get insight into decision making and reactions.

royalties Payments based on the number of copies sold or distributed.

royalty-free A copyright licence which allows the licensee to use the material without any further payment. A similar term is **buy-out**. See **clip art/media** and **royalties**.

run-length encoding A form of compression that stores the colour of a pixel followed by how many subsequent pixels are of the same colour. This works best with images made up of large areas of flat colour, such as a cartoon.

run-time The execution, or running, of a program.

SACD Super Audio CD. One of two new super-quality digital audio formats designed to supersede compact disk audio (the other is **DVD** Audio).

safe harbour A principle whereby individual American companies agree to comply with the principles of European data protection so that they can be legitimate recipients of data. See **data protection**.

sample rate The frequency with which an analogue signal is sampled on digitization. For accurate representation the sample rate must be at least twice the highest frequency in the signal.

scalability The ability of a website (or any other system) to function under very high load.

scan To convert a flat image such as a photographic print into a digital form by measuring the relevant parameters of sections of the image in an ordered fashion, usually left to right, top to bottom.

scanner A device that converts a flat image such as a photographic print into a digital form by scanning across it.

screen reader An accessibility tool that translates computer screen text into speech for visually impaired people.

screen resolution The number of pixels on a screen. The most common in multimedia is 800 by 600 pixels.

scripting languages Computer languages that are designed to be used without detailed knowledge of programming. They are specialized to particular tasks.

scriptwriter A person who writes TV, radio or film scripts for entertainment or documentary programmes.

seamless branching in DVD, a technique to allow users to choose different paths through moving video without there being any discontinuity.

segment An identifiable part of a market that has enough common needs to influence products being designed for it.

server In a local area network, a server is effectively the hard disk that is not on your own computer but elsewhere. You can use it to store your files or you can look to it to supply material available to the whole network. In a wide area network or video-on-demand system the server is the centralized repository for data. On the Web, a server is the distant computer that holds the web pages and responds to your requests for them.

server side A program or programs running on the server to dynamically produce, find and/or format information to be sent to the browser.

session fee A payment for performing in a music recording as a session musician or recording a voice-over. A principal performer would probably take royalties on sales, not a session fee.

set-top box A computer-based system that is designed to be like a piece of home entertainment hardware (for example, a VCR or CD player), and may actually sit on top of the television set. Satellite receivers and decoders for video on demand and digital TV are usually referred to in this way.

severance In employment, the terms under which the employment is ended.

sibilance Exaggeration of 's' sounds in a voice, sometimes natural but sometimes caused by poor acoustics or microphone placing.

sign-off The signature of a person given the authority to agree that a phase of work has been completed satisfactorily. Sign-offs are often linked to milestones in the project, which can coincide with staged payments.

simulation A technique used to reproduce a situation as realistically as possible to allow people to develop the skills needed to handle the situation. This is often used in management training. The easiest computer-based example to quote is that of a flight simulator used to train pilots, and in many ways this kind of simulation is better known as **virtual reality**.

site map Graphical or topographical representation of the structure of a website (see also **image map**).

slippage The amount of time that has been lost according to the agreed schedule and the present project position.

SMS Small Message System, a method for sending short text messages between mobile telephones.

software A computer program or computer programs in general. Usually used to differentiate from the equipment or hardware.

source code The human-readable version of a computer program before it is compiled into machine or object code.

spam Unwanted and unsolicited e-mails: junk mail. Named after a song in a Monty Python sketch.

speech recognition The identification of spoken words by a software tool. The words are digitized and matched against coded dictionaries to identify the words.

spider The agent of a web search engine that automatically surfs the Web, following links and indexing pages.

staircasing Appearance of lines on a screen that are almost, but not quite horizontal, and under some circumstances will appear jaggy. Also referred to as **jaggies**.

standards conversion In television, conversion of a video signal between the PAL and NTSC standards or vice versa. Changing from PAL to/from SECAM and between high and standard definition is usually referred to as *transcoding*.

standing waves In sound, self-reinforcement of a sound wave when it is reflected back on itself by a wall or the end of a tube. Between two walls this will reinforce certain frequencies and so colour the sound.

Star A configuration of a cable television network where there is a distinct path from the cable centre to an individual subscriber.

static web page A web page that is fixed and stored on the server as a simple text file.

storyboards A scripting convention that includes mock-up visuals; used in video production originally, and now sometimes used in multimedia projects.

streamer tape Magnetic tape, usually in cartridges or cassettes, onto which computer data is recorded or streamed for archiving and backup purposes. The most common formats are DAT; Exabyte and DLT.

streaming On the Web, playing of an audio or video file over the network so that it is heard or seen instantly as it arrives. The audio or video file does not usually remain on the user's computer, and it is possible to stream a live event, rather like a radio or TV broadcast.

style sheet A document that defines how the parts of a web page are to be displayed based on markup tags in the text. These could be a simple redefinition of the standard HTML tags or they could be completely unique to the page, possibly working in conjunction with **XML**.

stylus In computer graphics, a special pen without ink that is moved across a special tablet in order to draw a line or shape on the computer screen. In audio, the tip, usually diamond, on a gramophone pick-up that actually makes contact with the disk groove.

subcarrier A secondary frequency added to a signal in order to carry extra information, such as colour in a TV signal.

subjective evaluation Evaluation that is based on observation and analysis of non-quantifiable factors, and is affected by the experience and bias of the evaluator. See also **objective evaluation**.

summative Term used to describe evaluation processes used at the end of development. This can include testing but could also include such practices as the end of project review, or debriefing procedures. See also **formative** and **evaluation**.

SWOT A method of analysing a company's position against competitors by defining its *Strengths*, *Weaknesses*, *Opportunities* and *Threats*.

synchronization licence A licence to take music and synchronize it with pictures in a film or video.

synchronization pulse Part of a video or digital signal that identifies a position in the signal, such as where a frame of video starts.

take In a take, or a recording: an attempt to record something. If you have to try again, then you do another take.

talking head In film or video, a sequence which only shows a single person speaking, possibly direct at the camera.

task analysis Identification of all the processes and subprocesses needed to complete a project.

TCP/IP Transmission Control Protocol/Internet Protocol is the protocol used to pass messages around the Internet and in many ways defines the Internet.

technical specification Document describing a task to be undertaken in terms of the equipment and techniques required.

telco Shorthand term used generally for a telecommunications company.

telecine In television and DVD production, the machine that scans the film and produces a television signal from it. Now often working digitally and in high definition.

telemedicine Remote access to medical facilities using audio and, especially, video connections. The implementations can range from diagnosis assistance to remote participation in surgical procedures.

telephony Ordinary telephone traffic, in which people talk to each other.

teletype A teleprinter or telex machine, used to communicate with computers before monitors, or VDUs, were available.

TelNet System for remotely controlling a computer as if you were sitting at its own keyboard.

testing The use of methods and procedures to check the performance of an application according to predefined criteria. Testing is often confused with evaluation. It can form part of evaluation, which has a wider remit. See also **evaluation**.

texture mapping In computer graphics, adding a texture to the 'surface' of an object drawn in 3-D.

time and materials contract A contract for work in which the cost is directly related to the time spent and the materials used. It is the opposite of a fixed-price contract where the fee for the job can only be changed by renegotiation.

time code Information added to video and to audio for video, to uniquely identify the individual frames. This is a great help when editing. Time code can be displayed or even recorded on top of the picture in which case it is referred to as *time code in vision* or *burned-in time code*.

time-based media Media that change over time, such as audio and video.

time-lapse photography Photographic technique in which a camera remains fixed in position and records events in detail by taking pictures at intervals over a period of time. The film is then speeded up when shown, to allow people to see the changes take place in seconds rather than days. An example would be the change of a flower from bud to bloom to death.

TLD Top Level Domain. See **domain name.**

transcribe To make a written copy of a document or communication.

tree and branch A configuration for cable TV networks where there is no individual path between the cable centre (head end) and a subscriber.

trimedia Media production where content is produced for radio, television and the Internet simultaneously.

uncompressed Describes the original form of an image, sound or other data.

Uniform Resource Locator (URL) The full string that both defines the path to a remote service on the Internet and also says which kind of transaction is requested. The most common is to start the URL with http:// which means that the user wants a web page, but there are alternatives. A URL is a special case of the more general Uniform Resource Identifier (URI).

Universal Disk Format (UDF) A standard for computer storage directory structure (etc.) defining the dataspace on a DVD disk but which can also be used with other media. Optimized for large files.

Universal Mobile Telecommunications Services (UMTS) A plan for mobile telephony that includes high data rates and the use of multimedia. Better known as **3G** (3rd Generation)

Unix A computer operating system used extensively in tertiary education, industry and for Web servers. Linux is a version of Unix.

usability laboratories Specially constructed rooms where people are observed using applications and their actions are recorded on video, through the computer and on paper by the observers. The information is analysed to indicate the effectiveness of the program and to make recommendations for improvements.

usability testing The recording and subsequent interpretation of people's usage of a computer-based system through a combination of methods that can include observation, electronic records, and video taping. See **usability laboratories.**

UseNet groups A long-established system of bulletin boards distributed around the Internet. Sometimes called **newsgroups.**

user profile Information about the way a typical user would interact with the program.

user requirements The needs of the users; studied to determine how the application should be structured and how it should operate. Similarly *user specification.*

validation An appraisal of the methods that have been used to check that they are consistent with the results. It is sometimes used with the sense of evaluation but strictly it is part of an evaluation process. Also sometimes used with the meaning of field trial as validation exercise. See also **field trials.**

version control or **tracking** In software development, keeping track of changes to the software so that development is cordinated. This is especially important where more than one person is writing code.

vertical blanking interval (VBI) The part of a television signal between the bottom of one picture and the top of the next. Used for teletext, closed captioning, time code and test signals. In computing the VBI is useful because it provides time to change a displayed image.

video CD A compact disk, actually a Mode 2 CD-ROM, which contains MPEG-l video and audio, and can be played on a television or PC screen like a videocassette. Although this early digital videodisk has not been widely accepted by consumers in the West, it is very popular in the Far East.

video compression Reduction of the amount of data needed to carry something; also known as **bit rate reduction** to avoid confusion with dynamic range reduction in audio which is also known as compression.

video conferencing Basically the combination of a telephone conference call and television or a video telephone. Recent video-conferencing systems operate using personal computers, allowing both ends of the conference to work together on documents that each can see.

video on demand A system whereby a home subscriber can access television material stored remotely on a server. Some systems use high-bandwidth cable and others use ordinary telephone wires for the link between the server and the consumer's television. See also **set-top box**.

videodisk See **interactive video**.

virtual machine A layer of software between a computer program and the computer such that the interface between the program and this software is standard no matter what actual machine is used. The new software exists in different versions for different machines.

virtual reality A 3-D visual environment which reacts to a user's presence and input so as to give the impression of actually being there. Non-immersive VR uses a screen whereas immersive VR is shown using goggles to give a pseudo-realistic stereoscopic view.

voice-over An audio commentary that accompanies video or graphics. Hence *voice-over artiste*, a person who reads the commentary.

walled garden A self-contained mini version of the Internet which a service provider produces in order to provide a 'safe' web experience to its customers. This might be to avoid certain kinds of content (a school might do this to limit pupils' web access) or to make sure available material is in the right format for cable TV or **WAP**.

WAP Wireless Application Protocol – web-like system for use on mobile phones. Uses a mark-up language called **WML** which is based on **XML**.

waveform A visual representation of a signal, usually electronic in nature, that changes over time, such as recorded sound.

Web browser A piece of software that takes as its input a web page – with all its text, images, links and even sounds and moving images – and formats and displays it on the user's computer.

Web editor Either a person who is responsible for the content of a web page or a piece of software used to lay out web pages.

Web pages The individual documents, based around HTML, that make up a website. Analogous to the pages of a magazine.

Web Safe palette A set of 216 colours which will always reproduce correctly in a web page. It is not 256 colours because some places in the computer's palette are reserved for the windowing environment.

web surfer Person who accesses the World Wide Web and looks at websites.

website A group of web pages and possibly other networked resources that are designed to be viewed as a distinct entity in the same way a magazine is made up of pages and separate articles.

web-television Display of web pages on a television set rather than a computer screen.

white balance A setting of a camera to make sure that what is white in a scene is recorded as white by adjusting the relative proportions of the primary colours and so compensating for the inherent colour of the light source. Also known as colour balancing if carried out after recording.

WHOIS A part of the DNS which allows you to look up who owns a particular domain name. See **domain name system**.

wide area network Computer network that extends beyond the home or office building or complex. Often consisting of linked local area networks, as in the Internet.

wide latitude Of film, able to record a wide range of brightness levels in a scene, or cope with under- and/or over-exposure.

Wi-Fi Trade-mark name used to denote IEEE 802.11 standard wireless network as used by companies including Apple and Lucent. Has 11 megabits speed over a medium range sufficient for use in buildings or a close neighbourhood.

WML Wireless Mark-up Language. Based on **XML** and similar to **HTML**. Used to mark up web pages for **WAP**.

WMLScript Extension scripting language for **WML**. See **JavaScript**.

World Wide Web (WWW) The multiplicity of HTML documents on websites spread around the Internet. On a technical level the Web uses Hypertext Transfer Protocol (**HTTP**) for communication between web browsers and web servers, although other Internet protocols such as **FTP** (File Transfer Protocol) are also used in tandem.

WORM In data storage, Write Once Read Many, a type of computer disk that can be written to but not changed. Often used to denote a CD-ROM that has been written rather than pressed or replicated. The process is known as burning a WORM or burning a CD.

WYSIWYG Describes an application that shows you the end result of your work exactly as it will be seen by the end-users: What You See Is What You Get.

XML eXtensible Mark-up Language. A very versatile mechanism for defining ways of marking up documents which can be used for web pages and many other media.

zoom To increase the focal length of a lens in video or photography. It magnifies the scene and looks similar to, but not exactly the same as, moving closer to the subject.

Index

Note: When page numbers are highlighted in **bold**, the reference appears in the Glossary.